LIMITLESS

Nuala Moore is an Irish open water swimmer and adventurer. She has spent decades as a scuba-diving professional and has been involved in developing standards and procedures both in ice and channel swimming. She holds two Guinness World Records for extreme cold-water swimming. She is a pioneer, a cold-water safety specialist, a coach, a mentor, an event organiser and an endurance swimmer who has pushed the boundaries for women in extreme sports. She is the first swimmer in the world to swim a mile from the Pacific Ocean to the Atlantic Ocean, in the Drake Passage, and the first Irish swimmer to swim 1,000m at 0 degrees (as well as the third woman in the world). Nuala was awarded the Frank Golden scholarship for her work on cold water safety education. She founded the Ocean Triple R, a water safety initiative for sharing information around messaging. She has been listed three times in the World Open Water Swimming Association's list of top 50 most adventurous women in open water swimming and twice shortlisted for the World Open Water Woman of the Year.

LIMITLESS

FROM DINGLE TO
CAPE HORN, FINDING MY TRUE
NORTH IN THE EARTH'S VASTEST OCEANS

NUALA MOORE

Gill Books

Gill Books

Hume Avenue

Park West

Dublin 12

www.gillbooks.ie

Gill Books is an imprint of M.H. Gill and Co.

978 07171 95886

Designed by Bartek Janczak
Typeset and print origination by O'K Graphic Design, Dublin
Map illustration by Derry Dillon
Edited by Rachel Pierce
Copy edited by Alicia McAuley
Proofread by Sally Vince
Printed and bound in Great Britain by CPI Group (UK) Ltd.
This book is typeset in 11.5/16.5 pt Adobe Garamond Pro.

The paper used in this book comes from the wood pulp of sustainably managed forests.

A CIP catalogue record for this book is available from the British Library.

5 4 3 2 1

CONTENTS

Prologue: Bearings   vii

1   The Source   1

2   King of the Hill   14

3   Seven Frogs and Clydesdales   27

4   Taking on the World   37

5   A Unique Expedition: The Round Ireland Swim   48

6   Treading the Maelstrom   94

7   Criss-Crossing the English Channel   108

8   Trough   120

9   The Donegal Ice Mile   139

10   Breaking the Ice: Tyumen   154

11   Making the Call   175

12   Digging Deeper: Murmansk   200

13   Unifying Nations: Swimming from Russia to the USA   216

14   Letting Go, Taking Hold   258

15   Journey to the End of the World: Tierra del Fuego   282

Epilogue: True North   307

Acknowledgements   322

PROLOGUE

BEARINGS

'I am that quiet place, the centre of the maelstrom …
The dangerous abyss, where few dare to tread.'
Virginia Alison

My breathing was heavy – laboured, even. As I knelt on the floor of the inflatable boat, I could feel a sense of panic starting to rise. My eyes fixed on the dark, iconic headland of Cape Horn. The Sailors' Graveyard. So remote.

My swim hat and goggles on my head, the cold wind stripped what warmth I had from my body. The movement of the seas was frustrated and excited at the same time – three oceans mixing and meeting, racing around the world without resistance from any land mass. At this point in the world, there was no land either east or west. I was about to expose myself to the wrath of the Furious Fifties and lower my body into the notorious Drake Passage.

Closing my eyes tightly, I tried to visualise my swim. I rotated my arms and calmed my breathing. *This is why you are here.* My mantra played in my head. My mind flashed to the sacrifices I had made to get to this point, but mostly to the privilege I had of being here, of being strong enough to take on this swim. I was the first swimmer in the world to do so.

If you can't breathe, you can't swim, I told myself. *So, breathe.*

I inhaled and calmed myself a little. I tried to close down my world to this moment only.

The fishing boat took a wallop from a rogue wave and the Zodiac, the inflatable boat, jolted as it was slapped against the side of the fishing vessel. We all fell forward, grabbing the ropes from the side of the tubing. I could sense the team's urgency, but I was not ready to let go.

The water was darker than I had imagined and bitingly cold, but it was the size of the waves that was upsetting me. I searched to find a pattern, some movement in the water that would allow me to see its intention, but there was none. Just undulating waves, coming from all directions at once. Some breaking, some billowing and then swirling. I wished I had more time to study their movements.

The reality of my swim was not matching my plan. How could I swim without my team close by in these conditions? What if I panicked and couldn't get my breathing right?

Adan Otaiza Caro, the Cape Horn lighthouse-keeper, had indicated over the VHF radio that my command boat would be a few hundred metres away, because of the size of the swell. My skipper, Roni Olivares, also insisted that the safety team could not accompany me with the small Zodiac.

The uncertainties of this swim were now huge.

I felt the fear of letting go and not making progress, the risk of being tossed backwards and twisted by the waves, vulnerable to its power and failing to cross the meridian between the oceans. I wondered if I should have taken the swim from lighthouse to lighthouse instead, which would have been certain progress. I was scared of going home having failed.

I stared high into the headland, which was a few miles north of us. I had chosen to swim the meeting of the oceans, this far south – not for glory, but to find that person inside of me who was willing to risk everything. If the team and crew were to lose sight of me while I was swimming, with waves breaking and flipping me in another direction, in 7-degree water, with 4-metre swells of rolling ocean, the question would no longer be whether I would make land, it would be whether I would survive. I could stay alive for two hours at most in these conditions. The sense of fragility, of vulnerability – those weaknesses that I had trained and worked so hard to push away – was creeping back in.

This is why you are here, the inner voice repeated. *You are on the cusp of your own greatness. Breathe and trust yourself.*

You only have to swim and stay alive.

Keep breathing.

Look what you are capable of.

You are built for this.

I tried to block out the feeling that this was a risk too far.

Suddenly, the tears welled up. I was glad I had my back turned to the crew. Loud words fell from my mouth.

'What am I doing here? I have to be home for work on Monday. Maybe I'll take the easier option and swim closer to the headland.' I could not figure out how I could make progress in this ocean.

Catherine and Chris, my dive-safety team, were kneeling inches from my face, watching me.

Catherine said firmly, 'Nuala, you have to go now. We've got you and you can do this. Trust us.'

'Tell me again how you will get me out of the water.' My eyes darted between Catherine and Chris. 'How long will it take you to get to me if I need help?' I was asking for the tenth time.

The fishing boat had its engines in neutral. We were tied to the side, suspended. I could hear Roni's voice. I don't speak Spanish, but I understand urgency: we were bobbing with the engines ticking over, at the mercy of three oceans, all fighting for freedom as they raced excitedly around the world. These rogue waves could topple the boat and land us all in the water. I knew the vessel needed to get her engines started. She needed to gain control.

Catherine replied in a stern tone, 'Look at Chris. He is ready to go. We will not take our eyes off you, but you have to get into the water now. The wind is changing, and our window is closing.'

I wiped away the tears, still hiding my face. I lowered my goggles over my eyes. I now had just two tiny windows to see out of.

'Steady your ship and drive into the storm.' My father's words fell from my lips.

I turned to look at the iconic headland of Cape Horn bearing down on us.

'Please give me passage,' I said.

With one last intake of breath, I lowered my body into the dark, ferocious waves, maintaining my death grip on the rope.

Seven degrees is a battle even in calm water; in rolling oceans, it's an entirely different story. My breath was ripped from me as I tried to conquer the cold shock.

When I let go of the rope, I will be alone. The boat will have to steam away to gain control. She will disappear in the waves. I will be at the mercy of this water, this wind, my own weakness. I am the storm. I am the challenge.

I looked up at the crew. Three albatross circled above my head, their wingspan greater than the length of my body.

'I know why I am here,' I said, with a breath that was now broken and ragged.

Catherine stared into my eyes, stern. Chris had the same stare. Silence.

'Let go, Nuala. Let go,' her voice repeated.

The Zodiac banged against the timber side of the boat, bouncing from side to side. With all my will, I struggled to uncurl my white fingers, knowing that once I let go, I would be alone in the Drake Passage, the most dangerous and volatile body of water on the planet.

I had to let go.

THE SOURCE

'It may take courage to embrace the possibilities of your own potential, but once you've flown past the summit of your fears, nothing will seem impossible.'
Michael McKee

I pinched my nose and squeezed my eyes shut. The beach seemed so far away. *Why did we say this far out? I'm the youngest; I've never swum this distance. What if the boys don't wait? What if I can't swim that far? The water is really deep. What if I panic, or drown?*

Stop it! I screamed to myself. *If you cry, Dad won't let you swim to shore.* I put a huge grin on my face, the kind I put on to pretend I was fine, mainly because showing any fear or tears could mean being told I couldn't do it. *You're too young.* I was always too young.

Today I was nine years old, and I was going to jump into that crystal blue water.

Focusing on the castle, I jumped up high. I hit the water so hard it felt like I was sinking for ages. It was deep. I could hear the bubbles. I kicked my legs and put my arms out as if grasping for the blue sky. I opened my eyes. Everything was blurred. The salt water stung my eyes, but I was determined to get to the surface. My cheeks were bursting from holding my breath.

Keep smiling. Don't panic. You can do this.

I turned around, gave a big thumbs-up to my dad and started my slow swim to the beach, which now seemed like miles away. The small, choppy waves were mountains in my vision. I stared at the stone tower high in the sky, at the people standing at the bathing box (a concrete structure built in the 1900s for ladies to change in because the main beach was men only at that time). I reached out with each stroke, as if pulling it all towards me.

Behind me, standing on the side of the boat, was Gerard, our neighbour's nephew, who spent summers in Dingle. I heard him jump. The splash was followed by shouting from my father.

'Nuala! Nuala! Come back! Gerard! Hey! Grab the tyre.'

I flipped over on my back and lifted my head to see my father, two arms holding the boat hook, reaching for Gerard's arms, which were grasping at the air, directionless.

No, no, no, no! was all I could think.

I screamed at the boys gone on ahead, but my voice was lost in the distance. I turned back to the boat and focused hard on Gerard. At this stage, he was closer to the boat and seemed to be okay. Should I go back or forward? I was half afraid that, if I looked at my father, I would be in trouble for bringing a friend who couldn't swim.

He was shouting at Gerard, who was now panicking. He caught Gerard with the boat hook, a long pole that he used to pick up ropes for lobster pots. A seasoned fisherman is always accurate with a boat hook. In that minute, Gerard, his curly hair draped over his face, wrapped his arms through the black car-tyre fender, holding on for dear life. I tried not to show any emotion as I breaststroked towards him in case Dad took us both out of the water. He was angry. We were always supposed to check if our friends could swim.

'I thought you could swim!' I screamed at Gerard, deflecting my father's anger and doing my best to ignore his frozen stare and his clenched mouth, recognising the accident that might have happened.

'I can,' a squeaky voice replied. We were both more afraid of looking up at my father than the challenge of the deep sea and the waves.

'I got a fright. No one waited for me. You were gone.' Gerard was shaking from the experience. We didn't tell my father that Gerard had never jumped off a boat before.

'Come on, swim with me to the beach,' I said as I grabbed him by the arm, pushing my feet off the timber side of the boat. I shoved him ahead of me into the water. He was 13 years old, but he didn't live by the sea, so I made allowances for him.

'We'll be fine, Dad,' I said with a big smile, as my legs worked hard underwater to keep me up.

I turned to face the beach. The boys were standing on the sand, staring back at us. I was tired, but there was no way I was going to get back onto that boat and miss my day. Getting Gerard to shore was a better plan.

'You'll be fine. Just keep heading for the castle.'

I started slowly beside him, convincing him he could make it to the shore, all the time praying I could swim the long distance myself. I could hear the engines of the *Bridget* as my father prepared to leave, so I relaxed.

It was only fear of the deep water and being left behind by the group that had frightened Gerard. About five minutes later we joined the others, the sand clearly underneath us. Once we were all together, everything was forgotten. That day, pushing Gerard the whole way to the beach, changed so much for me. I realised that not everyone had the same experience as we did. I also gained the confidence to look beyond what I was capable of when I needed to. I needed to get Gerard to shore; I needed my father not to realise

I was afraid; I needed to be strong. And I was strong because I was more afraid of being told to leave the water than of facing my fear.

The engines revved and the *Bridget* steamed away out the bay, rounding the head. We watched her get smaller in the distance. In a few hours, she would return to pick us up.

Our Sundays in summer were all about this trip to the beach, while my father went mackerel fishing out in the bay. The boat was a 30-foot timber fishing boat with the wheelhouse up front. It was painted blue and named after my mother, Bridget.

My father was a fisherman, as were the rest of my family on both sides. The sea has always been a way of life in our family. As a very young child, my job was to sit at our back window for hours, watching, and tell my mother when my father's boat came around the headland so that she could put the dinner on. Then we ran to the pier to carry his bags home and help him tie the ropes. Catching the ropes on the pier as they were thrown from the boat was such fun. I could never tie the knots, but I could hold the boat until another fisherman or my father got up the ladder.

As children, we spent a lot of time in and around boats on the pier at Dingle. Some children were not allowed on the pier, but it was our playground. We jumped from boat to boat, pulling ropes and helping unload boxes. My mother would not tell my father that we jumped from the pier and swam around and through the islets. The fear of being given out to and stopped was far greater than any fear of the risks.

The *Bridget* was a small vessel, so she was always tied outside a line of larger boats. When the larger boats came in, the fishermen would untie the vessel next to the *Bridget* and slot into position, so that a smaller boat was never closer to the pier than a larger boat. This prevented damage. Sometimes it meant our boat was five or six boats out from the pier. We loved pulling the huge ropes, feeling the strength of dragging five or six huge vessels, often falling on our bottoms on the concrete as the huge line of boats drifted towards us on the pier. These were the jobs we were given.

Once the inside boat came close to us, we jumped fearlessly from one boat to the next, always from bow to bow, using the handrails as guides. Sometimes we climbed up high ladders, holding our bags, never dropping anything. This was considered a thrill, one that would be viewed as highly risky today.

Our beach, where we all swam as children, was beside a working harbour. Dad always told us to stay on the rocky side of Sláidín Beach, the east side, the side of the lighthouse. We had been warned to stay away from the 'channel' on the west side because this was the deep area where the boats travelled in and out of the harbour. Dad would bring the boat to a stop and point out the deep, running water where the trawlers travelled in from fishing.

He always gave the same warning: 'If you swim out here and get caught in this flow, you will get swept around the point to the Crow Rock, and you won't get back in.' Getting swept away was always a huge risk. 'I can't see you in the water under the bow of the boat when I'm in the wheelhouse steering her in. So don't come over here.' He always spoke in a tone and manner that made it clear a response was not required.

As the summers passed, I swam out further. In a small town like Dingle, the older children always minded the younger ones on the beach. We would all go there together as a group. I tagged along into the water, too, and the boys always ignored me, hoping I would go away. Around the headland is another beach called Beenbawn, past the lighthouse, an area my father warned me not to pass, but we would walk there every day and swim from the beach. Past the lighthouse, the water is deep, making the tides very dangerous for swimming.

One particular day, the boys decided to go swimming around the headland. My brother told me to wait on the beach. I nodded and sat down on my towel, abandoned. I watched like a prisoner planning an escape. I stared at the rhythm of their arms as they pushed out into the glassy sea, their bodies moving forward silently, the reflection of the green cliff grass clear on the surface of the water. Five heads, staying close to the rocks on the cliff side where it was calm, passing the bathing boxes. They all stood on the rocks and chatted for a minute. Sometimes I could hear a few voices. I waved. I hated being left behind.

They started their swim to the point. They had practised this swim for many weeks, taking it in stages. Often, I used to walk to the lighthouse and look down at them in the water, to study the rocks they sat on, where they could hold on. I knew that once they turned at the lighthouse and headed to Beenbawn Beach, the water changed. Knowing they would not look back; I decided that today I would sneak into the water after them.

I was 10 years old.

I paddled over to the bathing boxes and moved with the silence and secrecy of a snake, hiding out of view. I could not see them, and they would not see me after they'd rounded the first crop of rocks. I was clear for now.

I swam to the bathing boxes every day. No one on the beach paid any attention to me, a young girl going out into the water on her own, because this was what I always did.

I pushed my arms out and eased myself along. The sun was shining on the water. There were jellyfish and I picked up some stings, but I was afraid to scream. Once I passed the crop of rocks, I could see the boys in the distance ahead, near the lighthouse. They were sitting on some other rocks, so I had time to catch up. My plan was to be as quiet as possible. I was nervous.

I knew if I could get to the lighthouse without being spotted, the boys would not turn back with me – by that stage, Beenbawn Beach would be closer. One of the swimmers was Tom Long. He was our next-door neighbour, much older than me, tall, with huge shoulders and very strong. He could do the butterfly stroke. We all thought Tom Long was the best swimmer in the world. I knew he would save me if I needed help.

When the five heads turned by the rocks at the point of the lighthouse to swim towards Beenbawn, a shout went up. They had spotted me. The water was no longer calm. I took in some gulps of water and a few waves hit me in the face and took my breath away. This was why I had been warned not to come here. I was working hard, doing a mixture of doggy paddle and crawl. I was panting from trying to catch them but trying to smile. I wondered for a second if I should get out, climb onto the rocks at the lighthouse and walk back, but I didn't want to. I was so proud of myself. I wanted to see if I could make it.

From over the cliff face, I could see the silhouette of Paddy the Lighthouse – local man Paddy Ferriter from Beenbawn, who lived in the lighthouse. He was staring down at me. His cap covered his head, and his pipe was, as always, in his mouth. Leaning on the wire, he waved down at me. I waved back.

It was scary, rounding the point. The bright sun was beating down on the water and it was hard to see with the glare. *What if I hit a current? Is this where Dad said I would get swept around?* I was halfway there, swimming like a puppy, arms rotating and legs kicking, keeping my eyes on the cliffs in the distance.

Then I heard the shouting. It was the boys.

'What are you doing? What if you drowned?' one voice yelled.

I could tell they were not happy. 'Hold on to that rock,' another shouted at me.

'I can swim,' I said firmly, trying to hide the fear in my voice. I grabbed hold of the rocks.

'You can't swim out here,' another said.

What am I going to do? Give up? It's only swimming, I thought.

It never dawned on me that I could not swim well enough. *What do they mean, I can't swim out here? I'm here.* I really hated being told that I was too young, or that I wasn't able to swim that far. I was not turning back.

'We're not waiting for you. You'll have to keep up,' a voice said, not happy at having a young girl at the back of the group.

Once we left the rocks at the lighthouse behind and headed to Beenbawn Beach, the water was different. The cliffs on the other side now seemed far away, so small in the distance. I was very tired, and my mouth was full of salt water. I knew I was in trouble, but I was used to being in trouble. The boys started to go far ahead of me. At one point we had to leave the cliff and swim out in the middle of the water to get to the beach. I looked down into the deep water. It was dark blue, and I felt like I was on the edge of a huge hole, a great abyss. I looked to the sky to find a point on the other cliff to swim towards. I followed the heads in the water and, once we were close to the beach, the waves began their roll to the sand. We loved riding the waves so, once we got close, we all surfed our way to the sand.

There were so many friends on the beach, watching us. I felt so important. I started running back through the fields in my bare feet, in my swimming togs, while the boys were talking to the others on the beach. That was over 40 years ago, but I can still picture myself looking down at the rocks, knowing that I did it. I would never tell them how scared I had been.

I called out to Paddy, who was still standing at the gap down to the rocks. This was where he watched the boats go by and always made time to talk to us all.

'You're some girl.' He smiled, lifting his pipe from his mouth.

'Thanks, Paddy.' I smiled back at him, and my bare feet bounced through the grass, my hair drying as I ran across the fields, back towards the other beach, where I could see my towel on the sand.

The total distance of that swim is no more than 700 metres, but as a child, it felt like crossing the infamous English Channel.

Once we all got back to Sláidín Beach, we sat and ate our sandwiches filled with jam and bananas long since blackened by the sun. Hours later, despite our bodies being purple and blue with cold and hunger, we made our way home, the setting sun slipping from the never-ending sky.

Around that time, there was an ad on television for Bovril. It was promoted by Wendy Brook, who was shown swimming the English Channel. It was night-time. Wendy covered herself with Vaseline and drank this thick, brown liquid. I was sold. I convinced my mother to buy me Bovril. It was a horrible, thick, gravy-like drink, but I drank it each day. I took a jar of Vaseline to the beach and, despite not knowing why, I put it on my face and legs and started to plan to swim my 'channel'. My father had said that the place where the trawlers came in and out of the harbour was called the channel. I would start there.

I did cross my channel that summer. It was a short swim and my father sat in the boat while I did it. I was 11 years old.

A swimming race at the Dingle Regatta, at the pier. I was 12 years old. The wind was blowing hard, and the rain had turned the sea to a murky brown. It looked horrible, with seaweed floating on the surface of the dirty water. My eyes were riveted to the pier wall as the three of us were driven out for the swim start. No one asked how far the race was or whether we could swim. It was the first time they'd hosted swim races at the pier.

The engine went silent.

'Jump!' was all I heard.

I leapt into the water and started plodding for the wall. There was seaweed all over the place, my hands striking it, my hair getting tangled in it. I'm not sure if I took a breath, but I kept going for that wall. The distance was no more than 150 metres, but the feeling of excitement when we finished was as if we'd summited Mount Everest. We were all clapping, holding on to each other as the waves beat us against the concrete pier. I know I was nervous telling my father and mother about it that evening, admitting that I'd jumped in off the pier, but they were so proud of me and my shiny trophy. I still have that trophy; such is its importance to me.

One day in 1982, when I was 14 years old, our childhood was made all the richer when a fin appeared close to us when we were swimming at Beenbawn. A huge shadow of grey moved under the water, broke the surface and jumped again, so close to us.

'Shark, shark!' were the screams, as we climbed over each other to get to the rocks.

People on the beach stood up and stared. Shouts and panic filled the air. Then came the words 'dolphin', 'porpoise'.

The shadow appeared to follow us. The fin was the length of an arm; the body was twice the size of any of us and so shiny. It was a dolphin.

As we walked home past the lighthouse, we decided to drop in. Paddy was sitting on his chair by the stove, the cat beside him. What I loved most about Paddy was that he wore his white Aran jumper inside out, to save the clean side for the days the tourists came. Today, it was blackened by the stove fire.

'Paddy, did you see the dolphin?' we asked.

He lifted his cap back on his head, took out his pipe and looked up at us.

'Sure I know. 'Tis I that spotted him a few weeks ago, coming and going to the harbour. He's following the boats in the evening. He's resting over in that cave.' He pointed to the entrance across the channel.

Our eyes opened wide.

'He was here, swimming with us?'

'He was, following you around. Sure I was watching him. That's why I was watching you – he followed you to Beenbawn the last day. He was right behind you, Nuala.' There was a huge smile on his face. We were so excited. Our very own dolphin.

'See you tomorrow, Paddy,' we called, and we ran off home.

Fungie the Dingle dolphin had arrived to fill our summers, to fill our lives for the following four decades. Swimming daily with Fungie was such an amazing privilege. For me, his presence, his bubbles, his grace, his patience and his beauty were the forces that carried me through the longest and darkest swims in the winter. Sláidín and Beenbawn remained my places, where dreams were born and where life was reasoned through.

The sea was a way of life. It was where we played, and where we learned to understand the risks that life presented to us. It was where we learned to be able to ask for help.

I was exposed to the sea's dangers, living in a fishing family where discussions often centred on boats and lives being lost. Even so, when storms occurred, the boats continued to fish. My father often told us about the events of 1961 – Hurricane Debbie – which, to him, was a 'bit of a breeze'. In 1939 my grandfather Ned Moore took a timber boat from Dingle to Killybegs, County Donegal, where the Moores began their fishing lives and where I was born. My grandad on the McGowan side was also a seafarer.

The sea is where I have always found my peace. That feeling was there from the start. I remember being told, in an effort to dispel my curiosity about the birds and the bees, that I had been discovered floating into the harbour in a scallop shell. This image remains cemented in my mind and to me it has always accounted for my passion for the sea. Never a petite child, the whole concept of the stork was far too romantic and impractical for me to believe, but the notion that I was of the sea felt right and true.

My mother insisted that we completed every water-safety course, every sea-survival course, all the training available. We learned how to take off our jeans in the water, make floats out of our clothes and tow people, and do resuscitation and CPR. I had every certificate. Some courses I completed twice, even the senior ones. My mother insisted it would give us confidence. The greatest lesson it ever gave me was never to underestimate the power of the water. Looking back, I can see that my childhood training prepared me for an amazing sea journey.

I remember, as a very young child, the sinking of the trawlers the *Evelyn Marie* from Killybegs in 1975 and the *Carraig Úna* off Rathlin O'Beirne Island in 1976. I remember the feeling of loss in the community. As a young child, I knew all the victims' names. Families I had met, crews my people on both sides knew well, had lost members. My mother and father never sheltered us from the risks of the sea, but being exposed to that sense of loss was one of the greatest teachers. Accepting the danger was a way of life, but deep inside we held that respect. Each day my family and the rest of our coastal communities returned to their ocean.

In my early 20s, I trained as a member of the Irish Coast Guard Dingle Unit. The need to be prepared to rescue was always embedded in me. If I could help anyone, I would have the skills. Very early on I completed a coxswain's course to drive the rescue RIB. We worked on areas like casualty recovery and cliff removals, controlling the rescue boat on the transfers of casualties from inshore RIBs to the RNLI vessels, which I loved – that race against time. I always trained for all outcomes. I trained to be strong in the presence of fear and worked for many years in the rescue services.

My mind has always screamed *I'm nearly there* as opposed to *I can't do it*. I believed in myself even back then. Those experiences of my youth taught me to trust myself and gave me a gut instinct to embrace risk and danger. I think there was always salt water in my blood.

The sea is a way of life. I was born to it.

2

KING OF THE HILL

'You can keep going and your legs will hurt for a week, or you can quit and your mind will hurt for a lifetime.'
Mark Allen

Living in the south-west of Ireland, in the Dingle Peninsula, cycling long distance was an enduring passion of mine. I cycled the 40 kilometres around Slea Head several times a week and took part in the annual 120-kilometre-long Ring of Kerry cycle challenge. It was just how I spent my spare hours. The freedom of the open road and our countryside. The wind in my hair as I enjoyed the rolling coastlines. Combined with my love for the sea and swimming, it led to a yearning to give a triathlon a go.

I had read a book called *Iron Will: The Triathlete's Ultimate Challenge*, in which Mike Plant talked about the beginnings of the Ironman Triathlon, and it fascinated me. I felt that, with my background in swimming and cycling, it would be a good transition to make. I always believed I could do an Ironman Triathlon. Or, at least, I could try. I was invited to take part in the 2002 Chicago Triathlon, in a fundraising team. This was the world's biggest triathlon, hosting 7,000 athletes. Without a thought, I signed myself up.

The first thing I did was to purchase a new bike for racing.

Secondly, I thought entering a triathlon event close to home would provide a good focus before I travelled to Chicago. I had never done it before, but I viewed myself as a strong athlete, so it was only a matter of putting three sports together.

In July 2002 I registered for the King of the Hill Triathlon in Kinsale, County Cork. It was a sprint-distance event – a 750-metre swim, a 20-kilometre cycle and a 5-kilometre run – half the distance of the Chicago event, which was five weeks away. The Kinsale triathlon was part of the Triathlon Ireland series, an event that involved a technical course of hills and challenges. The plan was to try out my new racing bike and find out how a triathlon worked. My swimming was my strength, so for me, this was all about finishing and learning from the results.

I drove down to Cork the night before with Tania, my friend from Tralee. When we arrived at registration, as I collected my race packet, I was asked for a previous finish time. I joked that I hoped I'd finish before they took down the bunting. Silence. Sensing they were still waiting for an answer, I replied, 'This is my first triathlon. I have never competed before.'

The woman looked at me.

'No one chooses the King of the Hill as their first event. This is a Triathlon Ireland series event and there are points for competing. It's not for first-timers.' She wasn't being dismissive, just matter of fact.

The athletes milling around looked very fit. I have a good level of confidence, even a bit of cockiness at times, but I felt intimidated by my surroundings. Suddenly I was filled with doubt.

'Thank you,' I said. I was only here to try.

The following morning at the car park, a field between the beach and the road at Kinsale, the activity was manic. The sound of triathletes on turbo spinners and the vibration of the static training devices cyclists used to warm up filled the air. Standing there with my bike, I was frozen. *What do I do? Where do I put my bike? How do I organise my area? What do I wear for swimming? How do I get to my bike after the swim? What do I eat?* There were so many issues that I had not thought through. There was no camaraderie and no direction, just athletes focused on winning. In fact, the more I questioned myself, the more I thought, *What am I doing here?* I was strong but I had never been lean. I didn't look anything like these athletes.

The transition area was where we put our bikes. Beside the bikes, the athletes laid out all their things in their own special ways. Some had a small towel and on it, they placed socks in shoes, a T-shirt and a pair of shorts. Their helmet was attached to the handlebars and in the helmet lay sunglasses, a bandana and sunscreen.

I looked around and realised two things: first, the laying out was to speed up the transition from swim to bike, and second, the key thing was for everything to be visible and easy to pick up.

I chose a space and lifted my bike onto the rack. I laid out my stuff on a towel, all the time watching the people around me and trying to mimic their organisation.

I thought about the tyre pressure and put exactly what was needed into the bike tyres. I wandered down to the beach, the sand soft underfoot. I memorised the route to the field and had a good look at the swim course. It was only 750 metres. I looked at each of the buoys from different angles, so that I could visualise my route, but it was so short I knew it would not cause me any difficulties. There were 126 entrants, and they all wore wetsuits. Many were already in the water, rotating their arms and warming up. I was the only entrant on the beach in a set of swimming togs. Tania was with me all the time, convincing me I would be fine.

Competitors entered the sea to start to acclimatise their bodies to the water temperature. I was quite content to breathe in and breathe out and save my energy for what I would be doing later. I was glad I could not see myself because I could feel every pore exuding fear and doubt.

I heard that other voice, the one inside my head that got me here, saying, *I'm not here to race. I'm here to learn. It's okay to mess up. There is no such thing as losing, just results we learn from.*

I had been training using the three sports together for three months. I was a strong cyclist and a fast swimmer. I could understand the theory of triathlon. I had read the books and watched the videos. I had spoken to a few people. Now I had to present myself as a competitor.

I wandered over to the race marshal on the beach and asked, 'Shall I go in at the back of the group? How do we go around the one yellow buoy? This is my first event.'

He looked at me in disbelief and said, 'It's a running start. It's a race! Everyone runs in together.'

My eyes turned back to the yellow buoys. They were so small in the distance. I could not understand how that was going to work.

The triathletes were now all out of the water, and we gathered close to the marshalled area. The whistle blew: the race was on.

Over a hundred athletes ran together, splashing, arms moving in all directions.

It was an out-of-body experience. Caught up in the crowd of rubber-clad bodies with the momentum of a wave, I felt like I was in the Pamplona Bull Run. We were all vying for the same inch of water. There were bodies moving over me, slaps flying, and I couldn't think what to do. I was in survival mode.

The concept of controlled breathing was gone. This was sheer physical intrusion. The inner voice screamed, *This is your turf! This is your rough water and you're bigger than this. This is your battle. The swim is what you are good at. Get yourself out of this mess.*

I was physically strong in the water and, when bodies tried to swim over me or give me a slap as they swam by, heck, there was no wanting in me. I looked up and decided to swim outside the group, to find some clean water, as we call it, adding to the distance but making for a better swim. I pushed hard and swam to the beach. This was the fastest I'd ever swum, and I was so proud I was in the lead group. We entered shallow water. Getting my feet under me wasn't easy, but I was upright and moving.

Running up the soft sand to the transition area, my legs were wobbly. I couldn't get my breathing back on track. This is why people avoid standing up quickly after swimming. I was lightheaded. I could have trained for this if I'd known about it. I almost fell twice on the way up the field. People I'd passed in the water were running by me now. You don't tend to forget the faces of other athletes as they run past and look at you. Something in that glance stays in your mind. *Do I look defeated?* It's a question you ask yourself, of course, but it is very different when you see it in the eyes of others.

I found my blue and yellow bike. Then I had to figure out how to start the cycle. I really had not thought this through. I got a towel to dry the salt and sand from my body and change into my shorts and top. Athletes ran past me, jumping on their bikes, water dripping from their triathlon suits.

One athlete shouted, 'What are you doing?' as he ripped off his wetsuit, running at the same time. He didn't wait for an answer.

What about chafing? I wanted to scream at them. *Should you not change into dry underwear?*

I held up my towel and, right there in the transition area, I took off my swimming togs and put on my underwear. The other competitors ran past me in utter disbelief. I thought I was doing the right thing. I had never once considered the notion of cycling with my swim togs on, nor had anyone suggested any other attire for swimming. Shoes and socks on, I was finally off, just as two slow swimmers were making their way up to their bikes. At least I was not last.

There was a wonderful group of marshals on the bike course, and they gave such support. I smiled back at each of them and thanked them. The road out of the transition area to the bridge was uphill straight away. My legs were a ton weight and wobbling like jelly. The cycle was gradually uphill for 10 kilometres, so I stood on the pedals and tried to get some momentum. I began crying because I felt so weak and because I couldn't go any faster. But I knew it wasn't about the fitness – it was about the mind. Everyone else was so fast; I had not trained to race. Trying to steady myself, I said aloud, 'There's no going back.'

I managed to get into a rhythm. I had trained on so many hills at home. I closed my mind to my surroundings and visualised the Conor Pass, a route I had cycled so often. That was 6 kilometres of a tough uphill, and this challenge was just a little further.

At the 10-kilometre turnaround, I was feeling brilliant. The struggles were behind me, the wind in my face as I headed downhill. Only 3 kilometres to go, but something felt wrong with the way the front tyre was going around. Suddenly, *bang*. I got a puncture. I couldn't believe it. I couldn't fix the puncture and, even if I quit now, I still needed to get back. The only choice was to run the remaining distance down to the transition area with the bike. I began the slow job of jogging while holding the handlebars of my racer. I burst out crying. A voice inside asked, *What's with the crying? How weak am I?*

I was beginning to see that crying and sport were not compatible. It is so hard to cry and think at the same time. Anyone who has ever had a tantrum will know that they take a lot of energy.

Now was not a good time! If I was ever going to get control of my breathing, I needed to stop crying.

I screamed at myself. *There is no medal at the end of this, no certificate and certainly no one who cares about it more than you. Do this for you!*

When the transition area came into sight, I got so excited. The faces of the people I'd left behind an hour ago were still there. I was so happy, but then I saw that some of the people who'd started this race with me were packing up their bikes. The clapping people at the finish line were applauding competitors as they came to the end of their run. I was only finishing the bike leg.

I threw my bike on the ground in the transition area and my body followed it, pride denying me another crying fit. Muscles aching, frustrated, angry and confused, I sat there.

'You are well able to finish this. Loads of runners are out on the course.' Tania was leaning over the railing, trying to convince me to keep going, to push myself through the last section.

'For what? Why would I want to get up now and run-walk-crawl another 5 kilometres? The other triathletes are all finished, and I haven't even started the run. I'll be mortified,' I replied.

Inside, I was thinking, *If I stand up now, all these people will know that I hadn't yet finished the race. If I sit here, they will think I'm finished.* I did not recognise this fragile, insecure person I had become.

Why would I embarrass myself by continuing? Being accepted as a triathlete, at that moment, meant being equal to them. Instead, I was thrown to the ground, half-finished.

'Will these people remember you next week?' Tania said, trying to get me going. Probably not, but would I remember that I quit? Most definitely. I had no reason to worry about their opinions of me. This was about my own standards. I always finished.

I stood up. I was going to finish. Tania smiled as I walked past her.

I started my walk up the hill for the second time. *Just 5 kilometres and this is over. You only have to walk out to Beenbawn Beach and back again. You do this every day. Don't make it more than it is. It's only a walk.* There was nothing difficult about it, except for my embarrassment as I passed the race marshals and remaining supporters.

One lady smiled and said, 'You will love yourself if you finish.'

I smiled and said thank you.

There were very few athletes left out on the road. I started jogging, then walking, not breathing because, once again, crying had taken over and everything was now foundering in anger. I was not as fast as I thought I was. I had envisioned this being a much easier event.

Triathlon was not for me. It was so hard to jog when it felt like the event was over. I grimaced, gasped and pumped my legs up that hill. I tried to remind myself that I didn't need any applause. I could clap myself on the back any day and a medal, if I wanted to have one, would cost all of €2 in a shop. Being out there on my own, with only 3 kilometres to go now, became personal. Strangely enough, as I plodded on, I started to jog slowly, and I got a small but effective momentum going.

I arrived at the 2.5-kilometre turnabout, now only visible by a mark on the road. All the marshals were gone. There was evidence of a water stop, where a hundred athletes had jogged by long ago and grabbed water as they raced. Now, just a sign remained.

I could have cheated and turned a few metres short of the mark. I didn't. I went to the exact spot, despite being there alone. I turned by doing an exaggerated circle. Giggling to myself, I was nearly there. Suddenly I raised the tempo. I was able to jog and sing. I think this was the first time that I really understood that the mind is the main obstacle to progress. My legs moved once I understood that it was possible. Training can't help much if the spirit is weak. With a small smile, singing to myself, I looked down the hill. There was the large clock with the finish tape. I was last in the field, but I was also swollen with pride. I should have driven the route last night, to find out where I was going. Maybe that would have made it easier.

An older man shuffled ahead of me. Like me, he was struggling to cover the last 50 metres. Further ahead were his supporters, urging him on. I decided I couldn't pass the man. Where would be the glory in that? I stood in the ditch until he came close to the line and then I made a dash for it as if I had a huge reserve of energy.

Crossing a finish line has different meanings for different people. Some athletes do it for points. Some do it for money. Some do it out of obsession. I was doing this for fun, but it was not fun. I realised that being self-conscious about how you look when you are competing is the enemy of achievement. *Are they thinking I'm not fit enough?* I was thinking. *Or that I don't fit in?* I did not fit in. I did not look like any of the other triathletes. I had no idea how to compete on their level. How could I enjoy anything when I was worried about so many things? The person I was that day worried me. I was doing it – I had finished it – but my concerns about how I looked had taken so much energy from me.

As I crossed the finish line of my first triathlon, the tears welled up in my eyes – again. It was a relief to be still standing and a very proud moment. Tania was waiting. I was a big hero in that moment, both to my friend and to myself. I had done it at my own pace, but the point was that I had done it. The lady who'd wished me well was still there too, ready to take my timing chip.

'Aren't you proud?' she smiled again.

I nodded.

'Are they all gone home?' I asked because I could see only two bikes left in the transition area and five cars left in the car park.

'They're all gone, but you're fine. This is a fast race,' She smiled as she took my timing chip from my ankle. I was officially last.

I nodded and walked to the transition area. Tania and I gathered my bike and other things into my car. We were the last car to leave. There was no sign left of there ever having been a race.

A 750-metre swim, a 20-kilometre cycle and a 5-kilometre run. My entire sprint triathlon was 1 hour 40 minutes. That time would be so acceptable today, but 20 years ago coming in after 1 hour 40 minutes meant that the banners had already been rolled up and the transition bars removed. It was an elite sport.

From then on, my training for Chicago took on a personal element. The physical side of the triathlon was not my obstacle. Dealing with the mental and emotional side was going to be the real test. I needed to create a sense of belonging, to figure out how I could fit in.

Standing at the starting line of a race is a battle when you believe you don't fit in. I had trained but, without the feeling of having the right to be there, I felt shrunken and embarrassed. I didn't look like an athlete, but I was certainly strong and athletic. I had covered the exact same route as everyone else. How could people like me get a start in triathlon?

To win this war, I would have to conquer the enemy within. I needed to figure out how to beat my weakness, and how to compete. During the following weeks, I trained to be better between the bike and the run, dropping the bike at the Skellig Hotel and starting to jog out the three fields, even for five minutes. I practised standing up from the swim and running back to the beach. They were small changes, but they were giving me confidence. I would be better in Chicago.

I learned so much from that first triathlon. I accepted that defeat was a momentary thing and that winning was personal. I was so strong when I was cycling, and I could run when I felt I was close to the finish. The King of the Hill changed me as an athlete and shaped my future in sport. Coming home afterwards, I had so much to think about, but I had one certainty: I was not going to carry this feeling. I would create a path forward. I would figure out how to fit in.

Six weeks later, as planned, I arrived in Chicago with the team representing Our Lady's Hospital for Sick Children, Dublin. My next triathlon challenge was double the distance: a 1.5-kilometre swim, a 40-kilometre cycle and a 10-kilometre run. An Olympic-distance triathlon.

Somewhere in my mind was the thought that the longer the distance, the more time I would have to steady myself. I would need time. Distance was not my enemy, speed was. This event would be, first and foremost, about finishing. I felt that would help take the focus off my time and put the emphasis on the event itself.

I was part of a team with everything organised for us, which was a welcome change. I met amazing triathletes like David Adams and Miguel Gernaey, all great fun. A few days before the race, Dave brought us around the swim and run routes. He spoke about the need to train, to visualise the run route, to know when challenges would occur, and to keep hydrated. It seemed so much easier to take on the race when we could visualise it, all the turns and loops. Had I driven the run and cycle routes in Kinsale, it would have been easier for me. I still had not figured out how to change out of my swimming togs for the bike, so I decided to do the cycling and running in my togs and just pull up my shorts over them. I was a lot more comfortable in the longer events.

Chicago put all thoughts of King of the Hill out of mind. I passed the finish line in 3 hours 30 minutes, still wearing my swimming togs. My 10-kilometre run was a walk, but my 40-kilometre cycle and 1.5-kilometre swim were excellent. I was so proud. The team were waiting at the finish line with the Irish flag, clapping like maniacs for everyone. This was the sense of belonging that I loved.

Watching world champions and Olympians complete the event in under two hours was magical. Barb Lindquist was the first professional home, and it was unbelievable to me that we had completed the same course and that she was beside me. I walked straight over to her and asked for a photo. She obliged with a smile, as I unwrapped myself from my Irish flag and placed it in front of us. How I wished I had put on a T-shirt! I was standing there in my swimming togs and cycling shorts, chatting with one of the best triathletes in the world. I explained it was my first international distance event.

'Any tips?'

She smiled as she held on to the Irish flag, then turned her petite frame towards me and said, 'You got to lose the belly for the bike and the run to be faster. Still, your time is good. If you race as a Clydesdale or an Athena athlete, there are records to be won for you.' A wink and a smile. I smiled back.

It didn't seem realistic to believe I could ever be a runner, but her words, 'there are records to be won for you' were ringing in my ears. My 40-kilometre cycle only took 1 hour 30 minutes, and my swim was 19 minutes per kilometre. I was still losing time on transitions and the run, but I had improved so much. My time was strong. What was a Clydesdale? Or an Athena? I had to find out.

I spotted a bright yellow tent with loud music blaring from within, and inside was a festive atmosphere. I had found the Clydesdales. A group of larger athletes were milling around. It turned out to be an athletic association for triathletes and runners, in which athletes competed within weight categories. The colossal banner of triathlon records hanging on the wall, showing the ages and weight categories, gave me a huge sense of excitement. I could compete in the weight category of 180 pounds and over, giving me a 20-pound cushion. I could enter the 200-pound category, but I had dreams of losing weight. Nothing sharpens focus more than a deadline. A man walked by wearing a T-shirt that said, 'Caution: Wide Load'. I smiled.

I studied the banner again, thinking I was mistaken. My age group and weight category showed a time of 3 hours and 43 minutes as the present world record. I had just competed faster than that. I was shocked, but then I was invigorated. I walked forward and registered as a member there and then. I could visualise my name on that banner. I could have a world record.

Returning to Dingle from Chicago, I remained energised over the following weeks as I researched and developed training plans. I started cycling and running, swimming and cycling, training to be faster between each of the disciplines. Triathlon was a sport that demanded intelligence. Chicago had filled my mind with new words, like 'commitment to the outcome', 'enthusiasm', 'persistence' and 'determination'. It was the first time I realised I could be breathless and keep running. Before, when I became breathless, I stopped. I felt like I had never really challenged myself before. In Ireland, most athletes, at least those taking on Olympic-distance triathlons, were lean and muscular. It was hard for me to connect with those people. In Chicago, I saw top-tier athletes who looked like me.

I was going to be a winner.

3

SEVEN FROGS AND CLYDESDALES

'Our limitations and success will be based, most often, on our own expectations for ourselves. What the mind dwells upon, the body acts upon.'
Denis Waitley

I was very reluctant to re-enter the Triathlon Ireland series after my experience at King of the Hill. I was genuinely afraid to have another negative experience, especially now that I was in a really good place emotionally after my experiences in Chicago. I knew what I had to train for – the Clydesdale national event – and I knew how to train, so I set my own goals.

There were so few triathlon events for athletes like me. I always viewed myself as competitive, and I was certain there had to be more athletes who just wanted to be better, to find a way into the sport, to be accepted and to race in the Olympic distance event. I realised there was nothing for it but to become a race organiser.

I decided to create my own triathlon race. I wanted to offer an ethos similar to our swims, where it was fun based, and show others how it is possible to succeed in the body you already have.

I spoke with many friends, sold the dream, gathered some willing competitors who could swim, cycle and run, and in June 2003 I organised the very first sprint-distance triathlon in Ventry, County Kerry. We were happy to figure it out as we went along, to have a good day out. No medals, no expectations.

The morning of the triathlon, my friend Maryann and I stood on the beach with sheets of paper and stopwatches. I drew maps of the routes and briefed everyone. The local gardaí had been informed of the event and many had volunteered to marshal. In total, we had 28 competitors.

The sun was shining as we walked back to the beach, Maryann holding the rope and buoys and me carrying a concrete block to create the swim route.

'I think here is fine,' I said. I walked into the water and threw the block to the seabed, then repeated this 750 metres away. Swim route decided.

The bikes were all at the car park. Our cycle was 20 kilometres to and from Dingle and the run was an easy route to Cuan Pier. It was a group of athletes having fun. Some were fast, some were not, but everyone finished and enjoyed the sandwiches and soup and, more importantly, applauded each other.

The funniest part of the day was watching my friend Mags O'Sullivan propping up her fold-up chair in the transition area, taking out a bottle of water and a small dish and washing her feet. Her excuse was that she could not cycle with sand between her toes. She wasn't trying to win. She was happy to finish the event a triathlete.

That was the beginning of the annual Seven Frogs Triathlon (named after the Seven Hogs, the Maharee Islands off Dingle, which happen to be home to the natterjack toad). My aim had been to show that we could compete in an environment without judgement and still achieve. Sometimes the best version of ourselves sneaks up on us when we are not paying attention.

The success of Seven Frogs and the anticipation of competing in a Team Clydesdale event had me completely fired up. I turned into a tireless advocate for the sport of triathlon. I was convincing so many people that triathlon was a sport for everyone.

Over the winter months, I spent a lot of time answering emails and meeting people who were thinking of starting to train for the triathlon but didn't know how to go about it. Everything I had learned in the Chicago triathlon, I was sharing. I decided to risk organising the first Olympic-distance triathlon event in County Kerry. Even though I was not a particularly accomplished triathlete myself, people had confidence in me.

I love to log my workouts. I was never going to be fast, but I charted my plans. I created tough cycles with easy runs and easy cycles with tough runs. Mostly, I worked on my transitions. I had a huge appetite for information on nutrition, physiology, training models and how to not get injured. My friend Maryann, herself a strong cyclist and runner, agreed to travel to Chicago with me in 2003 to compete in her first triathlon. She was not a swimmer, but that was her challenge.

We trained so hard over the winter, doing 40-kilometre cycles over and back to Inch Beach, cycling through Dingle, dropping our bikes over her garden wall and then running 5 or 6 kilometres. In spring, we were cycling 40 kilometres around Slea Head in 1 hour and 20 minutes. We parked the car in Cuan or Ventry and jogged to Dingle town, having left water bottles in ditches in case we needed fluids. Our goal was always to run 10 kilometres inside an hour.

That June, I organised the second Seven Frogs Triathlons at sprint and Olympic distances. Word had spread and this time I had over a hundred athletes competing. It meant so much to me to have so many people sign up and trust my event. I contacted every single one of those people on the phone or by email. I explained the process, the transition area, what to do, how to excel, and mostly how to enjoy the event. Strong triathletes also came to support our event. I wanted them to inspire the beginners to achieve.

We didn't have a timing clock, as they were too expensive. Instead, I had six volunteers with sheets of paper, charts, stopwatches and race numbers. The work involved was horrendous. I had to calculate each person's time by adding together all the race times for their swim, run, cycle and transitions, divide the results up and make charts and then contact every single athlete with their total. But the event was a huge success. I was creating a triathlon for people who just wanted to find their way into the sport in a supportive, non-judgemental environment.

In our own triathlon training, Maryann and I never once talked about how hard it was to cycle 40 kilometres followed immediately by a 10-kilometre run. We never thought about the hardship, about being wet and cold in the wind and the rain. We thought only about how wonderful and how brilliant we had become. Training was always fun. There was pure excitement that we had become athletes. We were so prepared for Chicago.

It was August 2003. Finally, Maryann and I were in the lobby of the Hyatt Regency Chicago. My heart was filled with so many emotions. This year felt so different. It was my third triathlon, and I was excited.

There was a field of 7,500 triathletes. You could sense the dreams that were on the cusp of becoming reality. I genuinely thought I was fast enough to win my category, though I did not tell anyone that. There was such a huge sense of occasion – so many supporters, people wearing T-shirts emblazoned with the faces and names of their friends. For the first time, I felt I wanted to compete.

Once in our room, the time had come to open the bag and check that my bike had survived its maiden journey. First, the frame. Hanging from the body, very neatly taped and heavily wrapped with packing, were the gears and the chain. The back wheel and the front wheel were both flat. The saddle was in a bag. The pedals were lying loose in the bottom of the bag. The handlebars were twisted so the bike could travel. Pieces everywhere.

Now what was I supposed to do?

After about three hours, with spanners and Allen keys and help from Dave Adams, a fellow competitor from Pulse Triathlon Club in Dublin, Maryann and I were wheeling our bikes to the lift to get them checked by a bike mechanic at the Expo. I was once again with a lovely team from Our Lady's Hospital for Sick Children, and everyone was so helpful, all stepping up to help those of us newer to the sport. I met with Ian Claxton and David Ward, two triathletes from Dublin. Ian was a swimmer and, as we talked about open water, I discovered that he had represented Ireland competitively. His smile was infectious.

The professionals had their own stand, where they gave inspirational talks and answered questions. I pulled up a chair and sat there for hours, listening to Barb Lindquist, last year's winner, who had finished in under two hours. She looked at me for a long moment. I felt she remembered me, as her eyes came back to me again and again. Many other professional triathletes also took the microphone. It was surreal to listen to their stories of the Olympics and the World Championships. The atmosphere was electric. I told Barb that I had registered with Team Clydesdale. She smiled and wished me luck.

The truly exciting thing was that Team Clydesdale was using the Chicago Triathlon as its national triathlon event. The following year they would hold their World Games in the city. I was in a spin at the thought of competing in a US national event. The downside, though, was that it had attracted many more entrants than usual. There were 24 women in my category.

The next step was to weigh in. I had entered the 180-pound-plus category and I weighed in at 210 pounds. Despite all the training, I had gained weight. This meant I would only be competing against women 30 pounds lighter than me. My heart was racing with excitement. It was at that exact moment that I vowed I would return the next year to compete at the World Games. I would train more seriously next year. I would lose weight.

Back up in our room, we practised pulling off our new wetsuits and running out of the bathroom into the hallways, falling once or twice.

At 3.30 a.m., my alarm clock beeped, and I lifted my head. It was race day.

The plan was to meet in the lobby at 4.15 a.m. Dawn was creeping in as the sun slowly rose over Lake Michigan. The streets were lit up with the voices of thousands of vivacious people, carrying their equipment, all streaming down to the transition area on Lake Shore Drive, a short walk from the hotel.

Volunteers were using black markers to write race numbers on muscly bodies; people were turned away at the gate if they had forgotten their timing chip. Maryann and I had decided where to put our bikes in the allocated racking station. I moved my bike up the rack, looked at it and moved it down again. I laid out all the other pieces I would need: towels, race numbers and helmets, which had to be attached and clipped before leaving the transition area. So much to remember. I was aware that, once I left the area, I would not be allowed back in until after the swim.

We practised locating our bikes. We would be amidst 7,500 other athletes, who would be running from all angles. It's one thing being able to find the exact spot where your bike is after the swim, and quite another finding the same spot after the cycle, and then finding the right place to start the run.

Three hours later, the sound of the race was electric. With all the clapping and cheering, it was like being in the centre of a Mardi Gras parade. There were bangers, flags, deckchairs, and masses of people lining the routes, holding up banners of support for their loved ones. It was all much more exciting than the previous year.

The swim was a deep-water start, with 150 people jumping into the lake every 5 minutes. Supporters were screaming, 'Don't give up!' at those already swimming. I started clapping to encourage one man, who was close to the wall, hanging on for dear life. It was quite emotional to see the effort these athletes had to go to when I took the swim for granted. Thinking of the fears they were overcoming made tears well up in my eyes. I was proud of their efforts in the face of real risk.

It was important to position ourselves in our group so that we were where we needed to be. Too far back and I wouldn't be able to pass the slower swimmers. Meanwhile, the fastest swimmers from the group behind us would be trying to get around us or over us.

Despite all the waiting, the start came quickly. Waiting in the water for the buzzer in my group of 150, I focused on my route. I breathe to the left, so I planned to go as close to the rope as possible and not allow anyone on my inside. That way, I would always have an air pocket to breathe. It was all the strategy I could think of in the moment. Knowing my speed, I started to breaststroke to the top of the mixed group of men and women. Many were unhappy as I continued to propel myself to the front. There was some rough pushing. I closed my eyes and wished for the clear, open beaches of the south-west of Ireland, where no strategy was needed.

With the rope to my inside, the buzzer went. I couldn't regulate my breathing. I felt a body rising on my back. A swimmer was climbing over me. Each stroke brought him higher up and pushed me further down. I had to slide to the left and allow him to fall off my back. If he went fully across my body, he would kick me in the head.

I braced myself and thought, *If I kick harder, it will make it more difficult for swimmers to climb up my back.* My feet connected with a few faces, but better that than my own face being pushed under.

I tucked in behind a swimmer who was right in front of me, and we swam in tandem. I reached for the feet wiggling and breaking bubbles, making it difficult for any swimmer to come between us. The person's toes led me to believe it was a woman. Once the first 1,000 metres were over and we turned at the buoy, I slipped to the inside and made space for myself to make a sprint for the finish line.

Arm over arm, I scrambled for the steps. It was a deep-water exit, where volunteers reached in and helped pull you out. A lovely lady reached in and caught both my hands. I pulled to get out of the lake, but our balance was off, and I pulled her over my head into the lake. I could not believe what I had done. I turned to apologise, but she surfaced, fully dressed and laughing.

'Go, go, go!' she screamed through floppy hair.

I ran off, slow as a prisoner with two ankles shackled together, such was the weakness in my legs. Eight hundred metres later I headed into the transition area in search of my bike. I pulled off my wetsuit and felt a sense of elation when I found it.

The 40-kilometre cycle was easy – four loops of Lake Shore Drive. I forgot my water bottle and therefore had to stop to take some water from the marshals along the route. I gave the bike everything and imagined myself racing around Slea Head. I had such fun counting down the four loops.

I checked my time coming off the bike into the transition area: exactly 1 hour 30 minutes. I was so happy. I could take a few minutes to sit down and drink a good amount of liquid. Even if I walked the run, I was inside the fastest time on the wall. The pressure was off.

Sitting down was not the best idea, it turned out, because when I stood up again my legs seized up. No matter. A gulp of energy drink, a sports gel in my pocket and I was away again. This was where the suffering began for me: leaving the bike behind. I ran in between the hundreds of supporters lining the route.

'Looking good, 4194!' a voice shouted out.

'Keep it going – nearly there!' said another.

Even though my head wanted to droop, even though I was feeling tired, it was impossible not to be energised by the crowds, each one of them taking time from their day to help us through. I took some little walk breaks in the race, just to give my legs some recovery time. I was in the middle of one of those breaks when a woman came jogging alongside me.

'Will you run with me for 5 minutes?' she asked.

'I'm not able to. This is only my third triathlon. I'm happy to walk – this is my strategy,' I replied.

'I'm here for you. Just take a few steps with me and we can finish this together. Five minutes of your time. You're doing this!' she added, as if she had not heard me. She was an angel runner.

I started to stumble forward, in my mind jogging the three fields at home. I took in the scenery and thanked all the volunteers who praised me. I was so proud of what I was achieving. As I approached the last kilometre, I remembered the challenges of the previous year's finish.

Take a quick break for one minute. Get your breathing under control. Make sure your race number is hanging cleanly in front of you so the race commentator can identify you and call out your name. Hold up your head, shake out your hair and smile, because somebody will be taking a picture of you. Maybe you're a winner – so, no matter how tired you are, find some energy. Put on your biggest smile.

The Irish team and Maryann were standing at the finish line, the tricolour flying high. I crossed it. Done.

Ian Claxton came over with some drinks and a banana. Ian was a speedy triathlete. I was so proud as I stood under the fire hoses to cool down. I was not exhausted, just elated. I was much stronger than I believed.

I had won the US National Championships in my Team Clydesdale category – 180 pounds and over, Olympic distance. I had come first.

I was a winner.

At the presentation ceremony, all I could see was the time on the wall. It was 20 minutes faster than the world record for my age and weight category. I turned to Guy East, the president of Team Clydesdale. Guy was a very tall ex-triathlete with a huge smile.

'If I win next year, Guy, will I have a world record?' I asked, just to be sure.

'Yes, Nuala. You can have your name on our wall, but you have to win first. It's lovely to have international competitors,' Guy replied.

There was no stopping me as I walked back to the hotel, draped in medals saying 'Winner' and holding a trophy with 'National Champion' on it. All I could think about was the lure of the gold. I was going to be a world champion. And I was going home to convince even more people that triathlon was the sport for those of us who wanted to achieve within our own limits.

4

TAKING ON THE WORLD

*'Our deepest fear is not that we are inadequate. Our deepest
fear is that we are powerful beyond measure. It is our light, not
our darkness, that most frightens us.'*
Marianne Williamson

The chairs were placed in a semicircle in a suite in the Hyatt
Hotel. I sat quietly. Now that the Team Clydesdale World
Games 2004 had arrived – and I was actually here – I felt excited
and confident. I was about to race in the Athena weight category in
a world event. The atmosphere was all about achieving, about being
the athletes we could be in the bodies we had.

'Is there anybody here who feels that they could break a world
record?' Guy East, the president of Team Clydesdale, opened the
question to the room. 'Tomorrow we are hoping that there will be
several world records broken in different age and weight categories,
so raise your hand if you feel one of these records has your name
on it.'

My arm shot up in the air. It was an instinctive reaction. I
knew it was possible for me to be faster than the world record, but
I had not intended to tell the world. Thankfully, many others also
raised their hands.

Guy passed the microphone around the room to those of us
with our hands in the air.

One lady, a supreme athlete in her youth, had gained 60 pounds. She wanted to compete again. There was a rapturous round of applause for her. A gentleman, there with his son, spoke of a life of drugs left behind and how the two of them were now competing together. There were harrowing stories of illness and how sport had allowed a wonderful journey back to health.

Then the microphone was handed to me as the eyes of the room smiled at me. I didn't have a story of rising from the ashes. I hadn't anything prepared.

I stood up slowly and the words poured out. I talked about my competitiveness and my personal need to achieve, how I felt finishing the race and completing the same course as every other competitor and how we had to redefine winning. I talked about how, when I am racing, I believe I am so much faster, sleeker and fitter than in reality, that when I close my eyes, I see a very different body from the one I'm living in. When I race, I feel so competitive. I want to win for me, even if I don't line up with the sport.

The applause started. They loved my accent; they loved my honesty, and I got the biggest cheer. I grew a thousand feet taller. I was not being judged. I was being supported. Others had accepted me, and I had accepted myself.

'Nuala, you can be the athlete you want to be in the body that you have today. Everyone here is a winner because you have all taken on the challenge. You have chosen to start.' It was a tall, athletic man speaking directly to me. He was a member of the US Olympic triathlon team and an ambassador for Team Clydesdale. I smiled. He passed around his medals from the Sydney Olympic Games. My eyes were swirling as the shiny pieces of metal dangled in front of me. I was invigorated. He was right, and he was speaking to my soul.

'Could everyone who thinks they could break the world record please step up for a photograph and weigh in?' Guy continued, and the queues began to form. I joined them, smiling at the other women in my weight-category line, who all seemed quite athletic. So many people wanted to break the world record.

'Hi, my name is Courtney. I'm from New York.' She reached out to shake my hand. 'This race is mine. I am going to whip your ass!'

This woman was in my category and age group. I stood there, transfixed at the thought of having an adversary. I had only ever competed in three triathlons in my life, and I was still not a runner. What had I done? Why did she want to whip my ass? I had trained to beat a time. I had only thought about beating the time and getting a medal. I had not entertained the idea of beating another triathlete.

It was my turn to be weighed. I was 200 pounds in the 180-pound-plus category. Courtney weighed in at 181 pounds. She deliberately weighed into my category so that she could beat the world record. She was 1 pound over the minimum weight level. She probably ate her way in.

'I trained to take this world record,' she told me in her confident New York accent. 'I look forward to beating you.'

With that, I walked away.

The biggest challenge of travelling to any triathlon is ensuring the bikes make it safely. Maryann was with me again and we were trying to reassemble our bikes. Maryann's husband, Frank, had packed her bike and seemed to have a better system than mine. Her bike, except for the handlebars, was intact!

I looked at mine, in pieces before me. Why did my bike shop do this to me? Not even a diagram. *Okay, I can do this.* I was excellent at jigsaws as a child. I was certain I could put it together, albeit nervous that it might fall apart during the race. First, I put on the wheels, saddle and pedals and twisted the handlebars. Yes, everything was looking great. A bike is built in such a way that there is only one option for each piece. But a problem could occur if I damaged the thread of the screws by forcing the action. At this point, I had lifted out the chain and the gear derailer onto the luxury carpet, which I had dutifully covered in plastic.

After three hours, two cups of tea and a lot of laughing, our bikes were assembled, but we decided to do a final test by taking them for a spin in the hallways of the Hyatt Hotel. We cycled up and down the carpeted corridors of this lavish hotel, a mix of exhaustion and jetlag making us laugh hysterically. Time to bring the bikes downstairs and check out the symposium.

The elevator door opened. Inside were three other athletes with their bikes.

'We'll wait for the next one,' I blurted, mostly out of fear that there wouldn't be room.

'Not at all, ladies, there's plenty of space,' said a very fit, smiling American guy. He lifted his bike up on its back wheel and reversed into the corner.

My face reddened.

'Okay,' I said through a forced smile, well-practised from years of working in the tourist industry. I lifted my blue bike up on its back wheel and manoeuvred it into the tiny space, followed by Maryann and her white bike.

'Are you ladies getting your bikes checked or taking them for a ride?' a friendly American competitor asked us.

'We just assembled them for the first time, so we're making sure they work,' Maryann replied.

We all smiled.

I listened to the athletes' chat as we descended to the lobby. The words 'less resistance', 'more fluid', 'time-saving' and 'aerodynamic' were being bandied about. Downstairs at the symposium, the courtesy and helpfulness of the triathletes and suppliers were overwhelming. After an hour of passing up and down the Quintana Roo bike stall, I finally got the attention of a nice gentleman. Without a moment's hesitation or a whiff of judgement, he turned my bike upside-down and started spinning the wheels, running through gears that I had never seen before. He went through all the different tests and complimented our bikes. We bought two wetsuits from him as well as a bag.

The race was 48 hours away and now, instead of merely getting to the finish line, I knew I needed to push harder than I ever had before. The word had spread through the group that the woman in the queue had challenged me. I was being teased incessantly. My vision of winning was being disrupted by visions of Courtney. The more I saw her circulating at the hotel, the more I went into a tailspin.

We cycled the run route with David Power from Waterford and his Microsoft teammates. I was super-vigilant, watching for landmarks by which I could identify turns and water stops. David had a T-shirt saying 'HP'. I wasn't sure if that meant 'higher power' or 'horsepower'. Either way, it meant he was fast. I wished I'd thought of a T-shirt.

'Know your race objectives,' said David. 'Write the times you want on your thighs. Break down the 40 kilometres on the bike into 10-kilometre loops. If you can keep ahead of or close to your goals, you'll stay focused.'

I worked out the times I needed to achieve to win. That way I could push harder and keep track of my progress. A great tip.

The evening before the race, Maryann and I set up our morning transition area in the bedroom. I had accumulated so much new equipment at the symposium, I now had to figure out what to do with it.

Whatever came next, we were as ready as we were ever going to be.

At 3.30 a.m. the alarm clock woke me up. I looked over at the bed beside me.

'Maryann, why are you holding your cycling helmet?'

'I got up 30 minutes ago and thought I'd get dressed and be ready,' she replied. She was fully dressed in her shorts and T-shirt, lying there in the darkness.

We burst out laughing. We were so excited for race day.

'It would be great to be beside each other so we could monitor each other,' Courtney said, placing her bike next to mine in the transition rack. It was difficult to remain calm. 'When we get out of the swim, we'll be able to see who is ahead,' she said with a smile.

I had come to race, but not in an aggressive manner. I'd never tried to beat any particular person in my life.

Maryann, who was listening nearby and who is by nature very calm and collected, walked over to me. I had grabbed my bike, deciding that I would move it away from Courtney.

Maryann put her hand on my handlebars and said, 'Rise to the challenge. Courtney is only trying to aggravate you.' We walked away.

We counted trees, trying to memorise where we would go running in during the race, but also where we would come running out with our bikes from the opposite direction.

Maryann and I decided to go back to the hotel for a breakfast of porridge, toast, fruit and a lot of goading from the guys, who were sure Courtney would let the air out of my bicycle tyres. It was 5 a.m.

'Come on, you are nearly there! Keep your head up!' a woman screamed at a swimmer who was struggling in the water. It was energising to remind ourselves of the beauty of this sport – everyone trying their hardest, with their own limits.

It was clear that these swimmers were barely capable of the distance, but they were never going to admit defeat. Their belief was stoic. Swimmers, overwhelmed by the occasion, were scattered on their backs, trying to float their way to the finish point, but not giving up. Their chins stretched upwards to the sky; they were breathing and closing their mouths, moving their arms and legs in jerky movements, using up every ounce of their energy trying to reach the finish line.

'And you think *you* can't swim?' I reminded Maryann, who until three months ago could not do a mile with a front crawl and was still only learning to put her face in the water.

We were standing in the holding pen, waiting for our swim to start. Four minutes to go. My peripheral vision was suddenly invaded by a face that brought my heart shooting up into my mouth. I felt nauseous, my breathing was laboured, and I started to sweat. Courtney had come into my personal space.

'Best of luck, Nuala,' she said.

I was numb. The only response I had was to give her a big hug. I was so relieved to jump into the lake and start my race. Thirty minutes later I cleared the water and jogged towards the transition area in the blistering sunshine, energised by the thousands of cheering supporters.

I was stunned when I spotted Courtney's bike hanging where she'd left it. I had beaten her out of the lake! I felt a huge pressure to go faster at a moment where I could barely stand up. But I owed it to myself to push as hard as I could.

I had 2 litres of water, a carbohydrate drink and a power bar.

Once on the bike I sipped all of the liquid and ate the bar, pushing my body the 40 kilometres up and down Lake Shore Drive, monitoring the times on my leg for every 10 kilometres against my watch. It was very scary experiencing bikes whizzing past at huge speed, all the time shouting, 'On the right!' I was slightly nervous about moving out of my lane, but I dearly wanted to overtake another bike. I wanted to shout, 'On the right!' myself. My legs burned and my feet hurt from pushing the pedals, but it was so much fun. I decided to indulge in a little bit of Meat Loaf and sang 'Bat out of Hell' at the top of my voice.

The road surface was so fast. With 5 kilometres left, Courtney went flying past me. I could see her face.

Entering transition, I dismounted and ran with my bike towards my slot. I followed the vibrant colours of a helium balloon that was tied close to my bike. As I approached my space, I saw Courtney on the ground, looking tired and sweaty. I acted cool. With my sweaty red face, I started to dream of a medal. Why was she on the ground, and could I win? The pressure hit me like a ton of bricks. She looked at me and said, 'You smoked me in the water. You're a great swimmer.'

I smiled as I readied for the 10-kilometre run section. Courtney picked herself up off the ground and I watched as she waddled out of the transition area. I have no idea why but, looking at her, I decided I could beat her. I was not a runner but, from what I could see, neither was Courtney. I took a few minutes and gathered my mind. Did I want to win? Was there another woman out there who could beat either of us?

I picked up my body, drank more water, put a few glucose sweets in my pocket and walked off. I decided to begin slowly. The run route was crowded with supporters, all clapping to push us on.

'Good job!'

'Looking good!'

I kept thanking everyone as if they were talking just to me. I started my slow shuffle, running from the knees down, red, sweaty and swollen from the heat. How I wished I had trained more for the run! Despite the self-pity, I remained focused on Courtney, still ahead by about half a mile.

Damn your competitor! Stop looking – you're not a runner! I screamed at myself.

A lady at least 30 pounds heavier than me jogged by. She was not graceful, but she was fast. There went my theory that weight was my biggest obstacle. I decided I would tag a runner in front of me and pretend I was at home. My legs were burning, and my breathing was wheezy.

The balls of my feet were swollen; there was a burning sensation as each foot hit the ground and the cramps were setting in. The next minute, an Adonis-like body in little Speedo swimwear was running towards me on a return run loop. Despite feeling it was wrong to be running with so few clothes on, I was excited by the vision.

'Hi,' I said, and he smiled.

I started to panic because I could no longer see my challenger. *Never take your eyes off your mountaintop, Nuala.* Where did she go? I needed to track her. My legs ran away with me, and I suddenly felt possessed. Courtney's body appeared ahead at the 4-kilometre mark, walking as if she had nothing left. Had she given it all to pass me on the bike? Was she done?

I hobbled up to her and told her not to quit. She asked how I was feeling. I decided to try and talk to her. I didn't have to lie or pretend. We chatted. She was very low in energy. I was exhausted too. We had already been racing as fast as we could for over 2 hours and 30 minutes, in 30-degree heat. But finishing meant more than pain. I discovered that, when the pain reached that level, I just accepted that it couldn't get any worse. I was so glad we had cycled the run route the day before. I knew my landmarks.

'Good luck,' I said, starting to pull away with the grace of a hippopotamus doing a ballroom dance. I turned under the bridge with 500 metres to go.

I was ahead of Courtney, but still not aware if I was first. There were thousands of people lining Michigan Avenue, a massive fanfare. There were athletes running by me, but I was managing to pass people who had stopped dead. I burst out crying. I had been swimming, cycling and running for 3 hours 20 minutes now. The last 50 minutes had been surreal. I tried to give it a burst of speed like they do on TV. Bad move. I seized up. My body went into one big cramp. Then I heard 'Nuala Moore, Ireland' over the loudspeaker. I started waving like a lunatic.

I saw the Irish team with the tricolour. My eyes picked up Guy East, standing at the finish line with a camera, giving me a thumbs-up. I had won my category. I had come first in the World Games. I had broken the world record by 23 minutes.

Courtney crossed the line 16 minutes after me. She didn't see me, and I didn't make myself known. Secretly, I knew that if I hadn't had an adversary, I would never have pushed myself into the Twilight Zone. There were so many angel runners, people who ran alongside us but weren't in the race themselves. They were purely there to talk to anyone who was slowing down or who wanted to stop, to get them going again. This was the way to race. There was so much to learn from it. Maryann had a great race too and we celebrated into the evening, excited by the potential for the future.

The professional athletes also ran the same course, starting hours after us, and I witnessed the world numbers one and two finishing. They completed the same course in 1 hour 57 minutes.

How we view ourselves and our goals is so impo Winning for me was very different than for the next person. I was so enthusiastic about the future of my events. Sitting with David Power, I was all smiles. I thanked him for his advice and invited him to race in my Seven Frogs Triathlon. As the night progressed, we laughed because, despite the fact that he had completed his race 50 minutes faster than me, his medal said 'Finisher' and mine said 'Winner'.

That finish line showed me that I had a choice. I could go into the serious athletic world, where I might never be accepted, or I could work within my limits and try to push forward. I could accept that I did have a weight issue and be honest and realistic about it.

I committed to creating a pathway for others to race. Four weeks later, in Castlegregory, David and his friends came to race my Seven Frogs Triathlon, as promised. The numbers had grown to 200, all chasing their dreams. I was now mentoring triathletes, some going on to national events, facilitating dreams without judgement. My goal was to allow people a way into the sport, and I was doing that. What they did beyond that depended on their own path.

The Seven Frogs Triathlons brand was born. Between the open-water swims and the triathlons I was organising, I was hosting and mentoring hundreds of athletes, helping them all to be the best version of themselves and to find value in the bodies they had. The 'nualamoore' brand was born. I had redefined success.

5

QUE EXPEDITION:
UND IRELAND SWIM

'Whenever feasible, pick your team on character, not skill.
You can teach skills; you can't teach character.'
Ranulph Fiennes

The Round Ireland Swim 2006 was planned as an 800-nautical-mile relay swim, but it would become so much more than that. It would be an expedition and an unprecedented adventure, as pure as adventure could be, in that it would be the longest ocean swim ever undertaken by open-water swimmers in water temperatures as cold as those around the Irish coastline.

The marine perimeter of Ireland is roughly 800 nautical miles (or 1,482 kilometres as the crow flies) but we would probably swim twice that and more. The plan was to swim a GPS coordinate measured route of 20–25 miles of open water each day as a team. We would travel out to a selected point by boat, drop into deep water and swim in a clockwise direction. The back-to-back immersions in water this cold would be a constant challenge. The expedition would demand huge amounts of passion, expertise, trust and humility, as well as the ability to quickly reassess and change plans and, perhaps, to accept defeat. The fact that we were even attempting it was thanks to a strong team who all believed it was possible.

We were a team of six main swimmers, the command-boat skipper, a dedicated marine-rescue unit, a marine coordinator, a head of safety, a communications team and a land operations team. We had a command cruiser vessel and three Zodiacs. The daily logistics would involve the allocation of Zodiacs – three RIBs, the *Rachel Marie*, the *Dive Áine* and the *Abhainn Rí*, each with a dedicated marine unit – by the Marine Coordinator, Derek Flanagan. The marine-rescue units were divided into four groups: Alpha, Bravo, Charlie and Delta. They would operate for one full week each, with a changeover every Sunday.

The command vessel, the *Sea Breeze*, captained by Brendan Proctor and a marine team, would carry Henry O'Donnell, the expedition leader, who would also take part in the swim. The majority of our swims would be up to 10 miles offshore, to avoid many of the tidal flows and currents and give us the straightest line, even though this would increase the overall distance we had to cover.

As we faced into 18 months of team training for this monumental task, our focus was on being strong. I adopted a motto that would hold true throughout: *You can only swim the water in front of you, so dig deep and remember that every swim is only arm over arm.*

In reality, it was impossible to plan for the journey ahead, which only added to the excitement. How do you plan for an expedition for which there is no blueprint? No one had ever swum the mileage or undergone the same back-to-back cold-water immersions in the time we were planning.

As the Round Ireland Swim got closer, I found myself going to the sea for comfort, to think. One evening in April, on Ventry Beach, as the sun was setting, my fingers struggled to grasp my thermals in the car park, after a two-hour swim.

An accented voice asked, 'Is it cold? What are you training for?'

I turned to face a tanned, composed gentleman, speaking to me through the half-opened window of a rental car.

'I'm part of a team planning to relay swim around the island of Ireland. Just doing a bit of cold-water training.' Balancing precariously to get my socks and shoes on, I explained the distances involved.

His smile was never-ending, but at first, I didn't know if he was smiling with me or laughing at me.

'It's a big commitment. How do you balance your life?' His steel-grey eyes were fixed on mine. I could see a warmth in his eyes now, an understanding, something that forced me to engage despite the cold shivers I was now experiencing.

'Are you an endurance athlete?' I asked. 'Endurance' was my new buzzword.

'Suppose you could say that. I've done Deca Ironman. I've done ten Ironman Triathlons back-to-back over two weeks,' he said, quite nonchalantly.

My jaw dropped. I had read about these athletes. The distances are a 39-kilometre swim, a 1,867-kilometre cycle and 10 marathons – that is, a 422-kilometre run – over 14 days. This unassuming man was one of the most elite distance athletes in the world. The challenges these athletes seek are beyond understanding, bordering on the insane. They do not know pain – not pain as we mortals would acknowledge it, at least. He looked so human, so normal. I was suddenly energised.

Think of questions! I heard a voice inside my head screech. *Don't let him leave. Get in the car with him. Think. Think!*

He trained 4 to 5 hours a day while still working full-time. He would only compete at one or two events a year and considered the training part of his day as much as work. I was nosy about his relationships and how they worked, but I didn't cross that barrier. I could not get my mind around the 1,867-kilometre cycle and then ten marathons one after another.

'If you're on a bike for a thousand miles, running is a pleasure,' he said with a wink.

I was in love with his enthusiasm. This was the energy that I wanted, the excitement that I needed. Curious, I asked how he made himself continue through the distances.

'I take it mile by mile. The bike is a break from the water and the run is a break from the bike. For you, the boat will be a break from the land. The swim will be a break from the boat and the silence will be a break from yourself. It's completely up to you. What a great opportunity. Use it wisely.' I really wanted to get into his car so that he couldn't leave. 'What are your risks?' he went on. 'I hear swimmers have died from hypothermia. You have a super crew, I bet?'

I had not yet talked about the risks. We discussed his experiences hydrating during his long swims. It was like attending a talk, like he had been sent to motivate and encourage me.

'It's fuel and recovery, fuel and recovery,' he said. I knew that already but, hearing him say the words, now I knew it in a different way. 'Don't expect your body to ignore the signals just because you decide to ignore them. You have to be your own fuel light. Know yourself and your team.' Learning to trust was vital.

We chatted about options, stomach upsets and recovery. It was his eyes, his piercing grey eyes, that got me. There was a devilment in them, a certainty of who he was and what he was capable of. A true feeling of power oozed from him, a look that did not acknowledge the fear of failure. I wanted that look in my own eyes.

I bombarded him with questions, mainly because he had been deep inside his own mind multiple times, in the place where we were going but had not been before. I couldn't believe that this was all happening in a car park, a random meeting.

His greatest gift to me, though, was when he spoke about the huge opportunity I'd been given. I would have to meet the real me. I would get to know myself and see my worth to myself. He said that events like this are a mirror for the soul.

'You're going to hit some major lows, and getting through the lows leads to the real highs.'

'How do you cope when you break, in pain?' I stumbled over the sentence with the awkwardness of a teenager trying to impress. I could picture his body contorting in agony, muscles seizing in spasm, still with three marathons to go.

'You will need to be stubborn. You will need to bundle up all your negative energy, all your doubts, and put them out of reach. Your mind can be your biggest enemy and logic is not your friend. Hey, I watched you in there. Look at you now – it's freezing but you're not shaking.' He pointed at the now-dark sea. The wind had lifted, and the sound was fierce. He smiled as I grasped my cold, empty cup.

'Pain doesn't matter. It can't matter – it's only cold,' I replied with a smile.

'It's wonderful to meet you, awe-inspiring. I'll keep an eye out for you. You'll be fine,' he said. 'You got this.'

He shook my hand with a grasp that was so strong and so prolonged, I felt it for hours afterwards.

How I wished I could take him home with me. There was no substitute for experience. We had a lot of work to do.

As I drove home, I tried to rerun the conversation in my mind, trying to salvage as much as I could. I was trembling like a child. I kept repeating his words: 'You must transform yourself into a human machine.' I couldn't be connected emotionally to this task.

That was the day my approach to training changed. I was in love – not with the man I had met, but with the choices I had made and the adventure that was ahead of me. I knew now why I was doing this. I was going to find myself. I was ready.

Round Ireland Swim 2006

Objective: To be the first team of swimmers to circumnavigate the island of Ireland.

Expedition Leader: Henry O'Donnell (Donegal)

Swimmers: Anne Marie Ward (Donegal), Ryan Ward (Donegal), Tom Watters (Meath), Ian Claxton (Dublin), Nuala Moore (Kerry)

Marine Coordinator and Navigator: Derek Flanagan

Command Boat Skipper: Brendan Proctor

Marine-Rescue Unit: John Joe Rowland (Head of Safety), Noel Brennan, Frank McRory, Mandy Blaney, James Doherty, Kevin Boylan, Timmy Boyle, Hugo McFadden, Anne Boyle, Eddie McFadden, Aidan McKenna, Liam Dowd, Paddy McGown, David McGloin, Kieran Doherty, Damien Kelly, Gus O'Driscoll, Ivan Irwin, Joe Devenney, Owen Fogarty, Donal McEleney

Communications: Kathleen King Media and Marine Unit

Land Operations Unit: Ben George, Brendan Hone, Sinead O'Donnell, Jim Keller, Neil Aherne

Vessels: *Sea Breeze* (command boat), *Abhainn Rí, Dive Áine* and *Rachel Marie* (RIBs)

THE NORTH-WEST TO NORTH-EAST COAST

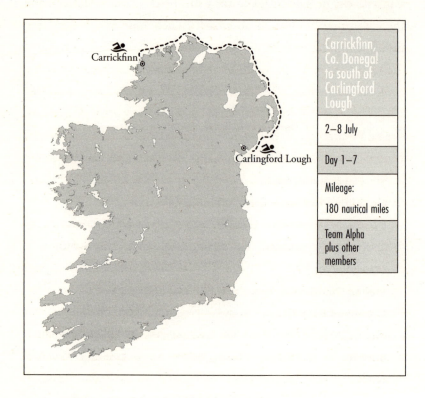

Carrickfinn

Carlingford Lough

Carrickfinn, Co. Donegal to south of Carlingford Lough

2–8 July

Day 1–7

Mileage:
180 nautical miles

Team Alpha plus other members

It was 2 July 2006 – start day. My eyes scanned the sun-soaked Blue Flag Carrickfinn Beach, County Donegal. Despite the wind, the crowds were gathering as our flotilla broke through the water. The thunderous flyover of the Rescue 118 helicopter signalled the start. A final wave to the crowds and we six swimmers turned and walked into the sea. The boats tooted their horns, and the air was filled with possibility as we swam to our individual boats, knowing that the next time we walked back onto Carrickfinn Beach we would be approaching from the south, having swum all the way around the island of Ireland.

At 400 metres from shore, our RIBs slowed up. The initial swims would be a continuous relay until we cleared the headland. Then we would work in a simultaneous relay, swimming set distances in different locations to cover the distance for the day. The moment we let go and eased our bodies away from the RIBs would be the beginning of our 800-nautical-mile swim around the island of Ireland. It felt dreamlike. This time last year we had been normal swimmers, swimming our beaches at home. Now we were striking out to swim around the entire coast of Ireland. We had no qualifications to undertake a marathon swim like this. Ordinary people doing something extraordinary.

The first day was due to finish at 7.00 p.m., with just a few hours' swimming to take us as far as Downings Pier. But the sea had other ideas. The wind was from the north-east and the tide was flowing easterly, giving us challenging swim conditions. Over the VHF we heard that Anne Marie was having a tough time coming out of the headland. That was the downside of an official start: we had to accept the swim conditions. We had no idea what lay ahead.

I lowered my body over the side of the boat. The water surrounded me as if it was holding me tight. Immersing my face in the liquid tranquillity immediately soothed my anxieties. I rotated my arms and kept my face underwater until every molecule of air was expelled from my lungs. This way, when I lifted my face, I would start with a new breath.

The water temperature was 14 degrees – warm, but with the north-easterly wind and an east-running tide, the sea conditions were choppy. After what seemed like the longest mile, the signal came from the boat.

'That mile took 50 minutes. Nuala are you all right?' asked James, one of the marine-rescue team, sensing my frustration.

What was I supposed to say? I had never been this slow. I pulled my socks over wet feet.

'What way are the tides? Are we all over the place?' I asked.

'Anne Marie and the boys are getting the same times,' replied Kieran. 'It's just the way the north-east wind and the easterly tide are against us.'

Tom and Ian had 40-minute miles; Ryan, Anne Marie and I were on 50-minute miles. We had expected 20 or 30 minutes – that was 20 minutes slower per mile.

Between swims, the low sun offered some heat as the boats spread out on the mainland side of the familiar Gola Island. In the distance stood the commanding Tory Island. The sky was dropping low over Bloody Foreland.

'The boats are heading into Magheraroarty Pier so that we can steady ourselves and have a cup of tea.' And off we sped. Today was a media day, so there was that pressure to smile as well. We were only due to be in the water for 2 hours each, 4 miles at 30 minutes per mile, so we only had a bottle of water and a few biscuits with us. Instead of a 5-hour day, we were facing a 10-hour day today. Thoughts of food descended on the group.

I climbed out of the RIB and took hold of the ladder. Lifting my body up those 30 rungs onto the command boat nearly killed me. Once at the top, Neil Aherne, my boyfriend who came to assist us, peeled us out of our immersion suits – waterproof body covers designed to protect us from exposure – like onions from their skins. The sensation of the sun on our wet clothes was intense. We watched the steam rising from our wet bodies.

'How do we get food?' Ryan mumbled.

Our eyes darted to each other. No one had money with them. An apple pie was landed in front of us and a knife. The smiles disappeared as we had to divide it.

We were beginning to understand how this was going to work. Already the frustration was rising. But we did not express these emotions and questions as the boats tied up at the pier, where crowds had gathered, and my friends and family held green-and-gold Kerry flags and banners. Instead, we only smiled.

Henry walked over. 'Are you good to finish? It's 10 miles to Downings.'

Given that we had over 780 miles to go, 'no' was hardly an acceptable answer. We took a few deep breaths, nodded and walked back onto the RIBs. I reached down to take Ian's hand and squeezed it.

The convoy travelled out 1,000 metres past the entrance, then the boats split to go to the waypoints. It was emotional watching the other RIBs disappearing onto the waves. The darkness of the sky at 5.30 p.m. was foreboding. We were alone again.

At 8.00 p.m., after two hours in the water with Noel and Aidan, I was transferred to Ivan and Hugo's boat. More RIBs arrived to help us finish the distance, leaving Tom to finish his swim. I had been wet for so many hours it felt like my bones were soaked. There was no smiling, no craic – Ivan and Hugo were deadly serious, putting in their GPS points. This was incredibly tough. And it was day one of a month-long expedition.

'Are you ready?' Ivan asked.

'Ready for what?' was all I could keep repeating, over and over again. I didn't know.

I closed my eyes and slid over the side, reaching into the darkness for my fourth hour in the water that day. I pushed hard to finish my last mile.

After 30 minutes, I had only covered half a mile. My eyes welled up with tears; my breathing was raspy and catching.

'You're in a battle of tides. All of the swimmers are fighting,'

Hugo said. 'It's not just you. The wind and tides are directly against us.'

The ladder finally dropped from the RIB, my distance for the day was finally covered. I needed to breathe before facing the team. I leaned back into the water.

'Give me a minute,' I said.

There was no minute – two pairs of strong male hands reached in and grabbed me. My feet didn't even touch the steps of the ladder. I was planted on the floor at the back of the RIB with my towels. I decided to stay there. I didn't want to sit up. I wanted to be in a heap.

I didn't take off my goggles. I didn't dry myself. I needed to be miserable. In the last 10 hours, we'd had one piece of apple pie, some biscuits and water. This was supposed to be a 5-hour day. The boys stared forward, and a wall of silence dropped on the RIB as they steamed for Downings pier, passing Anne Marie, her arms rotating in a dark sea, still swimming at 9.30 p.m.

There was such beauty in being allowed the privacy to steady myself on a 5-metre RIB. The team knew I needed space. There were no answers, so why ask questions? There were tides to battle that day, the wind in our faces; there was distance to cover and damp recoveries to make. The reality was that we had to swim the water in front of us. We weren't able to wait for perfect conditions. But it was also a day of photos and ceremony, and, because of the cameras, we had to smile.

It was midnight before we reached Anne Marie's house for our overnight stay, after a very late meal at Downings. We had to be up at 5.30 a.m. to do it all again. Despite the late hour, we needed to dry our saturated immersion suits. We talked it all over and accepted that these were day-one frustrations. The wind and the weather had turned, and we had missed our window because of the cameras. There was no quitting and no going back. There was no room for emotion. There was no plan B.

'Let's use this week as a training week to ease our way into the expedition,' Anne Marie said, as we toasted with glasses of wine.

Day 2 began 6 hours later, at 7.00 a.m., from Downings Pier. Today's approach was very different: methodical, structured, details and tide dependent. A sense of calm descended on the group.

Henry and Derek stood side by side, informing the team, the marine rescue and land-operations unit waiting for their briefing, John Joe standing tall with his notes, Brendan waiting for his GPS coordinates. Lunchboxes were handed out – food at the ready, litres of water. The pomp and ceremony were over. The expedition had truly begun.

'Yesterday is gone. Today we focus on getting around Malin Head, east of the Limeburner Rock. There is a north-east wind gusting force 5, which will be pushing us backwards and to shore,' Derek said. 'Our goal for this week is to get to Carlingford in County Louth, that distance is 160nm.' Our eyes focused on the large map on the pier.

There wasn't time for discussion. The reality of what we were undertaking, there in front of us, seemed like an infinite amount of the hardship we had endured yesterday.

The water was vast, thick and green rounding Malin Head – the Atlantic Ocean, as it spread north to Iceland and Scotland. Our focus was to go from swimming north to swimming east. The wind was against the tide for much of the day and the conditions were rough for swimming, especially exposed to such a ragged coastline. We did another 10-hour day on the RIBs, and all we smiled about was that we would get 8 hours' sleep – our last night in Anne Marie's home.

It became a pattern: on days 1, 2 and 3 we were 4 hours behind our schedule each evening. This gave us a very clear indication that our projected swim times were only guidelines and that expectations would be determined by each day's conditions. Our key requirements would be patience and trust: trust in ourselves, in each other and, mostly, in the possibility that we could achieve the objective. There would be much greater challenges than the swim itself …

As we swam through Rathlin Sound, crossing into Northern Ireland along the Antrim coast, the north-north-east tide lent us push and speed, in contrast to the previous days. The tides through Rathlin were running at 4 knots and our speed was something to behold. Ian and Tom each completed a mile in 19 minutes. Our emotions were settling into acceptance.

The tides in Rathlin can have ferocious speed and my father's voice resonated in my head: 'If a fish box fell off the back of a boat, it would be whipped away miles around the headland in no time.' I lowered my body into the crystal waters. I felt so peaceful, gliding through the water as if home was firmly behind us and home was firmly ahead of us. We were now in the circle of life. After 2 miles, I climbed the ladder into the rear of the RIB. A cup of tea to warm my core. We readied ourselves to move to the next waypoint.

That first week, swimming four to six hours a day, we had the sense that the RIB was our office and the sea our new workplace. Despite the 16-hour days and our tired muscles, we felt strong. Progress was visible and we had just completed our first coast.

As we turned south, swimming down the Antrim coast and past Belfast Lough, the water temperature dropped lower, and the depth increased to 300 metres. The emotion of the swim changes with the depth of the water, because the water becomes colder and therefore thicker.

We were truly coming to understand the conditions we were working in. Constant jellyfish stings and hypothermia, accompanied by rain and wind, gave us our first taste of what it was like to sit on the boats, wet and tired, saturated between swims, with nowhere to shelter and recover as the cold seeped into our bones. It was so difficult to keep our bodies from losing heat as we waited for our next swim. The immersion suits were wet inside from our previous swims, and it was hard to eat out there in the elements.

The wind, too, was exhausting as our tired arms drove deep into the waves. The miles became longer and had to be fought for as the times for each increased to 40 minutes. It was becoming apparent that training for distance was not the same as training for expedition.

When I slid over the side of the boat south of Belfast Lough for my third swim of the day, the cold water felt like a steel rod penetrating my skin. The time on the boat between swims had heated my core a little, but my feet were still freezing. It was simply not possible to keep our feet dry on the boat, with the floor constantly wet from frequent wave incursions. I kicked my feet to force my blood to circulate.

As I reached into the dark water, short, sharp waves slapped me and walls of lion's mane jellyfish confronted me, intermeshed with each other, tentacles like spider webs. Their core can be up to a metre in diameter. I slowed my stroke and lifted my head.

'Is there any way past?' I asked. The crew scanned the water in front of me and shook their heads. The only way past was through.

I began to breaststroke, spreading my body out as flat as possible. I stopped kicking and tried to glide, hoping this would pass. The stings began like brushes from a nettle, tiny electric shocks causing shivers in my body. I had been stung before, but these were different stings, much stronger and much deeper. I was glad that my body was so numb with the cold, to dull the pain a little. There was no way to get out.

'You still have over a mile to swim,' Peter O'Donnell told me in his gentle manner. Peter was the owner of the *Rachel Marie*. He visited the odd day to man his boat and support us.

'Another hour of this?' I asked, trying to figure out how I could deal with the pain and keep my body as still and flat as possible, as we scanned the underwater. They gave a silent nod.

I was moving into a mental minefield. I had to ignore the physical pain. This was about accepting that the next hour would be hell.

A deep breath and I pushed into the water, keeping my leg kick as light and as fluttering as I could, trying not to disturb the web of tentacles under my body. I failed.

The electric shocks drove deep into my body as the tentacles passed over my arms, shoulders and legs. Theoretically accepting the pain and actively experiencing it were two different things. The tears formed inside my goggles. I forced my mind to focus on the fact that we were swimming to County Louth, tonight, and would be sleeping two counties away from Dublin.

Pain is an indication your body is working. The ladder dropped and my frozen hands and feet struggled to cling to the rungs. I pulled my body up, helped by willing hands. My body resembled a map of roadways. The shivering started and would not stop. Mandy helped me out of my togs, into dry ones and then straight into my immersion suit. The stings can stay alive inside a swimming costume. They told me the other swimmers were suffering just as much with cold and stings. We were all in the same sea.

'We've another slot of about 2 miles, but the tide is picking up now,' Noel said after putting down the VHF. 'Nuala, are you okay to get in again? Derek is looking for a few miles. Some swimmers got caught in eddies and tomorrow's weather is not good. We'll have only a half day. The lion's mane is gone.'

I felt the tears coming to my eyes as my body trembled. I was frozen. I looked at Tom. We were all suffering.

Tom tried to smile.

'The cold might numb our bodies again – maybe it will help. Replace one pain with another? A few more hours of suffering?' he said.

I stripped the wet immersion suit from my frozen body, looked at the tracks the stings had made across my skin, and then eased my body into the dark waters below the Mountains of Mourne.

That night, finally out of the water, we compared sting marks, raised a glass of wine and made a toast to being very special, after spending 12 hours on the RIBs that day. We had swum 280 kilometres in 6 days, with 1,200 kilometres left to swim. How each of us felt didn't matter – couldn't matter. There was only the final goal.

'Is everyone okay to swim?' Henry asked the next morning as we left the pontoon.

What did 'okay' mean? No one answered, but all heads nodded in an automatic response. We were grateful for the sunglasses to hide the looks in our eyes.

The south-easterly wind was increasing to gale force 8. The sea state outside Carlingford Lough was difficult and all boats would have to be off the water by 2.00 p.m. That meant a 10-kilometre route to share between us, but there was a 10 nautical-mile RIB journey to our swim start point. Our arms were sore as we held on tight to the seats as the RIBs bounced their way through the lough.

Sliding over the side, I was genuinely terrified, without knowing what the strange feeling was about. *Swim the water in front of you – that's all you can do.* With each stroke, I drove into the turbulent waters. Through my goggles, I noticed the activity on the boat increasing from observation to preparation. At the next stroke, I rotated my head to allow my peripheral vision to pick up the fury of the force-8 storm lifting on the horizon. In a few minutes, the water was sniping at me. I could feel a pressure on my arms as I tried to drive forward. I knew there was an ongoing conversation about being stood down for the weekend and coming back on Monday. What would it feel like to leave the team and come back? What would the break in our focus mean? Who leaves base camp and Mount Everest and goes home for a few days?

The ladder was being readied, but I wasn't finished with my internal conversation. I was in total conflict with myself. I wanted to swim; I wanted to rest. I wanted to stay; I wanted to go home. My back and arms were aching, but what if a break was not the answer? My mind was racing but, digging in, I pushed the last mile out of my body. Once again, my mind was proving my greatest adversary.

As Frank hauled me onto the *Dive Áine*, the ferocity of the sea was evident. The urgency of the conditions had seeped into the soul of the marine-rescue unit. We watched the storm gather. It was beautiful. It was behind us and coming from the south-east. Suddenly, the nose of the RIB dug deep into a wave, the impact causing a wall of water to curl over us. We were all hurled frontward. Tom and I fell forward; the seat back dug into my stomach and, for a brief moment in time as if the world was standing still, the water hung over our heads. Finally, its weight forced the seawater to collapse on us and fill the boat.

Someone jumped to open the bung, allowing the RIB to empty the water out the back as it travelled at speed. In that few minutes, the landscape had changed. The water was showing its power and supremacy. Sometimes the squall was behind us, but then it would swallow us up again. We were surrounded.

Noel was concerned that the storm would catch up with us on the journey in. We couldn't risk another impact. He radioed that all swimmers were to be transferred to the command cruiser with Brendan Proctor and Henry. We had learned the procedure: the bow (nose) of the RIB would be brought to touch the back or side of the larger *Sea Breeze*. On the command of both skippers, each one of us would stand up onto the side tubing of the RIB. There was no handrail.

There was a sense of insecurity on this handover, but also a sense of excitement. We had eight bodies to transfer to the command boat and time was of the essence in the rising storm. Our RIB bounced on the waves and, several times, though the boats were seconds from connecting, the nose of the RIB diverted as if to avoid a collision. In between waves, there was a lull of a few seconds; that was the moment the command came: 'Jump!' It was so exciting, like being a child on the pier in Dingle.

To uncurl your fingers from the railing and leap up onto the tubing is as daunting as a bungee jump. It's that letting go among moving boats and waves. An outstretched hand from the back of the *Sea Breeze* grabs you as another hand on your back pushes. For a millisecond you are flying through the air, frozen in focus on the fingers that will seize your own. If you were to miss your landing or the fingers were not to meet, the outcome would be grave.

We were so excited to get into Brendan's fridge for some chocolate and biscuits. The cruiser, though fast, was very spirited in turbulent waters. She tossed and turned as we watched the squall surround us. We were right on the edge of nature. I loved it.

Once all were safely on board, Brendan began navigating our journey to Carlingford. The water at the mouth of the lough was being flipped and chucked, like an egg being whisked. A blanket of fog covered the horizon. The rain was being hurled at the windscreen in sporadic spurts, making it hard to see ahead. Brendan peeled back the roof hatch and opted to steer by sticking his head out to face the elements. A rogue wave would have a more devastating effect on the *Sea Breeze* than on a RIB. It was imperative that he see it before it hit.

It was 1.45 p.m. and the storm had caught us. Jumping through a side window of the cabin, legs first, Henry piled in, dressed in his black immersion suit. He topped it off with a black beanie hat. He had the satellite phone in one hand and the binoculars in the other, twin lenses rotating like a heat-seeking device, tracking the storm. We smiled: he was in full expedition mode.

We made it back to shore and it was decided to reconvene on Monday morning. I decided that I would like to go home to Dingle for the 36 hours. Many of the team were going home too.

The reality of physical depletion, emotional exhaustion and the lack of a physiotherapist, a nutritionist and proper cover from weather conditions were all going to be major issues that would create layers of extra challenge. There was no plan B. How can you plan for what you don't understand?

DINGLE: HOME

D riving away from the team towards home was like cutting an umbilical cord. There was a strange sense of separation. I wondered what it would feel like to go home.

'You're coming back, aren't you?' came the parting words from Ian, who was heading to Dublin with Tom, Anne Marie and Ryan, who were staying in Dublin with family. I would be heading to Dingle with Neil.

I told him I was.

Waking up the next morning at home in my own bed was

traumatic. I faced my decisions with the stripping rawness of a cutting easterly wind. I strolled up to the small shop I operated in Dingle. The streets were milling with July tourists, and I should have been behind the counter, working. What was I thinking? It's easy to shut down your life for anything negative – a medical issue, for example, a breakup or a loss – for as long as it takes you to get through. But for anything positive, personal or otherwise, you toss and turn, justifying it. Why did I think I could give up work for the summer?

Back in the house, I curled up in the upstairs hallway, my legs up against the wall and my back against the opposite wall, as if I was on the floor of the RIB. I cried a lot. I cried at the cost of my decision, at the costs of my dreams and at the fact that I was struggling to deal with the pain of the expedition. But I knew everyone involved was the same. The sacrifices each of us had made were colossal. We had given up so much to achieve our moment of greatness. To take on this swim and risk everything – physically, emotionally and financially – took courage. We were in too deep to back out.

On Sunday night, I sat out in Beenbawn, in Mary's house with Neil. She had baked two loaves of brown bread, brownies and scones for me to bring to the team. We had banana bread, too, from Brian Lapan, a friend who ran a restaurant. I chatted with Mary about the fear of returning to the expedition.

'Once you commit, Nuala, you are in it until the end. Don't leave it behind you. Everything always works out. You were built for this. No regrets. Who gets to swim around Ireland?' she said with her usual smile, as she packed the food into a huge bag. I didn't know whether to laugh or cry.

'Give me a call, day or night.' A final wave.

She was right. I had to try and refocus. We agreed that I should not come home again until I swim into Dingle.

THE EAST COAST

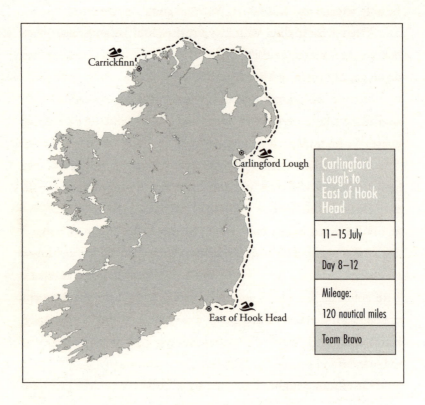

Carrickfinn

Carlingford Lough

East of Hook Head

Carlingford Lough to East of Hook Head

11–15 July

Day 8–12

Mileage: 120 nautical miles

Team Bravo

The map lay spread out on the concrete. Every pair of eyes was following its headlands closely as we readied ourselves to leave Carlingford Lough.

'Our objective is to get to Carnsore Point, off Wexford, in the next four days,' Derek said, pointing at the most southerly point of the east coast.

'That's more than 100 miles.' The words fell from my mouth. Our faces told so many stories.

'I know. I can see you all looking at the map. But trust me, the tides will be our friends.'

Welcoming Team Bravo to the expedition, Henry spoke about

the amount of support we would have on the east coast. 'Then we'll be able to turn and head west. Another coast done.'

'That is more than swimming an English Channel relay every day for the next four days,' Ryan said. So crazy. The energy was brilliant, as if we had forgotten the last week.

'I hope we can get our arms going. My muscles are so stiff,' said Anne Marie, as our eyes followed Derek's stick down the east coast. We knew the headlands, and, for Tom and Ian, it was home.

'Today is a training day for tomorrow,' we agreed. We all smiled in our huddle. I really hoped we were strong enough to take the physical beating every day.

We started once more. Ryan's arms drove through a body of water that seemed calm. The water temperature was 13 degrees. I lowered my body from the RIB for my turn. The texture of the Irish Sea was much easier to swim through. When the ladder was dropped for me, I wasn't ready to leave the water. On my second immersion, again my body felt strong. The islands just glided past me, gently and peacefully. I allowed my breathing to bring me to a meditative state as the sunshine heated our bodies.

The *Abhainn Rí* came alongside. Anne Marie had finished her mileage and Derek decided that I should finish my last 2 miles from his boat, leaving Ryan to finish with the *Dive Áine*. We would be finished early. Derek was always thinking of ways to make the journey easier for us. I gathered up my bag and jumped over to the other RIB and straight into the water. The stillness of the water was hypnotic – more like a garden pond than the raging North Channel. The fields were so close that I could see the animals.

'I can see the bottom! There are rocks underneath me!' I yelled in utter disbelief. 'It's only 10 metres deep!' The thunderous sounds of the Irish Coast Guard Rescue 116 helicopter were overhead, saluting us over the VHF. They were followed by a visit from the Howth Coast Guard. The energy was magical.

'I would be expecting you all to have a huge increase in your speed later today. Be confident and it will happen.' Brendan smiled as he headed off to the marina and we began our swim south, past Dublin Port. Derek had asked for 28 miles to bring us to Wicklow Head.

On my first swim, I felt that I was on a continual roundabout, trying to find an exit. I twisted and turned as the colossal Dublin Port emptied its basin of water at us. The Irish Sea was very frisky and fast, quick to change. It was frustrating and confusing, yet it was shallow and relatively calm. The water temperature was 2 degrees warmer than the north coast and we were reheating much more quickly between swims. The coastline was so close. Heading for Arklow was in itself significant: we were now two counties away from swimming westward.

'That was a 20-minute mile, Nuala,' Timmy said, staring at the GPS. For a split second, I thought he was joking.

We told ourselves that the first week's difficulties were teething problems and that we had come through them, that swimming around Ireland really was possible. A sense of calm filled the team. The east coast was a gift. In this Irish Sea, Ian and Tom were swimming 14-minute miles. Ryan, Anne Marie and I were all completing miles in under 20 minutes. Our days were sunshine and heat, with the Irish Sea light to the touch. Each swim finished with smiles. We were physically sore, but with the short days and early evenings, there was a spring in our step.

We counted off the cliffs and headlands as we passed them by. The energy was as exuberant as Bray Head, at 240 metres, was daunting. The cliffs there are high for a few kilometres until the land flattens out. We were swimming down the Wicklow coast, heading to Wexford – Cahore Point and then on to Carnsore Point. There was sheer excitement on the RIBs, watching the counties go by, then accepting that it was just us, our arms, making that happen. The pain always dulled when we realised our progress.

The wind turned north-easterly, so, with a combination of sunshine, the tide and wind at our backs and warmer water temperatures, we were able to complete Derek's request and cover over 52 miles in 2 days. Our final swims were at Tuskar Rock. I swam an 18-minute mile with an 8-knot spring tide. Directly south lay the Celtic Sea and our turn west. Despite exhaustion, the atmosphere was electric.

THE SOUTH COAST

Kilmore Quay was beautiful with the sunshine glistening on the water. We sat in the sun, aware of the increased breathing and physical depletions. We had Sunday off. Anne Marie and I spent time monitoring blood pressure and pulse oxygen, among other things. My blood pressure was high, 190/100 on my rest day, with my resting heart rate at 100 beats per minute. Breathing was elevated.

'Normally I would tell you to do more exercise,' Anne Marie said with a smile, as we pondered the medical impact of swimming hundreds of kilometres, on top of dehydration, exhaustion and stress.

The one area we decided to focus on was no longer battling what could not be changed. We would commit 100 per cent to the expedition, question nothing and let go of what we could not control. Our health depended on it. The impact of the anxiety and stress was starting to show itself. Reality versus expectation, cost versus sacrifice. The reality of what we had undertaken. Not knowing when it would end. We were not professional athletes.

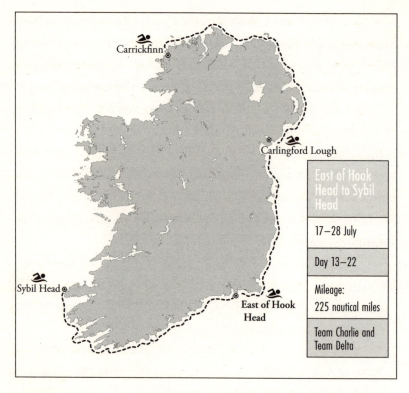

The following morning, the expedition restarted, and we were back in the game. All our emotions had to be suppressed as we accepted our next objective.

'Our objective for this week with Team Charlie is to get from here to Baltimore, County Cork, a total of 135 miles, over the next week,' Derek said. 'Cape Clear is the goal, but we will be swimming 12 miles offshore to minimise the tidal pulls. Tides run north to south, and we will be swimming west. Expect an increased swim time. If we can push 90 miles in the next few days, we will cross the halfway point at Kinsale.'

To avoid the bays, the plan was to swim well offshore. The tides, which had been our engine on the east coast, were now our enemy. A mile was taking 50 minutes and, with a considerable distance to complete each day, we had now a 16-hour day on the RIBs.

The recent sense of progress, accomplishment and capability was smashed by the fact that each mile was taking 20 minutes longer. It was confusing: were the conditions against us or were our bodies getting weaker? The thought of what the next few weeks would do to us physically and emotionally was unimaginable. We blocked it out.

'Today is 18 July,' Henry said. 'We should be leaving Ballydavid in west Kerry; instead, we are just after reaching Cork. This is the reality of an expedition. Is everyone okay to swim?'

A unanimous reply: 'Yes.' How could we stop? How could anyone say no?

'We can do this every day without doubt. Maybe some days we will do less, but finding a reason is the biggest mountain today.' We were physically and mentally exhausted. This was our lowest point. But maybe we would rally again.

The hours were running into days, the days were running into weeks and the weeks were about to run into months. How long would this take? As swimmers, we were truly on the edge, but there was a new unity in the marine-rescue unit. There was a sense that the protective ring around us was tightening, as if a fragility was being seen.

It was big water today. The movement was huge, slow and meaningful, pushing from depths that we hadn't experienced before. Ian eased his body over the side. The swell was close to 3 metres. The troughs in the waves swallowed him up – only his arm was visible as the boat lifted and fell. A swimmer could easily be lost today. We had to accept another 14-hour day on the RIBs, calculating 50-minute miles.

My turn. I drove my arms into the waves. Despite the calm, there was power. As my eyes focused downwards the fog seemed to penetrate the water.

Afterwards, sitting on the RIB with a cup of tea, Ian said mournfully, 'Cork is a really long county.' We laughed.

My phone rang in my pocket. I pulled it out to see my home number. It was my father. I signalled to Damien, asking him to slow the engines for a minute so I could hear.

'Where are you now?' a sombre voice asked.

'We're south of Kinsale Head. We passed Cork Harbour today,' I shouted, holding my other ear shut tightly to drown out the sound of the engines humming.

'Is that all you've managed? I thought you would be in Dingle by now.' I knew he would be down at the pier daily and he would be questioned about our progress. I rolled my eyes.

'We hit bad weather and wind – 3-metre swells. It's a very tough swim,' I said, knowing he would understand that side of the sea. 'It'll be another week or 10 days, so, to Dingle. The wind is shifting around in the next few days.'

Before I had a chance to ask anything else, the line went dead. I could only smile. He knew every headland and he was tracking our forecast nightly.

The map was laid out; the stick followed the line. In the last 4 days, we had swum in relay 80 miles in thunderous 3- to 4-metre swells. We were now 14–16 miles off the southern coast of Ireland. The smiles burst through our faces at how amazing we were.

'If we can cover 45 miles between today and tomorrow, we will achieve our objective of 135 miles before Team Charlie leave us,' Derek said. That was doable, despite the muscular pains and aches.

The 14-mile journey to the waypoint caused huge stress in our knees, backs and arms. We struggled to hold on tight as the RIB bounced its way through the waves. The weather had turned. I was watching Tom's swim, his yellow hat. Now my eyes rested on the dark, troubled water as it batted the side of the boat. The wind was gusting force 4 in squalls, so we were operating on the very edge of our safety guidelines. Tom climbed the waves, arms flailing to gain height, and then disappeared for seconds at a time, swallowed in the depression, before popping up again. His yellow hat appeared very small today. I could feel the danger. His arms pushed into walls of water, but there was no rhythm, no beat to his strokes. The decision was to keep the RIB close enough to see Tom, but not so close that it might be driven on top of him by the waves.

Waves covered Tom, not allowing any rhythm or progress. I could feel his struggle. His head movements indicated that all was not well. His stroke changed several times. His pace was 40 minutes per mile. This would leave me in the region of 50–60 minutes.

I knew that, if Tom was struggling, I would be in for an almighty battle. There was a level of urgency in the boat that I had not felt before. The crew were in a constant state of readiness. The enormous waters were treating the RIB like a rubber duck in a bathtub. The crew were watching and waiting for that rogue wave that could compromise us. Engines stalled to reverse a little, so as not to be too far separated from Tom.

'Get ready, Nuala!' Kieran shouted.

My breathing got faster, and I could feel my heart race.

'Please stay close,' I said. Looks transferred between us that didn't require any comment.

Tom's hand touched off mine as I twisted into the biggest sea I had ever swum in. I was sucked downward. I was breathing to the left, into the southerly wind that was now starting to gust. David was working hard, trying to prevent the huge RIB from being blown on top of me. No one should be swimming in this sea. The boats were on the edge of danger as nature took control, lifting the RIB and dropping her colossal frame within a few feet of my head. The crash was deafening. I flipped onto my back and pushed my legs forward, knowing that, if the boat landed on my feet, there would be less injury. I was glad of the engine guards.

Steadying myself again, I drove forward into the mountainous seas. I felt I was making progress. A signal to stop. I lifted my head.

'We can't stay this side. We're being blown on top of you. I need to go to your blind side. I'll stay close,' David shouted from the RIB.

I returned the thumbs up. I trusted them.

I stuck my face in the water as the sound of the engines drifted away. The RIB was rounding behind me. For those moments, I was here alone, 14 miles offshore, facing the mountainous sea. If my team lost sight of me right then, I would not survive. There was such power in that thought.

I felt the courage it took to swim in water this powerful. I felt privileged. My father's words were with me: *Trust the crews. Don't add to their problems. Stay strong.* Battling to get my breath, I faced the waves rolling from the Atlantic Ocean. There was nothing south of my position but thousands of miles of rolling ocean. I could feel its power. I felt insignificant, yet comfortable with myself.

I heard my sister Mary's words: 'Whatever you want to be, be the best at it.'

The underside of the boat invaded my thoughts as her hull drove too close. I put more power into my left arm and drove south into the abyss. I wanted to be free, but I knew that they had to crowd me. I did not feel scared. Waves of darkness pummelled down on top of me and I heard the boat scream, engines revving to get my attention.

'We have to call it a day, Nuala,' David called, looking down at me. 'We can't stay with you safely. The *Sea Breeze* is under pressure with the weather. They're heading to Baltimore now.'

The team were 10 miles short today, but it was a battle we had to accept we'd lost. After all, we were tiny, vulnerable bodies, swimming past places like Fastnet Rock – places where lives had been lost. Our emotions were very fragile. Through it all, I tried to hold on to the absolute privilege of our experience. What had started as a physical challenge had become an expedition into a new understanding of human willingness to go to that place inside, where most do not dare to travel. To see beyond weakness to the strength of achievement.

The following days brought Team Delta on board, the fourth of the rescue units. Even though the weather was beautiful, I prayed for the Cork coast to end. The cumulative pain, the inability to manage our food and hydration and the lack of physiotherapy were secondary to the knowledge of what it would take to finish this. The emotional costs were mounting. I had started to question more loudly the value of being away from my life, since the accents on the VHF had begun to remind me of my home county. My phone started to ring more often with work questions. When you see the cost of your dreams, it can strip you of energy and will. I was afraid to ask when this would be over.

As we swam those big seas, I counted headlands. We had passed 11 counties since starting and the next headland was County Kerry. I could smell home.

My phone rang. My father again, checking my progress. Laughter in the boat.

'Yes, we are at Stags exactly now, in Roaringwater Bay,' I replied, shaking my head.

He was not impressed by how slow we were. He listed some marine advice for the crew and some tracks to avoid. I put the phone on speaker and the crew listened. Afterwards, I translated the Kerry accent for them.

'Dad said once we pass Mizen Head we will be released, and the tides will run us north. The tides at the moment are crossing us.'

Rounding Cape Clear, the most southerly point in the expedition, was a milestone. There were so many significant moments now. The swell was over 2 metres – huge troughs – with a force-4 or 5 south-east wind driving us further offshore. The waters were mountainous, but that was nothing to the emotion of progress. Mizen Head stood commanding. The VHF screamed with celebrations as Ryan turned the swim north-westwards.

My breathing was ragged as I eased my body into the walls of water coming at me. My entire body was swallowed up each time, my arms struggling to find a forward reach in the walls of the Atlantic Ocean that had last seen land on the east coast of America. Swimming here was about diving under the water and making distance, surfacing to meet a wallop and diving again.

The open-water swimming community would never allow any swimmer to venture into these conditions. We had developed our own safety limits, surviving on flasks of tea and sandwiches, breakfast and dinner. Our bodies broken from the daily challenges and emotions of spending 16 hours a day on RIBs, cold, sunburned, skin broken, muscles torn asunder, no privacy, holding tight with arms which felt long since ripped from their sockets. Yet there was acceptance in the team.

The VHF radio was active.

'Can you translate that?' Joe asked, smiling.

I perked up. Valentia Radio Station.

'Honey, we're home!' was the shout.

We had just relayed from Baltimore to south of Mizen Head, a strong 26-mile day. Another line on the map, another milestone.

We had completed 450 miles. The pain was paling beside the sense of progress.

We pushed on 18-hour days. It was unrelenting on our bodies. On day 21, Skellig Michael stood commanding in the distance. I heard the voice of my brother Ed across the VHF – 'This is *Misty Dawn*. Over.' Tears came to my eyes as I listened to the chatter. Home.

28 July, our emotions were so high leaving Skellig Rock through the Blasket Sound to relay north of Sybil Head. We were emotionally and physically exhausted but driven to keep moving. I was home. Heading north-west was another big milestone.

Thumbs up from the RIB and I dug deep to cross Dingle Bay. The waves hit my face with the power of an Atlantic finally finding freedom up the west coast. Breathing was such a challenge. Arms pulling on a superhuman scale, half wrenched from their sockets. Lower back constantly in muscle spasms from the four weeks of bouncing on the RIBs, holding on through the waves. Fingers reached into seaweed-green water as each wave projected huge power. Pain numbed by the sense of progress. I couldn't care less today, because tonight, by hook or by crook, I would sleep in my own bed. I was going to snuggle with my dogs, come hell or high water.

The waves grew heavy, and I changed stroke a few times, going lower with my head as the wind drove them over me. Each breath to the left was filled with a wall of water, so breathing was a chance occasion. The deeper I could swim under the water, the less resistance my body would meet climbing up and down.

The white horses on the surface forced bubbles underneath. The boat danced in and out of my view, but I could see enough when I lifted my head forward. The Blasket Islands were growing larger. Signal given, I turned unhurriedly and took a backstroke. I wanted to look at Skellig Michael drifting away into the distance.

Two more swims and I'm home.

Back on the RIB, the phone rang. My brother.

'Who's going through Blasket Sound?' Ed asked. 'Whoever it is will have to be in it by 1.30 p.m. today. It's rough at the entrance. The south-west wind will help, but you can't be any later or you'll get walloped.'

It was 11.30 a.m.

'We just took a spin through the sound and it's extraordinary,' Derek said. 'It'll be a battle. It's your own choice if you want to swim it. We can go around the islands instead – it's safer water. Your call.'

The silence was deafening.

'I think we should give it a go,' I said, knowing that swimming around the islands would add another 16 miles. 'We're between the devil and the deep blue sea.'

Tom agreed and Derek accepted the decision. The boats divided to complete the final stint.

Blasket Sound is the stretch of water running north-east from the northern end of the Blasket Islands. The Atlantic Ocean splits: some runs outside the islands, some circles around and the remainder runs inside. I knew this body of water. Swimmers did not go there. There was a feeling of foreboding as we faced it.

Tom decided to take the first swim. As he got ready, the wind increased to a strong breeze from the south-west. The *Abhainn Rí* revved and drove uphill over the swell – and that was no exaggeration. From my viewpoint, their bow was raised high. Kathleen and Anne Marie disappeared into the waves as the RIB was swallowed up. It was the first time I saw water running uphill. Tom pulled on his hat and goggles. His hand brushed mine as he looked at me, a look that said, 'Keep a close eye.' Then he was over and gone.

In the distance I watched a huge, fluorescent buoy, a tidal marker for the fishermen and boat users, bop high in the air, disappear underneath and then pop up 10 or 15 seconds later, jumping about erratically. The rip currents. This was an angry section of water. Gus made eye contact to tell me to notice the distance Tom had covered. A mile in 15 minutes. This was world-record speed. I leaned over the tubing, within finger-touching distance, as waves crashed against the side and bounced back over Tom's head. The sea on the outer side of the RIB seemed higher than on the inside. I wished it was an optical illusion, but Blasket Sound was a strange place.

'Get ready to jump, Nuala.'

My breathing rose so high that I was gasping for air. I piled my hair into my hat. I was 30 minutes away from home, from being wrapped up in love and celebration. Tom grabbed hold of the rope as I lowered my body into the tumultuous Blasket Sound.

The sea floor here is scattered with rocks that jut up from the bottom – not high enough to break the surface, but high enough to offer massive obstacles to the running water. This creates eddies and contraflows, water running back when it should be running forward. Today, the south-westerly wind was forcing the water forward faster than it could run, thus lifting the top layer and causing the eddy to reverse the under layer. It was the most confused water I'd ever felt in my life. Hands catching, fingers pulling, my body was pushed faster and faster. My breathing was very sporadic, and I was swallowing water. But I was willing to take whatever it threw at me. My mind focused on the distance we had swum from Skellig Rock across Dingle Bay to here and the greatness and courage we had to take this on. It had taken us 14 days to swim here from Rosslare.

Without warning, as I raised my eyes to face forward, I was hit head-on by a wall of water – a wallop so thunderous that it sent me waist-high into the air. A rogue wave. My torso was bent backwards, my arms thrown, as if the wave had dropped me when it no longer required me. It was a backflip. For a split second everything in my system stopped. I felt like I'd hit a solid structure. I was stunned.

'Don't take your eyes off me!' I screamed, my words half-lost in the water.

Tom was standing just feet from my head, still in his swimming togs, not even taking a second to change from his previous swim. With each stroke, I stared at their eyes. Owen was standing on top of the tubing, holding precariously on to the windscreen, ready. Gus was kneeling, his entire body on one side. They were risking everything. How could they not?

A second engine filled my hearing. It was different from ours, so I took a quick breath to the right. Bearing down on me was the Irish Coast Guard Dingle Unit, of which I had been a member for years. Frank, Seamus and John, fully kitted, watching closely. They would be able to get me no matter what.

Shrill sounds now, a piercing screech. I pictured the whales travelling just beyond the Blasket Sound. The picture changed and my head was brought to an accident our trawler had a few years ago. I got a call late one night, when I lived in New York, to tell me that our trawler, *Undaunted*, was on the rocks. The gearbox had failed in the sound. She couldn't go forward or back; she was helpless against the wind and water. It was in this very spot. The crew, my family, were waiting to be rescued as my brother worked tirelessly to restart the engine. The heroic efforts of the RNLI and local fishermen got them to safety as the 30-metre steel structure eased its way beneath the waves to its present resting place. A mile from where I was swimming now, she lay on her side on the seabed. Shivers filled my body, and my breathing became irregular. *I need passage*, I told the ocean. *Thank you for not taking my family*.

My heart was racing, my breathing high, as the waves turned me in every direction, I started to cry inside my goggles. I couldn't believe I was home. The *Abhainn Rí* and the *Rachel Marie* came alongside, and my head was triangulated into a calm comfort zone. Four boats kept the storm at bay, outside my space. I can't remember if there was a ladder, but brute force had me out of that water in a second. It was a professional extraction. My arms up in the air, three men hauled me onto the tubing, landing on my belly, then head-first inside the boat with the grace of a beached whale. Off we sped, out of the sound and into calmer waters.

As I scrambled to get my immersion suit on, I noticed everyone was eating doughnuts from Courtney's bakery, delivered by Irish Coast Guard Dingle Unit. The three RIBs came alongside under Slea Head.

'Where is my doughnut?' I asked.

'We ate them all,' Ivan said. Kathleen and Anne Marie were laughing.

I could feel the tears welling up. Minutes later, the entire team laughed so loudly as my jam and cream doughnut was passed to me. I couldn't believe that the thought of not getting a doughnut could be so upsetting.

We celebrated. Having completed a 24-mile relay from Skellig Rock across Dingle Bay that day, we were turning north. I was most proud of my swim through the Blasket Sound.

DINGLE: HOME AGAIN

It was three weeks since I'd been home, and arriving at Dingle Pier was magical. Despite the crowds, all I could see was Maryann standing with my Labradors, Beethoven and Hally. My exhausted arms dragged my bags upstairs. My room looked so strange after spending a month on the road. I frantically started to make the bed.

I hauled the vacuum cleaner upstairs. The lead got caught on the door of my room. I tugged and pulled but it would not release. The pain in my arms was visible, my strength was gone. The tears started to rise, and my breathing became ragged. I wept tears of absolute anguish and wailed like a banshee. I fell to the carpet. Both dogs ran to me, making their large bodies as small as possible, as only dogs can. Wet noses nuzzled deep into my neck, pushing with all their weight to stop my tears. A paw, outstretched, touched my face.

'What am I doing?' I shouted. 'What the hell am I doing swimming around Ireland?'

'Are you all right up there?' my father shouted from downstairs.

My tantrum was interrupted by a ringing sound. Mary's name flashed across my phone screen.

I closed my eyes shut and silently screamed at myself. A few regular breaths, in and out, steady and strong, and then I pressed the call-back button.

'See you and the team in an hour?' Mary said, her voice excited. She was hosting a barbecue. The evening would be filled with music and food, and we could all enjoy our achievement as we looked out over Dingle Harbour.

At home, I could not escape thoughts about the cost of my sacrifice. This was a painful insight into the cost of a dream. At that moment, I could not find the value in it; yet how could I say no to the team? I had to go back to the water.

THE WEST COAST

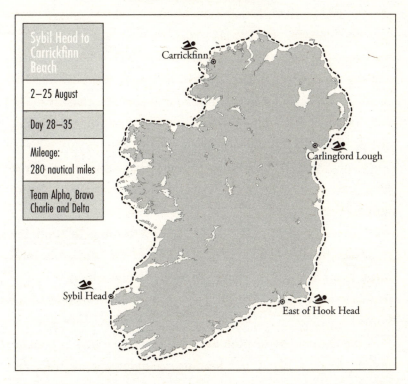

Sybil Head to
Carrickfinn
Beach

2–25 August

Day 28–35

Mileage:
280 nautical miles

Team Alpha, Bravo
Charlie and Delta

Carrickfinn

Carlingford Lough

Sybil Head

East of Hook Head

Leaving Dingle for the second time was the hardest thing, both mentally and physically. The water on the west coast was of a different nature entirely. It was green, strong water with a thumping heartbeat. Every immersion felt like a slide into thick, green soup. The Atlantic water moving under your body feels huge. Tankers dropped out of view, swallowed up in the mountainous seas, sometimes only covering one mile in an hour. Derek and Brendan had always said it would be impossible to gauge how this coast would be. After 28 days of swimming and an unknown finish date, our emotions were very fragile.

The 55-kilometre swim from Sybil Head to Loop Head began with our bodies being tossed about like plastic toys and ended with

60-minute miles and dolphins playing and jumping over us as we crossed the mouth of the River Shannon.

The following few days showed us the true nature of the battle we faced. The water 30 kilometres offshore was 300 metres deep, and the big waves and deep troughs meant we often lost sight of the boat. We swam for hours, only to find ourselves roughly in the same position. Swimming is the only sport where you can commit 100 per cent and actually lose distance.

On 5 August, the day we planned to finally get past Slyne Head, we were faced with towering weather systems. Derek's forecast was not good.

'There's a really bad weather system coming in from the Atlantic. The wind is now north-westerly, so if we can get beyond Slyne Head it would be a game-changer. That would leave us 130 nautical miles from Kerry and about 150 nautical miles from home.'

We committed to pushing hard as we travelled in convoy, passing Mutton Island and heading 14 miles west of the Aran Islands. But, after steaming 6 miles offshore, the sea became angry, the waves huge and the wind powerful. We were outside our safety limits and the unit was stood down. The RIBs danced back to Quilty Pier.

That night, my phone rang at 11.30 p.m. and the name 'Anne Marie' flashed up on the screen. I grabbed it.

'Come quickly,' Anne Marie said, her voice filled with stress. 'The boats are adrift. The ropes are undone, and the *Sea Breeze* is heading for the rocks. Come quick as you can.' Neil, Derek, Kathleen and I raced to the pier.

Within minutes we were standing on the tiny pier at Quilty, in darkness. The *Abhainn Rí* was tied to the *Sea Breeze,* and both were adrift, being blown onto the rocks on the far side. The tubing of the *Abhainn Rí* was acting as a fender, but the wind was driving the vessels towards a perilous outcome.

Neil and Eddie jumped from the lowest point of the ladder onto a small timber punt and rowed with one oar in the darkness, as the wind and rain howled around them. Head torches shining on the white cruiser, the three lads, along with Derek, took hold of the ropes, jumping from boat to boat. Huge, saturated ropes were hurled onto the pier. We reached and grabbed them, careful not to be pulled into the water, holding on to each other. The boats needed to be secured on the pier. Kathleen, Anne Marie and I reefed the ropes through the rings on the pier and then anchored them to ourselves by tying them around our waists. As the slack rope was made, the heave-ho of us three women against the wind pulled the huge vessel closer. I was living inside a childhood memory. Pull by pull, we worked the *Sea Breeze* and the *Abhainn Rí* off the rocks and back towards the pier.

The team arrived. Damien and Ryan went out to the two vessels to check for damage, bail out water and examine the engines.

At 2.00 a.m., our bodies fell down onto the wet, cold concrete of the pier. Brendan was confident that the *Sea Breeze* was safe and that Derek and the rest of the team had completed all the checks. Drained from the experience, we hauled ourselves back to bed at 3 o'clock, the relief and anxiety about what might have been still in our heads as we lay down for a few hours' sleep. It certainly reminded us that we were all in this together.

The tides around Slyne Head are complex at the best of times, and on day 27 there were spring tides. The boats navigated in convoy 10 miles south-east of Slyne Head. Our eyelids were stuck together with exhaustion, our hair was matted from the days exposed to the salt water and the muscles in our arms, backs and knees were shredded from the continued impact of the RIBs bouncing on the waves, the drops and the impacts. Our lips were cracked and bleeding and there were open sores on our feet from being wet for 16 hours a day. We were more like casualties to be admitted to hospital than swimmers to be released to the sea.

The water was rough – angry, even – the winds turned early from west to north-west and gusting force 5. Our brief was to swim the 20 miles north of Inishbofin. Once exposed, away from land, the vessels were swallowed up in the troughs of the 3-metre breaking waves. These were the most challenging sea conditions I had ever experienced. There was an air of anxiety. Both swimmers and marine rescue units were aware that we were all working within the tightest of safety margins.

The VHF crackled out a command: 'Stand down, over.' We were to return to Roundstone without any distance completed at all. The sense of failure was huge.

'If we all swim a half a mile each, it would only take an hour or so. We would get closer, or at least move,' we argued. We were willing to risk it all, as if nothing mattered more than passing Slyne Head. But the discussion was shut down – it was just too dangerous. We slumped into our immersion suits, hoods pulled tight as the wind and waves pummelled the sides of the RIB. In the last 6 days, we had succeeded in only swimming 50 miles of coastline as the crow flies. We had 150 miles ahead of us and the stress was building.

The VHF came to life again.

'*Sea Breeze, Sea Breeze*, this is *Abhainn Rí*. ...' The voice crackled in the wind. A rogue wave dropped and filled the stern and engines of the *Abhainn Rí*. Derek had to move ahead immediately to save the RIB. They had lost sight of Anne Marie and were rounding now to locate her. She was separated from the vessel in big seas.

The words fell like a concrete block in a bathtub. *Lost sight.* It was something that we all feared, a terrifying moment.

Silence fell as we all waited for word. Time passed slowly and the vessels moved tighter together. The wind began to howl, and the sea state became very angry, all in a matter of minutes.

'She's safe! The *Abhainn Rí* is heading to Cleggan Pier. They will come back by road.' Thumbs-up from Anne and Aidan. A colossal sense of relief. The call to halt was the right one. The engines revved and we made our way to shore as the Atlantic Ocean tossed us around like a plastic toy in a jacuzzi. Some days we just didn't belong here.

After a physically and emotionally bruising 10-day battle, Slyne Head gave us passage and our exhausted arms broke the back of the west coast. As we approached the final body of west-coast water, leaving the dark headlands of Blacksod Bay behind us, wondering if it would ever end, the team tightened like a ring of steel around us.

We had become institutionalised. Conversations became silent, words became expressions. Our arms and backs were no longer our own – they were numb or sore. Our ability to communicate in words was transmuted into the actions of holding and touching. The group of five main swimmers walked as one unit, always holding onto one another. We were fragile. We were sleeping in between swims on Zodiacs with their engines at full throttle. We were unable to stand up and sustain a conversation. We were unable to function as individuals. We were arms for hire, rotating on demand. Each day we eased our bodies into the cold water and rotated our arms to achieve an objective. There was no love left now. There was a vacant stare in our eyes, which was scary and a silence in our manner.

My father rang daily. I could picture him thinking, staring into the fire, chatting on the pier, knowing every headland and every risk that we could fall foul of. The west coast had worried him. He didn't like the way I spoke about being exhausted. Tiredness was not something he entertained. *The sea can take you tomorrow.* His words were the same at the end of each call: 'Don't you add to the problems of the crews. They need you to stay strong in that water. Keep your head focused. We would sometimes be awake for 30 hours, Nuala. You know the way of life. If you are weak, you are a bigger problem than the water. Push into that storm, Nuala, do you hear me? You can fall apart and sleep for a month when you get home. Didn't I tell you when you were a child? Don't ever take your eyes off that sea. It can take you tomorrow. You're nearly there. You're on the home straight now. Steady your ship. Do you understand me?'

His call would go dead without a goodbye. Being strong was all he understood.

We were facing the final stretch. The conditions never changed: we stood, saturated, at the back of an open RIB, pummelled by rain and wind, arms nearly pulled from our sockets from holding on while speeding to the next location. Water temperatures of 12 degrees. Soggy sandwiches abandoned to the seagulls. Water rushing along the floor of the boat, ensuring forever-wet, forever-cold feet, now broken from the salt. Staring into the sea, avoiding eye contact with the crew as we try to deafen our ears to the words, 'You're in next.' The long sigh as we dug inside ourselves for the strength to peel off our immersion suits when our bodies were freezing, not having had a chance to recover from the previous swims, days or weeks. Sliding over the side, allowing the dark sea to swallow us up as we took off for another swim. Nothing seemed to matter any more. Emotions were irrelevant – we had risen above them. How I longed for a mountaintop to aim for instead of these endless caverns of ocean. Beside throttled engines, our weary eyes closed, and our bodies slept often in the rain as others swam. Sometimes we had no memory of our own swims.

Physically, we were drained, emotionally, our eyes were void of expression, yet somehow we found enough each day to move, arm over arm. The reasons we had taken on this swim around Ireland were miles away from our reasons for finishing it. We were now 48 days into the journey and nothing mattered any more – whether we ate or not, whether we slept or not, the pain as we lifted our arms. Nothing. Leaving Blacksod Bay in County Mayo, we were aware that the west coast still had many cards to play against us.

The team worked night and day to try and understand how to get us across Donegal Bay. It was just as Derek had warned – unpredictable – and it was filled with emotions of all kinds. Mostly, though, it was filled with the strength that left us and flooded through us at the same time. We had crossed every bay, passed every headland and swum in every body of water that existed around Ireland. We had prevailed. As Brendan said leaving Dingle, it was as if five arms were pulling each arm. We would finish as a team.

We had battled hundreds of miles of rolling ocean and pushed our bodies into the abyss of danger and pain, but our greatest fear now, we came to realise, was finishing. What would that mean to us? What would leaving the group mean? There had been an emotional shutdown in us all, a sense that we no longer wanted to be in crowds, or groups – just in our small family, which had kept us safe. For each of us, the fear of going home was huge. What would reopening the door to my life expose? I was afraid of what would happen once I started to unpeel the whole event. The only way we could achieve this was to break it down – day by day, swim by swim, week by week, coast by coast. But afterwards, looking back on the whole, how would we deal with the sacrifice? The open-water swimming community could never understand what we endured out here. Would we ever be able to explain?

'We are not there yet,' Anne Marie kept repeating, as we drove, arm over arm, the 100 miles from Erris Head in County Mayo across Donegal Bay, the biggest bay in Ireland, in heavy sea fog conditions. The swim was managed over VHF marine channel 16 – an emergency channel – with visibility down to 500 metres. We vowed to each other to hold on tight as our emotions weakened. The end was in sight. It took one week of challenging swimming to get from Erris Head to Carrickfinn Beach. We drifted to become ghosts and paled into the background.

On day 56, 100 metres from the shore, we took the final swim, together with the rescue unit. We swam in formation, unable to maintain our breathing, onto the beach at Carrickfinn, County Donegal. We were the same team who had departed, going clockwise, 800 miles earlier, and it felt like we had left every ounce of our blood, sweat and tears in the ocean. If ever there was a moment where a team was responsible for the success of an event, it was this one. We became the only team in history to have circumnavigated this island by swimming. There would not be any applause. There was no podium, there were no medals. There was just pain and sheer and utter emotional release. We had completed 35 relay swims from headland to headland, each connecting the longest marathon staged swim in history (although the exact mileage we swam would be left as a secret to the oceans). It had taken only eight days to swim down the east coast, but it had taken one month to swim up the west. But it was the goodbye. So many of the team, I knew we may not see again. These events end so abruptly. Normal life beckons.

The cost of any event is the amount of your life you are willing to exchange for it. That statement epitomises the journey, the key words being 'willing to exchange'.

The Round Ireland Swim taught me what 100 per cent really

is – and that I had it in me to live at 100 per cent, trust at 100 per cent and deliver 100 per cent. It showed me that in weakness there was strength, that together we are more than the sum of our parts. It taught me patience. It taught me what sacrifice was and what it meant to be part of a team – knowing that, left to our own devices, we would not have survived. It showed what is possible, albeit at a certain cost, and how much I was willing to push to attain my goals. I knew that it would never be possible really to explain to anyone what it took to swim around Ireland. How could anyone else understand the value of the achievement? Going home was going to be one of the most challenging moments ahead.

Sitting by the fire the following days, Dad was relieved to have me home. I could tell.

'Didn't I tell you you could do it?' was all he said as I discussed the challenges of the west coast. There was no clap on the back, just the quiet knowledge that I came from good stock and good breeding. His shoulders shrugged and a smile crept onto his face, his eyes on the flames of the fire, which he always kept lit.

That evening, as I made his bed, I noticed newspaper cuttings about the last month of our swim on the locker – photos of me and the team, articles about Nuala Moore, laminated, alongside a magnifying glass. I smiled to myself. We were truly special.

6

TREADING THE MAELSTROM

*'People have a need to feel their pain. Very often pain is the
beginning of a great deal of awareness. As an energy centre it
awakens consciousness.'*
Arnold Mindell

After finishing the Round Ireland Swim, that 56-day marathon,
I struggled to enjoy swimming. I had broken each swim
we completed down to its mechanics – arm over arm – and had
become disconnected from my emotional response to what we had
completed. I was struggling to piece the achievement back together
again because I could only see what I had lost, what it had taken
from me.

A few short weeks ago, at the end of August, Neil and I had
left Donegal after swimming for two months. That car journey
home was traumatic and emotional: leaving the team, there was
a huge fear of going home, of facing my normal life, of seeing the
impact on it. We swimmers had been protected by each other. The
moment we walked onto the beach at Carrickfinn, we had achieved
our objective – we had stayed strong, physically and mentally,
long enough to finish. But, when we got home, it was like a dam
bursting. A flood of emotions rushed through. We no longer had to

stay strong and now the reality of our world had changed. Instead of the small, focused, task-driven day-to-day of the last few months, where nothing else mattered, everything else mattered. We realised how institutionalised we had become.

We didn't know how to celebrate – we just wondered how we could put our days back together in a manner that would allow us to function. For two months and longer we had closed the doors to both our work and our personal lives. We had existed purely to swim the next section of the coast of Ireland. We had accepted the role of being a link in the chain to achieve this swim, not knowing what the cost would be. Each moment of pain had been compartmentalised – the potential agony of failing far outweighed the discomfort of any injury. Each emotion – like anxiety about what it would feel like to reopen the door to our lives and see the costs of this expedition – had been pushed into the darkness, invisible to us, because we could not let it matter. Now the day had come to face it. The darkness was real and Pandora's box was open. How could we learn to identify feelings again? That question, 'Are you okay to swim?' haunted me. How could I relearn a normal response? I struggled.

It's over. What happens next?

The jubilation and excitement, the sense of euphoria at our success were brief. Normal life took over. I felt a sense of panic going back to work. How do I debrief and make sense of it all? I sat in the smallest of spaces in the hallway at home, again replicating sitting on the floor of the boat. The world was too big. I could see the price of my sacrifice everywhere. There was no glamour, no fanfare, no celebration; yet there was so much noise.

The pain increased; an injury that had been masked by adrenaline suddenly became undeniable. As the weeks passed, I faced the sheer impossibility of stretching my arms to the top shelf in my shop, or of holding my arms out from my body. Those arms that had battled the greatest of waters felt useless. My chest hurt. Everyone around me tried so hard to help me, but I just wanted to be with my team. Looking around my world, I simply could not balance the costs.

It was my mind that scared me the most. I wanted to talk about the Round Ireland Swim 24 hours a day. I was faced with an avalanche of emotions. I needed to celebrate and be told how amazing and how powerful we were. I wanted to tell the world what we had achieved, again and again – but the world had already moved on. Looking at a map of Ireland, I remembered what it had taken to swim each section of coastline, the powerful feelings we had experienced as we lowered our bodies into raging waters and how strong we were to have taken it on. I remembered the way, as swimmers, we had broken and rebuilt ourselves as part of the team. Those final weeks had been all about the team.

I did not want my normal life. I wanted the adrenaline. I wanted the excitement. But I also needed to feel that the challenge was understood. I kept looking outward, expecting the swim to be honoured by the swimming community, by the wider community and by the media. It didn't happen. The statement, 'We swam around Ireland,' was too simple for people to understand. The achievement was too big, yet all I wanted was to feel normal.

Recognition is a vital part of any journey. We had achieved the longest marathon staged relay swim in the world – with no medical and psychological support, just organic passion. Defining winning and success was something I had been focusing on for a long time. We Irish are not great at celebrating ourselves. That was one of the reasons I had set up my triathlons. I had become frustrated knowing it sometimes takes more for some people to start than it does for others to finish.

Two weeks after the swim ended, a lady walked into my shop. I was behind the counter, selling bed linen, head down. An unfamiliar face greeted me by name and congratulated me on our swim. I beamed.

She handed me an envelope.

'You don't know me, but my niece met you in Kilmore Quay in Waterford. She was following your expedition through her school, and you took photos with her. She is nine years old and loves to swim. You are her hero, Nuala. She wants to be like you.'

Tears welled inside, but a huge smile came across my face. I did not open the envelope. I waited.

'I remember her – a young girl with brown hair. She asked me if I would be getting a medal for swimming around Ireland. I said there were no medals.'

She nodded, quite impressed that I remembered her. In truth, I think we remembered everyone. The people we met were all so kind to us as we travelled, and we rarely forgot them.

I opened the envelope and a beautiful glass necklace fell out. A hand-painted disc on a chain. I felt unable to process the gift.

'She saved her money over the summer and picked this out herself. She asked me to bring it to you in Dingle. She said you deserved a medal.' The lady smiled as tears came to my eyes, a lump in my throat. I walked around and hugged her.

A nine-year-old girl was able to recognise our achievement, and that gesture meant the world to me. I still have that piece of jewellery today, because of the value it came with.

I knew that I had to figure out how to get recognition from inside myself. I had to find my own way through. I had monsters in my mind, whispering to me: *How can you reconcile extreme achievement, the value of sacrifice and the battle for recognition?* I could not find the why.

I had definitely broken something inside myself. I had dug so deep, the well was empty. Putting myself back together again and becoming my own biggest fan would be a slow process. Every evening was spent on the phone to Anne Marie, Ian and Tom, or messaging Ryan. We had broken the 1,482 kilometres up into small pieces to be able to achieve it, and broken ourselves up in the process. Now I had no idea how to step back and see the big picture, how to put myself back together. I was focusing on what we had sacrificed. I was at sea within myself. Even when people told me I was phenomenal, I could not accept it. I didn't feel phenomenal – I felt confused and emotionally scattered.

Maybe this was the 'expedition hangover' that people talked about. I was treading water in a maelstrom. I gravitated towards others who had sacrificed for expeditions like climbing Mount Everest, which had taken years from their lives. I could feel their pain.

One gloomy January day, Mary arrived into the shop.

'Now so,' she said, looking over her glasses at me. She sensed there was a problem, so she stayed quiet and listened to me.

I had been at a swimming awards ceremony, where I'd been described as one of the best marathon swimmers in Ireland who had not swum the English Channel. Maybe I should just do the English Channel this summer?

'Nuala, you need to work every day this summer.' Mary had looked after me all my life. She was a maternal figure to me, as my mother had passed away in my teens. She supported me through college and saw me through all my foreign trips. Everything had to be run by Mary, even when I was an adult. She had that effect on people – you wanted to make her proud. Mary had sacrificed a huge part of her life for us, so she was not shy to call it as it was. She was my sounding board.

She pulled open a duvet cover.

I knew Mary was right. No one in Dingle or any other tourist area takes any time off from May to September. She was telling me what I knew but hated to hear. I always worked the entire summer without a single day off. Two jobs, at that. But I really wanted to be part of this marathon swimming world. I could not get those words out of my head.

'How many channel swimmers have swum around Ireland? Is this 300-thread count? I think this colour would be lovely in my room.' She smiled, gently deflecting. Mary and I used to have awkward conversations which often ended in diversion, usually her leaving with bed linen or blankets. Two sisters sounding off each other. As usual, her message landed. She was right.

Mary was all about moving forward. She hated people to dwell on things.

'What about going back diving in the Maharees? Can you go back teaching with Sandra? I am going to dive next summer, and I want Patrick to do the National Geographic Open Water Diver,' she finished with a smile. 'Do you want dinner? I'm making a big pot of curry.'

I smiled. Mary's response to so many things when life was challenging or in an awkward conversation was to cook big pots of food and offer dinner.

'I do. I'll drop out after six o'clock,' I replied. Maybe I would go back diving. In the previous decade, since living in the Cayman Islands in 1990, I had continued my scuba diving education with the Professional Association of Diving Instructors (PADI) to the level of Instructor Development Course (IDC) staff instructor, achieving this standard only a few years previously in 2004. Diving was my passion. She was right, maybe it was time to descend into the blue and calm world away from the chaos, where so much stands still, and just breathe.

'Byesie bye,' she said, floating out the door with her phone to her ear and a duvet cover under her arm. Already moving on. Mary was always one of my biggest supporters. Her standards for herself and others were impeccable. She knew what sacrifices were, but she was a realist.

That evening, en route to collecting my curry with Beethoven and Hally, my Labradors, I stopped at Sláidín Beach and swam out to the rocks under the lighthouse. I watched the water dance in the sunlight as the sun dropped over Dingle Harbour. I saw myself as a child, being told to sit on the towel by my brother when I was too young to swim far; I heard the splash of the waves as we jumped off the side of my father's boat and struggled for the shore. Those were the battles that had brought me to this point. Being told to stay at the shoreline and not follow the boys into deep water; jumping off piers when I could not swim. I thought about the freedom I had been given to take those risks, at an age when other children were not allowed to be alone on the beach. The laughter burst out, the echo filling the air. I remembered drinking Bovril on that beach, the gravy texture making me retch, the sand on my legs and my arms covered in Vaseline, not knowing why. Preparing for the channel, without even knowing what it was.

I was afraid of missing opportunities. I was capable of so many other things, like swimming the channel solo, but my mind was not free to train or to take on the challenge. It was cruel to accept that I may miss that moment of greatness. I could not sacrifice the time.

It was a deep conflict inside me. I was unable to be the best version of myself. I was being forced to wait until I was free to succeed.

Mary's words came into my head: 'What's for you won't pass you by.' I just had to wait for the well to refill. I put my face in the water. Focusing on the slow movements of the seaweed calmly moving to and fro, I listened to my bubbles.

The sea had already given me so much. Now I had to have patience.

In July 2007, Kevin Murphy, the 'King of the Channel', arrived in Dingle. He had asked me to organise a crossing of Dingle Bay, an inaugural swim. He had completed 34 English Channel crossings at that point, earning his title. Kevin was an unassuming man. Physically, he was so strong. He was an amazing orator, a former journalist, with a CV of swims that raised the hairs on the back of my neck. I was so excited that he wanted to come and swim here in Dingle Bay with me. It was a big ask, but I stepped up.

Kevin's strong arms rotated across Dingle Bay in over seven hours. Today the conditions were not exactly favourable, but it was Kevin's final day. The complex tides played their part in the difficulty and Paddy Sheehy and Garry Kavanagh kayaked alongside him the entire journey. I was in awe of his accepting attitude when the tides went against us. He displayed a patience and calm which was wonderful to absorb, never once questioning when we had to change the swim because of the weather.

For me, it was so exciting to navigate, as opposed to being the swimmer fighting the flow. My mind visualised our 25-mile relay swim across Dingle Bay. Being back out in the boat, miles from shore, was so therapeutic. My brother Ed piloted the 12-mile solo crossing from Doulus Head to Coominole. Ed's guidance for this pioneering swim was crucial, as his fishing knowledge was so important. There was no guesswork, just a calm understanding from eyes that knew every ripple of this water.

Talking to Kevin afterwards, soaking up his knowledge, I was struck by all I could see in his eyes when we discussed the North Channel on the north-east coast of Ireland, the body of water between Ireland and Scotland. Mile for mile, it was the toughest in the world. I was captivated.

'I've done 56-mile swims. I've done 52-hour swims. I've done a high-altitude lake swim. I've done Loch Ness, where the temperature falls to 7 degrees. I've swum in an air temperature of −34 degrees. I've done a Norwegian fjord, passing the inflow from glaciers. I've swum in South Africa with great white sharks. When I'm asked what's the toughest of all, my answer is the North Channel. I've done it three times and it still frightens me.'

I was blown away. I didn't want to ask him about the fear because I felt it was too personal. But I couldn't stop wondering: what could frighten a man with such experience?

'Why have so few Irish swimmers taken on the North Channel swim, but taken on the English Channel instead?' I asked him. I was thinking of my Round Ireland Swim teammate Anne Marie, who was planning to cross the North Channel the following year.

He explained about the cold water, the short seasons and part-time pilots, and the fact that there were only one or two slots available per year. Then his voice changed. 'And, of course, there's what happened to Jason Zirganos and Alison Streeter. That frightens everyone.'

I didn't know what had happened to these people. Why did I not know? I made a mental note to look them up and find out.

I just could not get my head around it, but in the strangest of ways it excited me, knowing first-hand what it was like to lower my body into a huge body of water. What could make it so dangerous? I was burning to know.

After five days, Kevin was leaving Dingle, but before he did, we discussed the challenges of recognition and sacrifice. Speed was not his focus; it was an adventure of body and mind. Pushing his limits. It was so affirming to hear his appraisal of our achievements and his understanding of the post-swim emotions of work and life I was experiencing. Having his company for that week allowed me the space to think and listen at the same time. His advice was to give it time, to focus on the adventure and to enjoy it.

I accepted a double-crossing relay challenge in the English Channel for 2008, with a team of four other swimmers, based in County Cork, whom I had never met before. We would be the first Irish team of five to attempt it. It would be a huge sacrifice to be in Dover for a week in August, during my busiest working time, but I had to get the monkey off my back.

On 19 August 2008, with the sunshine beating down and the water temperature at 18 degrees, I stood on the pebbled beach of Dover, England. Though it was my first time standing on this beach, nestled between two harbour walls, it felt strangely familiar and exciting. This would be my home for the next week to 10 days. Swimming in the warm water, with the sun on my back, made me feel years younger. Not experiencing the cold changed my approach to everything. The water was warmer than we would ever experience in Irish coastal waters.

Outside the harbour walls were rows and rows of enormous channel ferries and ships, leaving and coming. The Straits of Dover is one of the busiest shipping channels in the world and swimmers have to negotiate the traffic. But the sound of the waves crashing over the pebbles was beautiful and very soothing. I stared at the opening of the harbour, knowing that beyond the lighthouse was the entrance to our body of water, the swim leading to France.

There were lines of swimmers, their arms rotating with military precision, swimming, touching and turning off each wall. A woman stood on the pebbles beside a sheltered tent, her eyes scanning the water the way a gannet scans for prey. She was taking note and standing guard. I knew immediately that this short, commanding figure must be Freda Streeter, or the 'Channel General', as she was known. In person, she was everything I had imagined: a strong woman of older years, her tanned face beaten by the sun and salt, with a gentleness about her. She would be willing to give of her time, yet her approach and stern tone were that of a woman who was in control on her beach. Many came here just to train with Freda.

Our swim-week slot opened on 21 August, so from today onwards we were on standby. Dave Whyte, our pilot, replied to our questions.

'The weather is due to break on the twenty-third and the wind may last a few days. If there is a slot for you, it will be the end of the week, your last day.'

Our team was looking for a solid window of 30 hours of calm water and weather. The possibility of only getting a single crossing of two one-hour swims each or nothing at all was taking its toll on my mind. I kept busy, but it was hard to fill the days. Waiting for the weather was a challenge. We were at its mercy.

I had decided to focus on gleaning some information from Freda about her experiences in the North Channel. At that time, Anne Marie was on standby in Donegal to do her North Channel solo swim, so I was in daily contact with her, excited for her. Freda's experience with her daughter, Alison, was truly chilling to listen to.

Twenty years earlier, in 1988, Alison Streeter took on the swim from Ireland to Scotland for the first time. She was an experienced channel swimmer and Freda, her mother, was in her crew on the boat that day. As Alison was swimming, Freda suddenly noticed that she had fallen unconscious in the water. She reached down and grabbed her and managed to hold on to her daughter for a moment before she disappeared under the waves.

Allison was hauled onto the boat and revived. Three weeks later, she returned to the North Channel and became the first woman to complete the crossing between Ireland and Scotland.

This story fascinated me. How had it happened? The temperature was the glaring difference from the English Channel – the weight of the cold water and the air temperature. It was a different swim, Kevin had said, but *how* was it different? And how could you train for it? I could not get my head around what had happened to Alison. If it wasn't a medical issue, what had caused the loss of consciousness? Was it the cold? I was aware of shallow-water blackout – a loss of consciousness caused by lack of oxygen. Could this be something similar? So many scenarios came to my mind. The risks and accidental outcomes were always at the forefront of my thinking. The fact that Alison recovered to try again had been a good outcome. With her mother, I was careful not to pry.

Apart from trying to learn all I could from Freda, I spent my days in the internet café and chatting with Kevin Murphy, who was there too. My mind was on Anne Marie. I couldn't stop thinking about what she was facing. I remembered Kevin's mention of Jason Zirganos and I looked him up online. I nearly fell off the chair as I read the information on the screen. How did one of the greatest long-distance swimmers of his generation, having swum the English Channel four times, meet his death in the North Channel?

> In 1958 at the age of 46 years, Zirganos attempted to swim the 22-mile North Channel of the Irish Sea (9.4°C–11.7°C). After 6 hours, and only three miles from the Scottish Coast, Zirganos became unconscious and blue; he did not feel 'cold' prior to

this. He was hauled from the water, and a doctor, using a pen knife, exposed Zirganos's heart to reveal ventricular fibrillation. Direct heart massage having failed, Jason Zirganos was pronounced dead at the scene.

(Tipton, M., 'Drifting into Unconsciousness: Jason Zirganos and the Mystery of Undetected Hypothermia', *British Journal of Sports Medicine* **53** (2019), 1,047.)

How did some of the best long-distance swimmers in the world succumb to unconsciousness while swimming in cold water? My mind filled with questions about what could have brought on the cardiac incident. I had so much to learn.

Looking out at the sea that evening, I knew that I was doing what I had to do, and Anne Marie was doing what she had to do. But I knew I would be nervous as well as excited about Anne Marie's North Channel swim.

The call came from the pilot, Dave Whyte.

'It looks like we will have a weather window, leaving the port at 6.30 p.m. tomorrow, the twenty-seventh. There's wind coming in late on the twenty-eighth. How does that sound?' All good, we agreed.

'What about our flights?' I said to David, knowing we had just lost four flights – but this was a normal hazard for channel swimmers.

We all headed to the internet café to book more flights for the twenty-ninth. Succeed or not, we would be going home on that day.

I rang home to let Mary know my plans, to check if everything was okay with my shop and to ask if she could pick me up at Kerry Airport.

'Book for Cork Airport,' she said. 'I will be there to meet the earliest flight and I will have you back in time to open the shop. That's no problem at all.' A silence. Her voice changed. She was in Treasure Island, one of her two shops, and I could tell a customer was in her sights.

'That is the Boat Bowl,' I heard her say, 'one of the heritage crystal collections. You have a great eye. One of the more prestigious pieces that Waterford makes. This piece is handmade, a superior product. The cut is much rougher, making it original, hand-cut...'

I giggled to myself, knowing that the heritage Boat Bowl cost hundreds of euros. Mary was on fire.

I waited for about 30 seconds; she did not come back to me. I understood that the customer comes first. I was still holding the phone, her other conversation in my ear. As a family, we knew the drill – just stay on the line.

I really should be at work, I thought, *behind my counter in the month of August, the height of the tourist season.*

'Call you back, Nuala. You have a great swim and I'll see you at 6.30 a.m. in Cork. If you need anything else, just give me a call. Now, would you like to see that piece? It will only take me a second to take it down …'

As her voice disappeared, I heard her telling her customer about her sister, the swimmer, who was in Dover, England, about to swim to France and back. I could picture her face, with a smile on it.

7

CRISS-CROSSING THE ENGLISH CHANNEL

'No pessimist ever discovered the secrets of the stars, or sailed to uncharted land, or opened a doorway for the human spirit.'
Helen Keller

The pilot boat, the *Ocean Breeze*, seemed a lot smaller once all five of us and our bags were on board. Including the pilot's assistants and the two official observers, we were 10 adults in a tiny space, but as we steamed out of Dover Harbour towards the white cliffs, the atmosphere was euphoric. In the corner of the wheelhouse, in front of the window, was a small teddy bear dressed in a little yellow T-shirt, with the name 'Kevin' on his chest.

'Kevin?' I asked Dave Whyte, pointing to the bear.

'Kevin Murphy,' he replied with a grin.

I smiled, content that Kevin would be looking over us during our long swim.

'May I have a look at these charts? I pointed to the large marine charts of the English Channel and the Dover Straits, positioned ready for the tracking of our swim.

I accepted Dave's nod as approval and reached across his space. Even though I had studied the channel before and read up on the tides and the coasts, I occupied myself by focusing on points and references, my presence silent and not intrusive. We passed the breakwater and headed south to the start point.

The swim itself was only 21 miles, but the distance would be covered in an S shape owing to the tidal pushes up and down the English Channel. Our team were called Siorcanna na Mumhain – the Munster Sharks: Amy Wolfe, Donal Buckley, David Tagney, Danny Walsh and myself.

At 7.30 p.m. on 27 August 2008, Amy Wolfe stood on Shakespeare Beach near Dover, raised her two arms in the air in a final wave and started our swim to France. The horn blew from the boat, the observer pressed the button on his watch and Amy disappeared into the white surf. I was so excited.

As the boat moved away from the shore, the gigantic, commanding white cliffs of Dover appeared to move and weave without end along the coastline. The chalk, along with the pebbles and the sand, gave the water in the Dover Straits its texture and its colour, a creamy, sandy, soapy shade of white.

The pilot played the most amazing, fun music, and for the first few hours, I was happy to be entertained. At 11.00 p.m. I prepared for my first swim in the English Channel. I was excited to feel warm water surrounding me, to experience the channel and to understand the concept of swimming in the Dover Straits. We gave the swimmer before me, Danny, the 5-minute warning, but then a sense of panic overcame me: *What if I'm not fast enough to pass him? What if he doesn't slow up enough?* The swimmer entering the water must pass the other swimmer from behind, but not before the hour passes.

It was time to jump. I was fifth in the rotation and happy to wait. I leapt from the back of the boat, feet first, focusing on the distance to ensure I cleared the engines, which were put into neutral. The water was soft to the touch – warm at 17 degrees, much warmer than any water I had ever swum in before.

My head popped up first, but in the dark of night, it was difficult to determine which way to turn. I picked out the lights on the back of Danny's head and stretched out with both arms, reaching towards France, legs kicking, as I tracked down the lights in front of me to take my slot on the team. It felt good.

We were in the shipping channel. In the darkness, I could identify a convoy of tankers. I wondered how the pilots of the ships could see us and I certainly didn't envy the job the pilot of the channel swimmers had daily, navigating one of the busiest shipping channels in the world.

I had a flashing light attached to my goggles and a snap glow-stick and light attached to the back of my swimming togs. I dipped my head underwater, into this liquid darkness, in a mini-dive, to check if my lights were reflecting and flashing. The blinking was visible. The darkness in the water allows you the sense that your only focus is on that little piece of space in front of you. Your vision and your concentration are brought down to the bare minimum: the split second when your hand passes your goggles. Nothing else can seep into your mind.

Feeling the water around my body was heavenly, and comforting. Every stretch of my arms, pulling the muscles from my body, relaxed me more and more. It's a stretch that can only be found in the water, as you reach your fingers to their endpoint and then twist your back and feel the lateral muscles pulled from the centre of your spine, your body doing a little dance. The tension and the uncertain waiting of the last 10 days, the emotions that had brought me here, the gnawing question of whether swimming across the English Channel would silence the voices, whether it would be worth the cost of coming, whether the sacrifice would feel worth it … all of that melted away and no longer mattered. With every turn of my spine, every stretch of my fingers, every out-breath of bubbles, the turmoil in my mind was calmed. I could feel each muscle losing its spasm. Nothing mattered now. What would be would be, and I would be home in two days. For now, it was just a swim and I was determined to enjoy it.

As the lights of the tankers drifted into the distance, I picked up movement in my peripheral vision, a signal with the light, in a circular motion, indicating an okay sign. Then the torch was focused onto the laminate form, giving the 5-minute warning that my hour was up. I strained my eyes on the activities at the rear of the boat. I could see Amy take those steps off the back of the *Ocean Breeze*, the splash and the leg kick, and with the power of a triathlete, she sped past me. I pushed to the rear of the vessel, engines in neutral, the ladder floating towards me, and climbed out as fast as I could. Within minutes I was wrapped in my towels. It was 12.40 a.m. and we were now exiting the first shipping lane.

Dave seemed very content with our progress as he plotted the GPS coordinates of our swim slots. There was a spring tide, which pushes swimmers north with the power of the water rushing from the Atlantic Ocean to the North Sea, through the Dover Straits. Our relay team was able to prevent the swim route from going too far north, and on the second rotation, we would benefit from the tides running south. The pilot's job is to track progress and determine the best route to get the swimmer to the landing spot. A lot of people believe that a pilot is in some way following the swimmer or travelling beside a swimmer, but a good pilot's job is to be ahead of the swim route.

I decided not to have a nap. Danny was preparing for his swim, to take over from David, and 45 minutes later, at 4.30 a.m., it would be my turn again. I was frightened that, if I gave in to sleep, it would be a deep sleep. I was used to swimming sleep deprived. I felt it would be better for my second swim in the darkness if I remained in that focused space.

At 4.28 a.m., lights flashed, the signal was given, and I jumped off the rear of the *Ocean Breeze* again. Dave had told us that, even though we were swimming south with the tide, we had to keep pushing east. Regardless of the direction we were facing, the French coast would always appear in front of us. As I approached the second half of my swim, the bright yellow sun peeped out to rise in the distance. In the dark of night, I wear clear goggles, and through them, I saw a lovely array of reds and yellows. This was the first natural light I'd seen in my two hours in the sea. There is a peace that comes with a sunrise. A new day is dawning. The shadows danced on the boat as bodies moved around and what was previously darkness became a half-light. My time passed so quickly. I watched Amy's silhouette move to the rear of the boat for the third stint, and with that, her arms and legs rotated past me at speed. Within minutes I was back on board. I was delighted we were not doing a single crossing from England to France because then my swim journey would have been over. The excitement was only beginning. I was looking forward to the challenges of the 24 hours and turning back to England.

The sea conditions were taking a toll on board and a few of the team were experiencing a little nausea. That's one of the challenges of getting in and out of the boat and swimming intermittently, alongside tiredness and the diesel fumes. Certain swimmers are more impacted by seasickness than others. It can be a curse.

'We are 5 hours into a tide running speedily south and, close to the coast, especially the French coast, the tides are merciless,' Dave said as I studied our progress.

I stood silently as he plotted the previous swim and the new GPS onto the chart, navigating the stretch to France. I was fascinated by marine charts, by seeing the route in front of me.

CRISS-CROSSING THE ENGLISH CHANNEL

'See this point? This is Cap Gris-Nez. Can you see the lighthouse? That light in the distance?'

It was hard to determine what was a tanker and what was a lighthouse from this distance, but I nodded. If he could tell the difference, that was enough for me.

Dave beckoned me over.

'This next section is the most challenging part of the relay. The tides will be pushing us south, which means we may have to swim another 5 miles east before we get another landing spot, down to a place called Wissant. The tides are turning north in the next hour. The next swimmer must get themselves turned north-east to the Cap very quickly because the coast is disappearing from us.' Dave was focused.

I watched as Dave followed the map with his pen, tracing it out for me.

The rocks, though jagged and posing more of a risk, were closer than the beach and they counted as the coastline. A last look towards the coast and David Tagney was gone, into the water. Sometimes you're like a crab, crawling sideways, swimming to stay still, pulling north-east and being pushed south. But David's legs powered like the motor of a boat and his swim style was that of a sprinter. A thumbs-up from the pilot. David had broken through and was clear of the flow. Ten minutes later, at 7.57 a.m., he hauled himself up to sit on the rocks of France, on the cliffs of Cap Gris-Nez.

The excitement was colossal. The *Ocean Breeze* tooted its horns and the group screamed. We'd made it.

A sense of relief and calm came over the boat. We were swimming home. Regardless of how it went, it wouldn't take us more than 15 hours to get back, so I would catch my flight. The sense of relief shifted our emotions. A huge pressure lifted. Now it was only about the grafting, the hard work and the physical side of the swim, the sunshine and the cliffs of Dover. There comes a time in each swim when the questions stop and the work begins, a moment when you decide that, from now on, the workload is only physical. We were on the home straight.

At 8.00 a.m., I texted Mary to tell her I would definitely be at Cork Airport at 6.00 a.m. the following day. An immediate reply: 'Okay, well done, keep going.'

My next swim was at 9.32 a.m. The water glistened in the morning sun and I felt the heat on my back. The visibility in the French waters was clear and crisp as my arms reached out to the fingertips. The water was so much warmer and lighter, too. The temperature, with the sun rising, gave me comfort. This was the first time I could clearly see our surroundings with each breath. It was a different channel from what I had imagined at night – a much bigger world. France was behind us, England ahead, and I felt the magnificence of what was being achieved. What was beautiful was that progress was visible everywhere.

The water in the English Channel is shallow, by swimming standards. Despite the 400-plus ships and tankers going north and south each day, it was an average of 50 metres deep. The next few hours were about getting into the water and pushing as hard as we could as a team while the clouds gathered. The spring tides were driving us north at a much sharper south-bend angle, meaning that we were swimming north-north-west instead of west-north-west. We were making small progress towards the Dover coast for all of our effort, but we were comfortable in the knowledge that, as a relay team, we just had to bide our time and we would soon be released into the southbound tides. The tides would weaken as they turned and that was when, as swimmers, we would make some gains.

I decided I had better lie down and take a quick nap. My mind and body were beginning to get very tired, the constant yawning bringing me to tears. I had been awake for 24 hours and I knew that a power nap would be helpful for my fourth and fifth swims. I set the alarm on my phone for 45 minutes.

My mind drifted to the days of crossing Donegal Bay and Dingle Bay and even the mouth of the Shannon. The tides there can hold you in position or send you off on a different route. I had learned that the tides release you when they release you. Sometimes you can drive against them, but sometimes you must be patient.

If my 56 days swimming around Ireland had taught me anything, it was that the swim is over when it's over. The moment a swimmer is on the shore is the moment there is no more swimming to be done. We can have our wishes and hopes, but the swim will finish when it finishes.

'That breeze is now rising faster than we thought and it's driving us up the channel,' Dave said as I studied the map. 'It is very important that the next swimmer pushes west.'

Coastlines can be very confusing. The Dover coast dipped and jutted out and was deceiving to the eye. There were landing spots that were close and others that would mean we had to swim further, just like Cap Gris-Nez in France. It was hard to tell the difference between them.

The wind had lifted and made for uncomfortable travelling at the rear of the vessel, with one observer and some of the team repeatedly vomiting over the side. But we were nearly home.

Down in the water, David's body was getting twisted and turned by the backsplash from the boat driving forward. Sometimes his arm was pulled back by the power of the water eddying onto him. He was swimming in frustrated water, a battle that was hard to watch, and much of the challenge was being created by waves coming from the boat. It was a horrible sensation, trying to breathe into that water. Yet even in frustrated, dirty water, there was always some type of an awkward rhythm.

The sun had set over the cliffs of Dover as I grabbed my goggles and hat. Despite being more about power than speed, today I really wanted to play my part and drive this relay home. All I could focus on was the fact that I would be back at work this time tomorrow. It gave me a sense of calm to know that this journey would soon be over. *Swim for home* – that was my mantra. *Reach the cliffs and breathe.*

I turned to Dave and asked him what I should be reaching for.

'Aim for that section of the cliff. Keep the lights there at a point above your head.'

The water was grainy, filled with sand, a texture that I had experienced off the Arklow sandbanks on the east coast of Ireland. It was also shallow and light to the touch. I focused my eyes high on the cliffs and kept the lights right above my head.

I was gagging. I was breathing into the backwash of the waves hitting off the side of the vessel. I made the decision to pull my body very close to the side of the boat and slightly further towards the bow. I had spent many days during our west-coast swims in this pocket, which allowed me the calm to breathe into the side of the vessel and a position on the inside of the crest of each wave as it rode out from the side of the boat. My swim strategy in this space was to drive my head far under the water each time I pushed my arm forward; then my breath would come from a very small air pocket I was creating at my shoulder by pulling my chin to my opposite shoulder.

Every few minutes I drifted back down the side of the boat. I could see the faces of my team as they passed me. The boat would kick into neutral and slow up, and I could drive up the side again into my sweet spot on the crest of the wave. It was a difficult job for the pilot but, if we worked together, I would be much faster in here than battling 3 metres further out.

I could feel the vibrations of the boat, riding up and down alongside it, being driven by the power and taking some momentum off the water. That light was so close now.

For me, swimming, the movement of my arms, had become so unemotional. I suddenly realised it was the passion I had been missing, the fun and the edge. During the Round Ireland Swim, we had become arms for hire, rotating to achieve a goal, which would pass; then the next goal would arrive. I had missed the excitement of being one with nature. That feeling of living on the edge of adventure.

Swim for home, was all I was repeating. The water was calming.

I noticed the lights running around the boat. I pulled myself away from the side to watch the activity. With a splash, Amy went flying past me, legs kicking as if her life depended on it.

I climbed the ladder, grabbed my towels and immediately started vomiting. Seawater came up, followed by empty retching caused by the amount of liquid I had taken into my lungs and stomach. I washed out my mouth with Coke and flat 7-Up and smiled. It was over.

Fifteen minutes later, at 8.47 p.m., Amy walked onto the coast of Dover. The emotions were a mix of relief and happiness all around. Amy swam back to the boat, got on board and dried off. We enjoyed a huge round of applause. Our split time for our record two-way relay was: England to France in 12 hours 25 minutes, France to England in 12 hours 50 minutes, a total time of 25 hours 15 minutes. I was excited – we had succeeded. Our pilot had done an amazing job.

Dave turned *Ocean Breeze* south towards Dover Harbour. It was a scramble to pack and dump our rubbish before making our way to the airport. We stopped at the White Horse pub in Dover, stood on stools and signed the ceiling, leaving our messages alongside all the others who had shared these dreams. Then a short goodbye and a wave. There was no more applause. We went our separate ways and that was that.

At 6.30 a.m., 8 hours later, I landed at Cork Airport and hauled my bruised and battered body through customs, barely able to carry my bag, laden with wet towels and clothes. I climbed into the back of my sister's van, shattered and exhausted. I could barely speak. In true Mary style, she had the back of the van covered in blankets and pillows. I had no memories of the flight from London – I think I slept solid from the moment I sat down on the plane – and I was still in a daze.

'Throw yourself back there and have a sleep,' she said, pointing to the blankets and pillows. 'Town is crazy busy. There's some fruit there, too. We can stop for breakfast if you want. When last did you eat?'

I had to think about that.

'Solid food? Probably two days ago.' We laughed.

The reality of my life awaited me again.

'We are the fastest two-way 5 person relay team ever, and the first Irish two-way relay of five – so, yep, I got my journey. I didn't sleep for two nights.' I grabbed the grapefruit and pineapple Mary had brought for me and was asleep in minutes.

We headed west.

'Do you want to turn on the lights in the shop and leave a note on the door that you'll open at 11 a.m.? Then people will know you are back.'

It was a good idea. Mary dropped me home. It was 8.30 a.m.

'Is that you?' my father shouted.

'It is. I'll be down soon.'

I ran up the stairs for an hour's nap, knowing I could catch up on sleep tonight. I had slept four hours in the last two days.

At 11 o'clock I was in my shop, starting a new day, the sun shining outside. I had a huge smile on my face because it was over. Not that it had been difficult – it hadn't. It had been great fun – a beautiful two days on a boat. I felt like I'd been hit by a bus, a pain in every muscle in my body, but that would heal.

'Can you show me that bed set?' a lady asked, pointing to the top shelf. I tried to lift my arms, but I could not. I started to smile. I could hardly explain that this time yesterday I had been swimming to France.

I grabbed the ladder, stood up and pulled down the bed set without reaching above my head.

'Has it been a busy week?' she asked. 'You look like you caught a bit of sun.' She was commenting on my wind-burned face.

'It has, and yes I did. I was swimming,' I replied, so tired that I was unable to go into any explanation. Our achievements would have been lost on the lady anyway. She walked out the door with her new purchase and I laughed out loud with my cup of coffee.

I had learned so much in Dover – so much about who I was as a swimmer, so much about what I wanted from swims and so much about teamwork. I had learned about the value of having the right people around me and knowing what I wanted from swims. We had completed the first Irish five-person two-way relay ever in 25 hours and 15 minutes. More importantly, we were the fastest five-person two-way English Channel relay on record and also only the second team ever in the world to complete one.

As I wrote on the wall in the White Horse pub in Dover, everything is sweetened by risk. I was a channel swimmer.

8

TROUGH

'And once the storm is over, you won't remember how you made it through, how you managed to survive. You won't even be sure, whether the storm is really over. But one thing is certain. When you come out of the storm, you won't be the same person who walked in. That's what this storm's all about.'
Haruki Murakami

Many athletes need the win to feel progress, to validate the months of training and sacrifice. They need to feel that glory, to experience that moment of crossing a line, to be faster, to stand taller. Many athletes need to hear affirmation that their achievements are great. Many athletes need to feel that they have beaten their previous time.

In the previous few years, I had been exposed more and more to this tunnel-vision approach to success. I had realised the personal sacrifices and costs of swimming around Ireland. I had slipped deep into a trough, into the abyss of a struggle to find a way forward. Nothing was matching up to the emotions and adrenaline of the challenge and achievement. I was still searching for that high, that feeling of challenge, that sense of adventure. Despite our Round Ireland Swim being the longest marathon staged relay in the world and involving the coldest immersions back to back, in some of the most difficult waters in the world for swimmers, it was just a swim.

I had become clinical. Despite the fact that the English Channel double-crossing relay was an Irish record, it was just another beautiful swim. At that time, I could not see them as any more than that. In hosting my triathlons and swims I was helping hundreds of athletes to find their way forward, mentoring those with fear. Yet I was lost.

In my search to find my self-worth and to balance the sacrifice and achievement of swimming around the island of Ireland, I hit on a plan. I got a large map of Ireland and drew the lines of the Round Ireland Swim, showing the 56 days and the GPS points. I added headlines from the newspapers, with a photo of us swimmers: 'Swim Team Complete Round Ireland Swim'. I laminated this huge map of Ireland and put it in the window of my shop for the passing world to see.

It attracted so many people. First, they came to find their location on the map (Dingle is a tourist area and people are always lost) and then they came in through the door. I would listen as it suddenly hit them: 'Hey, these guys swam around Ireland!' It was entertaining – their gasps of surprise, their incredulity that humans could do that. Sometimes I would run out, smile and tell them 'That was me'.

I needed to see the swim through their eyes and hear their joy and amazement.

Day by day, my sense of value and achievement increased. Recognition was so important – not on any grand scale, but on a scale of knowing that what I had sacrificed was worth the pain, that the years of financial and emotional cost had value. I could not explain it at the time, but I found such pride and solace in seeing and hearing my accomplishment through the eyes of other people. It wasn't an ego situation – it was not the need to be praised – it was a sense of hearing their voices. It gave me comfort. We had broken it down to make it possible, this allowed me to put it back together again.

That map stayed in the window for 10 years.

How do we accept that the win may not be at the finish line? How do we define success and failure? How do we define achievement? It takes a rare athlete to accept the battle with the greatest competitor in the world. Maybe that's why it's so difficult to see where or what a win is. We swam for days and made little progress on the south and west coasts of Ireland. We battled physically to cover a mile in over an hour. Some would not take on such a challenge without an expected outcome. How do we accept that some days we are moving to stand still, going backwards, stuck in a trough? How do we train and sacrifice to go far, not just to win? I remember telling people about the 800-mile swim over 35 swim days, and people looking at the map and asking me, 'How many hours a day did you swim?' As if they were trying to work out how fast we were. One person actually said, 'So you averaged 1.5 miles an hour?' I was stunned, but it gave me the opportunity to explain and to allow that person to accept that not all swims are about wins. I felt their awe.

At two o'clock in the morning, three weeks after our English Channel swim in 2008, Anne Marie lowered her body into dark, 12-degree North Channel water with the intention of swimming to Scotland. In the darkness of night, when risks will blindside you, this requires a rare and special type of swimmer, someone who will rise to the challenges of the sea. Understanding the sea – where it goes, how it feels and what it wants – would be crucial, as would having a dedicated crew, the heartbeat of the swim. But I remembered the 12-degree water of our own swims and my mind was with her as I tracked her journey.

She made great progress for the first seven hours. The team were happy. And then the tide turned northward. The tides in the Irish Sea race up and down the coast, excited water heading north-east. Tides get excited with power, especially spring tides, as we had discovered off Tuskar Rock and the Blasket Islands on the south-west coast of Ireland. Crossing spring tides is for fast swimmers; slower swimmers can be pulled and dragged at their mercy.

Fourteen hours into the swim, despite swimming strongly at a constant pace on a cool air temperature, Anne Marie's body was pulled 8 miles north up the Antrim coast by the tide, 1 mile back from where she had been 6 hours earlier. Anne Marie was not advancing at all.

All the boat and crew could do was stay with her as they watched her being driven back, not knowing when or if the tides would release her. What other sport pushes someone back, despite hours of effort? That's probably why so few swimmers undertake this challenge. The North Channel is a cruel taskmaster.

The darkness dropped for the night; the air and water were getting cooler and Anne Marie's stroke was getting faster, a sign of anxiety. After 17.5 hours of swimming, Anne Marie apologised to the crew for not being able to swim across the North Channel. She treaded water, touched the boat and accepted the finish.

'You did not fail to get there, Anne Marie. We failed to get you there,' Brendan Proctor said. It is the pilot's job to pilot. They apologised for not getting her to the coast. They had understood that north-east tide, but they had not understood the impact of the tides on Anne Marie as a swimmer and her speed.

It was the longest immersion by an Irish swimmer ever, and also the longest immersion in such cold water by any swimmer. In the following days, Anne Marie's swim was described as a failure to get to Scotland. I was so upset. How could anyone describe that swim as a failure? But that is how it is recorded. I wanted to scream that 17.5 hours in 10–12-degree water was no failure.

My Seven Frogs Triathlon, Olympic and sprint distance, now standing at 260 entrants, had been on the same weekend. I gave prizes to the triathletes who came last as well as first. We applauded effort. I could help to change the definition of success.

The summer ended with a group of Tralee Bay swimmers deciding to swim from Sandy Bay Beach to Fenit, north across Tralee Bay, a roughly 8-mile route. I was going to do it alongside my friend Mags.

The sea conditions were difficult from the beginning, but steadily the wind increased and many of the kayakers had to be removed from the water within the first two hours. The larger boats stayed in the water, but our drinks and our kayaker were gone.

A cruiser with a crew we knew very well came alongside Mags and me as we battled the waves, stroke for stroke. They asked if we wanted to abandon the swim. Our immediate reaction was to say no – we were fine to keep moving forward. Fenit was just across the bay.

The tide was going out and the wind was blowing hard from the west. We started the swim in the outgoing tide, so we would get the ride of the incoming tide to help us to Fenit, but it was not working out for us. Testing conditions were something we were used to and it was often fun to climb and surf the waves. The crews from the boats came alongside and told us they had to leave us to pick up more swimmers. We were given an orientation – swim towards a yacht that was moored west of Fenit Island. That seemed straightforward enough.

Lifting our goggles, we both picked out the top of the yacht's mast, lined it up against the landscape and worked out our point of direction. It appeared to be about 2 miles away. We started swimming towards the yacht.

'Sure we have nowhere else to be Mags, we will get there when we get there.'

We laughed as we headed off. Over the years, Mags and I would head off and swim from bay to bay. Years earlier, on a dive holiday, we had recced bays after our dives and then gone swimming for hours around the coast. We'd arrive up on beaches and rest, then swim home, neither of us interested in sunbathing. Our days were sometimes spent swimming for three to four hours, coming home when we were hungry. We were at home with this sort of swim.

Every few strokes, one of us would orientate and force a change in the other's direction by moving closer or further away. But the waves were such that one of us was high and one was low, like a see-saw. We laughed as we were hurled forward and dropped. Experienced swimmers react immediately by reorientating and adjusting their own swim, mostly by straining their eyes backwards or forwards on the stroke to pick up part of the other swimmer's body. It is a skill in open water and today was a battle.

'I think that yacht we're swimming to is moving – it isn't moored to stop at all. Look, it isn't where it was. It's moving out the bay,' I said, lifting my goggles to confirm that our waypoint was not lined up. 'We're following a yacht that's heading out of the bay!'

A silence as the waves continued to come. We twisted and turned around like periscopes, trying to figure out if we could reorientate. How long had we been swimming after a moving yacht? It was so hard to tell. Checking our watches, we could see the other vessels in the distance, managing the weather and the kayaks. We had been in the water now for nearly 3 hours and our drinks were on the kayak. There was nothing to do but keep swimming or stop. We adopted our usual response: we could do nothing about it. We knew where we were and we had the day long.

'Will we just sing a song?' Mags asked.

We burst out laughing. We lay on our backs, floated in the waves and sang a few bars of a tune.

'Is it right or left for Gibraltar?' I said, as we observed the yacht steer north, towards Kerry Head.

'I just don't want to miss the burgers at the barbecue,' Mags said.

Sticking our heads deep in the water, we started swimming again, arm over arm in a determined rhythm, our stroke always in unison, this time keeping a heading for the lighthouse. Wind and tide together made for a good combination. Underwater we heard rumbling and vibrations from engines. The boat, cutting through the waves, appeared nearby.

We told them about tracking a moving yacht, noting the yacht was now gone.

'Sure, lie on your backs and the wind and waves will carry you to Fenit!' came the shouted reply, followed by much amusement.

'We could have been halfway to the Shannon!' we said, laughing, and told them, as the waves hit us, that of course we were going to finish. Closing in on four hours of swimming, our only concern was that we might not get to Fenit Beach in time for the food at the Boat Club. There was no other pressure. The barbecue was our only priority.

Four hours and fifty-two minutes after we started, we walked onto the beach at Fenit, the others having all finished just ahead of us. There were some tales told of our swim across Tralee Bay. Some swimmers had been taken out, but no one person was greater than the next. There was no judgement and there were no medals. Just a fabulous reminder of why we swim.

I was rebuilding slowly. The cold seas and rough oceans of winter attracted me the most. The cold crisp still water became my place of psychoanalysis. I used the cold to clear my mental clutter, deal with my thoughts and empty my head. The fun was creeping back into the days – I could feel it. Adventures were starting their siren call.

I had this mantra when days were tough: *You can only swim the water in front of you because you have no mountaintop.* I took life day by day.

I focused on scuba diving and found calm in the stillness of the depths of the oceans.

One day, Mary dropped into my shop.

'Sandra Fitzgibbon is organising a dive trip to the Galápagos Islands and I'm going with her,' I said. 'Darwin's Arch and Wolf Island. A dream trip!' I was delighted that I had returned to PADI teaching with Waterworld Dive Centre.

Mary sat back. She looked up from over her glasses and propped herself up on the bed, putting down her phone to listen.

'I've always wanted to go to the Galápagos Islands. When are you going?' she replied.

'It's a technical dive trip, Mary. The water is really fast – drift dives, sharks – and we will have to jump off the boat while it's moving. The dives will be very tough, very physical.' Mary had done an open-water dive course many years before, but she was not experienced. The islands were not for recreational divers. 'It's a group of 10 other instructors, Mary. The level of experience would be very high,' I continued, trying to dissuade her. But she had such emotional intelligence that she was quick to spot a blindside. I had to move gently.

'That's brilliant – a load of people to mind me. I'll stick to the easy dives, but yeah, sign me up. I'll go to Galápagos. I don't mind sitting on the boat. Will you tell Sandra?'

I stared at her, unable to speak.

Mary's phone rang. She stood up. At the same time as she was speaking to the customer, she gathered a red Christmas throw into her arms, a nod that she was taking it. She waved back at me. She was coming to Galápagos with us, diving. Eleven instructors and Mary.

The following week, I collected Mary to do a diving refresher course at Maharees Pier before the water got too cold. We organised our equipment and started to get ourselves into the water.

'Don't forget your gloves!' I shouted up.

After entering the water, I did not know whether to laugh or cry. Mary was standing in front of us with a pair of yellow Marigold gloves on her hands – the kind you would use for washing the dishes.

'I couldn't find the ones you gave me, but these are gloves. They will do me fine. I'm setting a trend!' she said with her roguish smile. That shake of her head and those wide eyes that used to get her out of any challenge. Her hands moving like jazz hands. The scene was set for Mary's dive trip to Galápagos.

Landing in Quito, on the side of a mountain, was breathtaking and terrifying. We boarded our liveaboard boat – a beautiful vessel – and then travelled the 600 miles of ocean to the volcanic islands off the South American coast. We were 11 scuba diving instructors and Mary, my sister, the diver.

The water was pristine as the penguins swam across the surface close to Fernandina Island, at Cape Douglas. The iguanas lured us into their prehistoric world, skirting the surface of the water in their hundreds. The area's rich nutrients attracted every marine animal.

The first few days we spent acclimatising, snorkelling, watching and diving shallow dive sites, allowing our bodies to regain their energies from the flights as if sitting in the largest open aquarium in the world. We met lonely George, the world's oldest tortoise.

The intention was always to travel to Wolf Island and Darwin's Arch, two of the most remote islands in the archipelago, over 100 miles north-west of the main islands. This involved a 20-hour boat journey to a remote area of the Pacific Ocean, about 600 miles from the coast of South America.

Mary could not attempt these dives, as the water was so complex, but this didn't appear to bother her. Entering the crystal waters at Darwin's Arch, we descended into crystal blue waters 25 metres to a thermocline, a point where the warm water at the surface meets the cooler water below. Here the temperature would drop from 30 degrees to 16 degrees within 2 metres. Three large and strong sea currents influence the marine life entering the Galápagos archipelago constantly: the Humboldt Current, the Panama Flow and the Cromwell Current. The Humboldt and Cromwell Currents come up from the dark depths, along with massive amounts of nutrients. The Humboldt runs the length of South America from the Antarctic. It was a movie set of real marine life.

The water changed texture and, as I eased up through the thermoclines, breathing steadily, always in control, down again, then up again, just to experience the magnificence of being one on one with nature. I was at my happiest. Everything was calm down there, despite the fact that above our heads, hammerhead sharks swam anticlockwise against fierce currents, swaggering to make progress, their large heads, eyes on each side, a breathtaking vision. That was the most mind-blowing moment. When the currents became too difficult, the huge sharks turned and eased their pace and effort and their shapes eased themselves. A life lesson.

Below us was another species, the Galápagos shark, which was more common in cooler waters. We sat in the middle. Some marine animals were heading south, others were heading north. All insignificant in these vast oceans.

At moments like that, you realise that we, humans and animals, are all passengers in time. Life is precious. Our eyes expressed our smiles to each other through our masks. We were in absolute awe – fingers clenched, grasping and holding on to the rock in the huge current. I can still remember that feeling, as if the world was rotating around us and we were in one fixed position, holding tight. I felt like a child, eyes strained into the end of the tube as I watched kaleidoscope images pass in front of my eyes. If we let go or stopped moving for one second, we would be drawn backwards into the aquatic abyss, pulled backwards around the world in this huge movement of water. Keeping calm as a whale shark passed by and following the plan together during these moments of excitement was what made the underwater world so beautiful. It was a true sense of who we are. Passengers in time, our emotions so insignificant. (Plan your dive, dive your plan.)

Sipping wine each evening on the boat, watching the sunset as the penguins and iguanas flew across the water, Mary was so delighted with the photos. Tomorrow, once we re-entered the centre of the marine reserve and calmer waters, she would get the opportunity to dive.

The sun beat down as we prepared for our dive at Isabela Island, at the Roca Redonda. Giant manta rays were gliding under our catamaran, mouths wide open as they absorbed all in their paths. Their wings were huge and graceful in the crystal blue waters. We were in awe and excited to get into the water. I finished checking Mary's equipment and gave her the okay signal.

'That's you good to go,' I said. I turned to grab my tank and kit myself up, smiling with Sandra, excited about the dive into the crystal blue waters.

We heard a splash, and a scream from a crew member.

Mary had just turned around, shuffled with her fins and

jumped off the back of the catamaran without a look back. She was chasing a manta ray. We stared in shock as her bubbles and body became smaller to our eyes. With the visibility clear, we saw that she was moving under the boat. The scramble to get the equipment on meant the boys were ready first. A few jumped and immediately descended under the boat. The relief! Sandra and I followed within a few minutes, once I had calmed myself. From the surface I would see the divers calmly moving, an okay signal exchanged.

We descended into our liquid heaven.

A huge smile came across our faces, Mary was lying, relaxed on the seabed, hands supporting her face, her eyes wide with excitement as she watched two blacktip sharks shimmy their bellies on the sand, a type of scratching they do. She was transfixed by the watery world, oblivious. A green turtle and some barracuda passed by. I eased myself closer to her and we moved on with our dive, filled with spotted eagle rays, cruising, their wings gracefully moving. As we began our ascent, a huge manta ray approached, half the width of the underside of the boat. Its giant mouth was open and we stared through our masks in awe, all the time reminding ourselves to breathe. What a privilege.

Though I wanted to be angry, and I tried to discuss it, Mary was correct. I said, 'That's you good to go,' so she jumped. I had not been clear that she should wait for the group.

I learned from that experience to be more precise with my instructions.

The time away was brilliant and I fell back in love with adventure. I was thrilled with the blue and green shadows of the mountains, seeing them race across the water. I wanted to do other things, but I also wanted to train for something.

On 1 September 2010, Anne Marie tried the North Channel one more time. She touched the rocks north of Gobbins Island, filled with determination as she dug deep into the water. This was her fourth attempt.

After 9 hours of swimming in 12-degree water, she had covered a great distance. The cold was not her problem and starting at the slightly later time of sunrise meant the heat was on her back.

Once the tide turned, the tide that had driven her backwards, the crews watched and waited. In 4 hours she covered just over 3 kilometres – but she did not go backwards. At 11.00 p.m., after 14.5 hours' swimming, Scotland was only 8 kilometres away.

The boys will bring me home was her mantra. This was now personal for the team and for her. She had not lost ground. I was so nervous, knowing this was her last attempt. The tide turned in her favour and once again there was hope. The boats were so close to her as night dropped that nothing could come between them. You want the boat right on top of you, like an umbilical cord, so you can draw oxygen from the faces watching you. In the next 2 hours, she covered 3.1 kilometres. Anne Marie was making excellent progress. Inch by inch, she was getting there. The patience that was required was incredible.

They say you never know with the sea, but deep down Anne Marie and her team did know. An hour later, Anne Marie became the first Irish woman and the eleventh swimmer in history to cross the North Channel, having done so in 18 hours and 59 minutes. She had swum from the darkness of night to the darkness of night in water so cold that few swimmers worldwide could have survived it.

They wrapped her up and brought her home. Again, there was no fanfare and no medals, and no recognition in Ireland.

'Did you celebrate?' I asked her the evening afterwards.

'No. They dropped me home and told me to rest. Then the team went out to dinner.' She laughed. I decided that, rather than waiting for someone to recognise us, I would seek recognition myself.

The World Open Water Swimming Association (WOWSA), founded by Steven Munatones, had an award for the best swimmer in the world in 2010. I nominated Anne Marie for her North Channel swim. I began a campaign in the media, issuing press releases, and, over two months, spoke about her amazing achievements, including the Round Ireland Swim.

In January 2011, Anne Marie Ward was recognised and honoured as the World Open Water Swimming Woman of the Year 2010 for her North Channel swims. I was so, so proud. We were invited to New York for the ceremony. I was beyond elated. We were going to present ourselves to the global swimming community.

At the event at the United Nations in New York, Anne Marie spoke about her three-year journey to complete the channel swim crossing and the immigrant route from Ireland to Scotland, a route personal to her. They already knew who we were. I thought the world had not been watching, but they knew my name and Captain Tim Johnson, an authority on open-water swimming, had written about our Round Ireland Swim. We belonged without realising it.

The large North Channel marine charts lay on the centre table and some of the best swimmers in the world studied the route Anne Marie had taken. Their eyes then stared at an athlete who could swim in 12-degree water for close to 19 hours. Their surprise and awe, in a world of speed, certainty and expectation, was palpable. Being in a room filled with channel operators, marathon swimmers and organisers from the Tsugaru Channel in Japan and the Catalina Channel in California, all asking such technical questions, was fabulous. They questioned the organisation of the channel swim itself and the applications for it. It stimulated so much thought.

I had learned so much about the North Channel, its tides and its risks. It requires a swimmer who is willing to take defeat and success objectively. There is nothing personal in there. The North Channel is scary in a strange sort of way – dark in its heartbeat and movement. Tides and planning were the key. Yes, so much had been learned – but there was still so much to respect.

'What makes the swim difficult?' a voice asked Anne Marie in her Q&A session.

'The tides and the water temperature,' she replied.

'Were you cold after 18 hours in 12 degrees?' a South African swimmer asked, his accent pronounced.

'Hmmm … I was cold, but I don't think I was hypothermic,' Anne Marie replied with a wry smile. 'It's about training and preparation.'

So much possibility was being opened up in our minds about our future in open-water swimming in Ireland. It was wonderful to present our world to them.

The South African swimmer was studying the charts from the North Channel while Anne Marie was talking.

'How long would you be able to spend in 5 degrees?' he asked Anne Marie. She turned to me. A bizarre question.

'Forty minutes, maybe?' Anne Marie replied, and he jerked backwards, raising his eyebrows.

I didn't think I had ever swum at 5 degrees, so I kept my mouth shut.

'Are you cold afterwards?' he continued. Again, a strange question. *Define 'cold'*, I thought.

'Yes,' Anne Marie replied, but with a shrug, as if to say, well, cold because the water is cold, but not freezing. We didn't look at swims that way, at being cold or not. Of course we were cold – the sea was cold – but we were still fine.

The room gave a little gasp of surprise and a smile as we talked about our swim around Ireland. It was a heart-warming experience to feel so honoured. For years I had searched for this type of conversation – for people who were excited by our achievement. It wasn't about the medals or the accolades, it was about feeling there was value to what we had achieved. Being able to share our experiences with swimmers who had sacrificed so much to achieve their dreams was magical.

Two hours later, the South African swimmer who had asked Anne Marie those seemingly bizarre questions stood up and introduced himself to the room as Ram Barkai, president of the International Ice Swimming Association (IISA). He showed us a video featuring men swimming, visibly surrounded by snow and ice. He shared his vision for the future of the sport of ice swimming. The images showed acutely cold men recovering, shivering and shaking after swimming a mile in water 5 degrees or colder. It looked like a very intense experience, but it was fast. Their bodies were shivering and quite impacted by the cold, but they were alive. There were days during our swim around Ireland when we had been just as bad.

Ram Barkai told us that the ice mile had been achieved by only six swimmers in the world.

Only six people in the association? I could not figure out what the difficulty could be. It was just swimming a mile in very cold water. With what we had endured, how difficult could it be?

I raised my hand.

'How many women have swum an ice mile, Ram, and how many outside of South Africa in your association?'

'All men. No women have achieved an IISA ice mile – yet!' His face was half-smiling at us as my facial expression gave away my surprise. I was aware that Lynne Cox, a woman I was in awe of, had swum a mile in Antarctica in 2003, but what Ram was promoting was a specific standard set by the IISA, which he would certify. Lynne had finished her swimming career before Ram's association became established.

'You've met the right two women,' Noel Brennan remarked, knowing from our faces what we were thinking. Noel had travelled with us to New York.

We all laughed.

'You girls looking to try it?' he finished, as if challenging us.

Anne Marie and I were nudging each other, smiling as our brains were suddenly calculating more adventure – this time, adventure lasting only 40 minutes.

'Absolutely, we could do that,' I said with a smile. 'What's 40 minutes of pain?'

'How can we do an ice mile? Where is the event? What do we have to do to qualify or meet the standard?' Anne Marie fired at him.

'I can come to you in Ireland,' Ram said. 'You just have to swim a mile in water of a certain temperature. It is painful, and not that easy, girls,' he replied with a smile. He may have been joking, but we were not.

'We can swim it anywhere? As long as it's cold water?' I asked.

Pain was a path in life. Not succeeding was painful. Not finding my way forward was painful. Pain was not something to be avoided – it was something that formed part of the journey. Injury was different, but pain was something we could manage and understand. It was only pain.

'We could be the IISA's first women in the world to achieve this,' I said. All I was thinking was that it was winter and the shop would be quiet. I would not have to give up so much to allow for training. It was a win-win situation.

'We can stay alive for a mile,' I whispered to Anne Marie. 'He looks normal enough.'

Watching the videos on the screen of the swim and the recovery, I realised it was just about pain management and hanging in there. That required the very skills we had harnessed over the past decade: patience and resilience.

We giggled with excitement. The recoveries looked rough enough, but what could be worse than what we'd already endured? We were remembering swimming through jellyfish for 5 hours.

'Noel would be well up for it, too,' I said, referring to Noel Brennan, a man who loved all things water-related and who was always pushing for another swimming adventure.

We walked up to Ram and Steven Muñatones, took some photographs with them and asked for their business cards. Steven smiled and shook his head in amusement. I turned to Ram.

'Would you have an interest in coming to Ireland to swim an ice mile with us? We will be the first IISA women in the world, the first Europeans and the first Irish. We have the boats, the crews and the expertise.'

Time would tell whether we could or couldn't do it, but I felt it was possible. Noel was nodding. He was in.

I could see Ram's eyes light up. A man possessed by a sense of adventure. He understood now that we were serious. He could not refuse. He had his new candidates.

'Finding water 5 degrees or below will be dependent on the weather, but we should get it somewhere,' Noel said.

'I'll publish your story in *The Daily News of Open Water Swimming*,' a smiling Steven Muñatones said. 'Send me some stuff on your Round Ireland Swim when you get back, and we must chat about the North Channel. I will connect you with other channel organisers. I would be interested in learning more.

We can help you develop the North Channel swim.'

I could feel the energy lifting inside me. It was the images of the recoveries, the challenge of survival and the men's eyes as they fought their way back. I was intrigued.

Steven spoke about the concept of including the North Channel on a list of the most difficult channels. There would be a lot of work to do. I was delighted to step up.

I was excited for our future in the world of cold-water swimming. I felt free from all that emotion, from not knowing what was next or whom to impress. I could direct my own story instead of trying to understand where I fit in. I could create my own mould. I could set my own scene. There was a sense that people were watching and that I was free to succeed. People would follow. I could see the crest of the wave now. I could see my way out of the trough and into the clearing. The ice would be the adventure I was looking for. I was navigating my way out of the maelstrom.

9

THE DONEGAL ICE MILE

*'To do anything in this world worth doing, we must not stand
back shivering and shaking and thinking of the cold and
danger, but jump in, and scramble through as well as we can.'*
Sydney Smith

We sat at the table in Anne Marie's house in Creeslough, County Donegal, joking and laughing about the ice swim the following morning.

Ram asked, 'Are you girls nervous about tomorrow?'

A silence, a pause. We searched for a word to describe how we felt.

'I don't know,' we both replied. We were so confident. *It's only a mile*, we thought.

There is always a moment when we must be humble in our confidence. What excited me most was the huge day ahead – three boats, teams and adventure. I could not see any reason why we would not finish but, when so few in the world swam in ice, there always had to be a question mark. The physical pain of swimming in cold water was not something that bothered me: pain was something I viewed as a means to achievement. My previous swim a few months ago was 12 hours across Lake Zurich (26.2 kilometres). To prepare, I had completed swims of 3 hours at 8 degrees and Anne Marie had proven her worth. This water would only be a few degrees lower.

As long as I could identify the difference between pain and injury, I would be happy. The only thing that bothered me was not having any experience at this temperature. We went through some videos showing us the outcomes and impact of spending 30 minutes in ice water. It certainly looked extreme, but those people merely looked like swimmers who were acutely cold from being in the water. They all recovered, albeit shivering.

It is a sign of strength to discuss your weaknesses and it is important to explain your fears. Over the previous days, I had visualised the swim, right down to changing in the boat – every feeling, every movement I could picture. I could not see a minute where I would need to get out of that swim. Having swum multiple miles at 7 degrees and for hours at 8 degrees, I felt a soft confidence.

'Can we calibrate the temperature probes and show me what we need to get accredited?' I asked, being obsessed with the details.

We stood near the fridge with a bowl of ice water and dropped our watches and temperature probes into it. The IISA has strict standardised guidelines for the measurement of temperature. Standards were important to me.

'What's the difference between swimming in 5-degree water and 6-degree water? Why 5 degrees and under?' I asked as we watched the temperature numbers on our devices drop. We then had to ensure the three different devices were within the same range.

'I decided on this temperature range for the association,' Ram replied, 'to indicate ice water.'

Our test swim yesterday was 6 degrees. It was a challenge to get my breathing right at the start, but then everything settled and we swam fine.

At our safety meetings before meeting Ram in Donegal, we discussed the risks of ice swimming. We worked on casualty scenarios and took guidance from the experienced Sheephaven Sub

Aqua Club members, who not only worked in cold water in this area but also knew us from the Round Ireland Swim.

The crew can only look for changes in the swimmer – stroke count, body position, lucidity and fatigue. Dr Paul Stewart from Creeslough, who would monitor our attempt, requested medicals in advance of the swim. He would stay with us until we had recovered afterwards. We were delighted to have only one swimmer per team. Most of our physiological changes would be happening internally in cold water. We would need to be alert enough to identify them in ourselves, and then acknowledge and deal with them.

'Dr Stewart is bringing a defibrillator,' Anne Marie said as she wandered about, filling the dishwasher.

We started to laugh – nervous excitement. We had gone from watching videos of acutely hypothermic swimmers shaking vigorously in South Africa, to safety planning for casualty, to drawing veins on our skin, to intravenous fluids and defibrillation of an unresponsive swimmer in about 5 minutes. All because we wanted to swim a mile.

Noel Brennan pulled a rope from under the table and started creating knots. We stared as Noel forged a plan to ensure both Anne Marie and I could exit the water over the tubing of the RIBs when the cold had taken our strength. The boats would also carry a Jacob's cradle, which is a roll method to recover a casualty from the water. Noel thought of everything, and always in his own Noel style.

The Irish Coast Guard Mulroy Unit was coming on a drive-by to observe. In total, we would have fifteen marine-rescue personnel, four medics with two helpers for transportation purposes, and a land operations team with heated jeeps. All for three swimmers – me, Anne Marie and Ram – for just one mile.

Six months ago, we had not yet met Ram Barkai and we knew nothing about ice swimming. Now he was walking up Anne Marie's stairs, going to bed in preparation for an ice swim with us. Here we were, chatting nonchalantly about taking on the Bering Strait – swimming from Russia to the United States – with a group of extreme cold-water swimmers. Really! We burst into belly laughs. It felt so amazing – how so much opportunity can flow from saying yes.

'What have we got ourselves into?' Anne Marie said.

'If they can do it, we can do it,' I said.

'Maybe we should have had a glass of wine,' Anne Marie replied, laughing, and putting the last of the cups into the dishwasher.

'The boys won't let anything happen to us.'

Anne Marie looked at me and said, 'The pain doesn't bother me. I just hope my heart doesn't stop.'

That summed it up.

'Me too. I am going to take my time and enjoy it,' I said.

A final laugh and off we went up to bed.

The water was a dark, menacing grey, folding over on itself. Mulroy Bay was a cauldron of wind. It is a long inlet in north Donegal. Generally the deeper the water, the colder it is, and Mulroy Bay was deep. Thirty minutes bouncing through the waves, three RIBs in convoy, and we were at the start point.

We only have to swim, I kept repeating to myself.

I put my hands on the ropes, sat down on the wet tubing, twisted and lowered myself into the water, holding on. A few smiles from the team as they looked at the waterproof marker tracks on my arms to show where my veins were.

'What if I need a drip and you can't raise a vein? I'm being a really good casualty.' I smiled. They knew me well.

As the weight of my body dropped into the cold water, I was sucked in, my fingers holding tight to the side of the tubing so as not to go too deep under the surface. The icy cold grasped me, like a vice, like I was being choked. It grabbed hold of my ribs and squeezed the muscles tight. A real bite. We had to swim to the pink house at the end of the bay. A mile is the length of Ventry Beach. I only had to reel in the house, a 30-minute swim.

I tried to breathe calmly, but there was a reactive gasping and gulping, more from panic than from swimming. *It's only pain*, I repeated, trying to calm the anxiety.

Five attempts to get my face in the water as I released all the pent-up air from my system. It was a double-edged sword – gasping and breathing, neither successful, but my scuba-diving training had given me a strong pattern of control under stress.

Stop, breathe, think and act.

My arms rotated and my breath flowed more easily.

I was moving.

The islands in my rear peripheral vision were disappearing further behind me with each stroke forward. The blood started receding to my core to protect my organs. My feet tingled like they were going numb, the pain elsewhere a searing, cutting feeling. Nothing unexpected. As I pushed out my ankles, they felt clunky rather than featherlike. I could feel the pins and needles climbing up my legs. Though it was scary at first, I became aware that I was trying to have a pee, but no will in the world would relax my muscles. I could not pee, and I was afraid that that would stop me. I had been drinking warm water and maple syrup in the hours leading up to the swim to heat my core and add to my blood sugar levels.

My hands were starting to become tingly, as if there was no circulation as if I had slept on them, so I clenched my fists and stretched out my fingers. After about another 10 minutes the numbness that Ram had spoken of took hold and the waves began to lift over my head. I became aware of my lack of flexibility. My shoulders were tight to rotate, but I kept my focus on the crew.

Understanding the why of the pain and of the physiological changes I was experiencing made it easier for me to accept them. As my fingers trailed past my eyes, into the darkness, my breathing worked with my mantra – *You're on the cusp of your greatness. Push!* I watched my fingers return under my eyes to my belly. One of the most difficult challenges in teaching scuba diving to new entrants is managing their sometimes-irrational fear of the unknown. Once I am told of the expected outcomes and can understand them, I can tolerate any level of pain. I expected every change – the tingling, the freezing, the breathing. I was happy. There was nothing to fear as the pink house grew in size.

At times, my breathing became elevated and ragged. As the waves hit me I tried to keep rhythm in my stroke. *Stretch out, roll, arm over arm. Swim the dark and lumpy water in front of you.* I could feel the shortness of my breathing – quite a strange feeling, considering I was not racing and there was no pressure on me to go fast. The gasp reflex in my throat seemed to be building, and this could easily lead to panic. It was a mistake to get excited. I was careful not to open my mouth too wide. The ice water was piercing my teeth, my tongue was frozen. I needed to stop thinking and start breathing.

The end of the ice mile was in sight. I could see the windows of the pink house now – they were growing bigger with each stroke. Taking a few extra-long exhalations, blowing bubbles to calm myself (a skill I'd learned when I needed to steady my breathing during scuba-diving), I brought myself back to swimming the water in front of me, the next arm over arm, as the waves lifted and climbed back over my head. This was truly ice swimming, and it was so much more difficult than I had anticipated.

I took a few minutes to relax, repeating to myself: *Take your time. You can take the pain. This is why you are here.* The sound of the engines filled the water and rumbled into my hearing, coming closer. I darted my eyes around. It was the Irish Coast Guard boat coming into my peripheral vision and Dr Stewart giving me the pre-agreed hand signals.

I was excited to confirm with a hand signal that I was fine. Though my hands were freezing, I was so happy with how strong I felt. But it was not over.

The water was dark and heavy, but I tried to visualise heat. I pictured a flowing waterfall of gold that poured in through my head, spreading through my body with bright colour, warmth and glow. I had read that this worked when cold was the overriding feeling. I was not certain if it was working now, but it passed a few minutes. I tried several different waterfall images until I heard myself laughing underwater.

I was supposed to position myself under the waterfall, but I am not great at this type of visualisation. I'm more of a realist. Instead, I looked up at the brown eyes and big smile of David McGloin, who was staring down at me, making eye contact, and I smiled to myself. I closed my eyes and imagined David standing under the waterfall. I could see the water cascading over his body. I must admit, that did warm my heart! I smiled and heard myself laughing under the water again. Where the mind goes.

The green fields and pink house at the end of Mulroy Bay started filling my view, the dark water rising to meet the grey skies. My body gave a few shivers; the cold was starting to get to me.

It's 30 minutes of pain. It's a small price to pay for this moment of greatness. Focus on the positive.

The greyness dropped and, in that split second, the day changed. Rain set in and my stroke missed some rhythm. I started to sing a song to distract myself again; there was no going back to the image of the waterfall. I pushed deep into the water, watching my fingers trail into its cold darkness.

I kept my focus on my mantra: *You're on the cusp of greatness. Do not become complacent. Be aware of all movements.*

I was frightened that, if I stopped moving my feet or hands, they would be difficult to restart. A spasm might occur, such was the extreme of cold. *Be proud and strong*, I told myself. *Count it down.*

The pink house was close. I had reeled it in.

I'm there, I'm there! A mile completed.

My right shoulder was tight and my leg kick was becoming quite stagnant. I was over-analysing every pinch. My ankles felt locked in a square motion, my face tight like a pincushion. I felt that I could pierce my nose and my lips and eyes with needles and not feel a thing, but strangely, I felt alive. Behind me, as I turned around, filled with pride, I watched Anne Marie's hands rotating like seagulls flapping on the surface of the dark water. Ram was swimming towards me. We decided to stay in the water as Anne Marie approached.

Never one to lose a photo opportunity, I asked for my waterproof camera, which came everywhere with me. Eyes stared at me, my frozen hand outstretched, as if to say, 'Really?'

The mile was complete and we were alive. I was ecstatic.

'I told you we could do it!' I shouted at Ram.

I looked at my watch for the first time. The glance told me we had been in the water for 32 minutes. Anne Marie swam close, filled with smiles, and went straight to Noel's boat. We were the second and third women in the world to complete an ice mile under IISA standards, and the first Irish swimmers to do so. Or so we thought.

I took a few photos of Anne Marie reaching for the rope and Noel assisting. My fingers were numb on the buttons, but I really wanted some photos to remember this fabulous moment.

Hands came down and grasped my frozen shoulders and within

a few seconds, I was up at the bow of the RIB, scrabbling through my bags for my clothes. The cold wind started to cut through me, the waves making the RIB unsteady and a lack of balance making changing difficult. The severity of the cold wind became clear as my body suddenly froze solid. My tongue was so cold, I was speaking like I'd just come from the dentist.

One of the main messages that stayed in my head was: *Your swim is alive until you recover your body temperature, so stay in control.* Maintaining that level of control, while at the same time feeling out of control, is part of cold-water recovery and can be a dangerous issue.

I pulled my large survival suit on over my togs, put on a hat and gloves, threw myself down in the bow cover of the tubing and wrapped myself in blankets. We began the long journey back to the pier.

I started to go over in my mind what needed to happen next. I made huge, exaggerated exhalations to clear the cold air from my lungs while inhaling warmer air from inside my suit. That gave me some heat. I tucked my face and head low inside my suit and focused on keeping my eyes open and breathing, humming. We arrived back at the pier. A shiver started to run through me, an involuntary, forceful muscular movement. I could feel the cold moving around my body as if I was getting a little electric shock. My speech started to feel strange; my mouth was numb. But I was in complete control and in great form.

Wrapped in our immersion suits, we sat in the jeeps. Ram walked over to us.

'Sorry to say, ladies, I measured the water on my watch as I was swimming. It cannot be an official ice mile.' He looked disappointed. 'That swim felt just as cold as other ice miles I have completed, because of the conditions.'

We stared at him in disbelief and disappointment. I wanted to ask the boat crews.

Ram pointed out that the temperature had measured 5.6 to 6 degrees. The technical standard was important – 5 degrees or lower – and we had not met it.

I wanted to check with the boats and the crew to see if there was any chance he was mistaken but, as Ram kept talking, I could tell that the swim was not going to be accredited as official. However, it was close.

What is the difference between 5 and 6 degrees? In reality, very little, but for accreditation it was a vital standard. What was important was that the integrity of sport be protected.

We shrugged our shoulders and accepted the response. It was a good learning experience. Anyway, we were 1 degree away from achieving the ice mile. It was possible. Painful, but possible. And we were nowhere near the acutely frozen swimmers from the videos. We were very much in control. I was so proud. I supposed our experience and our immersion suits contributed a lot.

'We will do it again – and this time, get much lower,' Noel said, and we knew he meant it.

Foil blankets were wrapped around us in the Sheephaven Sub Aqua Club house. There were coffee and sandwiches, a great atmosphere. Two doctors and two medical students were loving the excitement of having hypothermic casualties who were not an emergency. My body was becoming much colder than when I was standing on the pier. The shivering was now quite extreme. I felt fine, but when I went into the ladies' I was quite surprised by how physically shattered I looked. I'd thought that I must look great, so that was a shock.

'We're like an experiment,' I said to one of the medical team. 'What would a 30-degree body temperature look like?'

I first met Fungie in 1982, right in the water where he lived for 38 years. On this winter's day in 2018, I was struggling both emotionally and physically and his face would come close to mine, his eyes connecting with me. The sound of his bubbles and Paul's presence were gifts when I felt alone. © *Paul Britten.*

Hanging with the pros at the Chicago Triathlon in 2004. I treated myself to walk the walk with the professional triathletes. I slowed up so they could walk with me. They were great sports when I explained that I broke the world record!! © *Maryann Heidtke.*

My father Benny Moore. Fishing was in our blood and the sea was a way of life in our family.

I had the most amazing childhood of roguery. Clockwise from top-left: my mother Bridget (McGowan) Moore, Mary, me and Edward at the Dingle Races. It was one of the most exciting weekends of the year.

Coming Home – RIS 2006. There was such excitement and emotion coming into Dingle Harbour on 28 July with a flotilla of boats and a welcome on the pier, knowing we had completed three coasts in 27 days and had only one coast left to climb to Donegal. It was hard to process that we had swum close to 1,000km at this point. © *Kathleen King*.

Blasket Sound – RIS 2006. The choice to swim through the Blasket Sound was fraught with risk, mainly due to the rip currents, conflicting tides and eddies, and exposure to the Atlantic Ocean. Risk and trust were what we engaged with on a daily basis. Team was everything to us. Tom did not even get changed after his swim, it was all eyes on the swimmer and readiness was vital. I was swallowed up multiple times. © *Kathleen King*.

1991 at the Cayman Wall, Cayman Islands. I have always felt at home in and under the water, an absolute balance of mind and body. Once we descend, our focus narrows and our body breathes in perfect harmony with the movements of the sea. These moments are when we are truly one on one with nature and when our decisions are all about survival. We never fight it, instead we move with it, dance and adjust our rhythm. Just as life should be.

In 2018, I founded Ocean Remote Recovery Rescue Emergency Care, an interagency initiative. It is fantastic to share, develop and create value to messaging around making the call, preparing safety plans and managing outcomes and risks. The main objective is to create an environment where safety is a culture of discussion, constantly evolving.

'If we can't get you out of the water, you don't get in.' Slyne Head – RIS 2006. The west coast was a daily battle to get into the sea. On 10 August we travelled in convoy 3 miles south-east of Inishbofin, the winds were north-west, force 4. We all wanted to try and swim 500m each to get past Slyne Head. She did not want us in her waters that day. © *Kathleen King*.

Teelin Pier – RIS 2006. Left to right: Henry, Tom, me, Ian, Anne Marie and Ryan. Day 31 – exhaustion was visible. After swimming 50km from Broadhaven Bay in Co. Mayo across Donegal Bay to south-west of Rathlin O'Beirne Island, we then had to steam 24 nautical miles to Teelin Pier. Our arms felt like they had been pulled out of their sockets and our bodies were truly starting to weaken, but we were delighted to be back on Donegal soil.

Lake Zurich, 26.2km, swimming Rapperswil to Zurich, August 2011. 18-degree water. I finished second in my category. Frances Lynch was my crew. I lived in Switzerland in 1990 so it was a fabulous day out swimming and revisiting the familiar towns. After my first freshwater lake swim, I was happy to return to the energy of the ocean. © *Frances Lynch*.

Anne Marie and I invited IISA President Ram Barkai to Donegal to complete the ice mile with us in December 2011, in Mulroy Bay. However, Ram measured the water temperatures at 5.6–6 degrees during his swim, so the mile didn't meet the standard of 5 degrees or under. It was a superb day out and fabulous to finish an event within an hour!

The team had come full circle. Our final night – RIS 2006. Brendan Proctor, Command Boat Skipper on the *Sea Breeze*, Tom, Anne Marie, Ian, me and Ryan. We celebrated in Anne Marie's kitchen, after two months of swimming thousands of miles around Ireland.

'Meeting of the Oceans' – Cape Horn, 2018. Me, Catherine Buckland and Chris Booker. It was surreal to climb the steps onto Cape Horn Island after my swim and receive my certificate, stamped on Cape Horn, confirming my coordinates and exact location in the Drake Passage. As my team, Catherine and Chris were the gold standard in allowing me the trust to let go. Adan Otaiza Caro observed the swim with PatagoniaSwim.

The first 1,000m at 0 degrees by an Irish swimmer – Murmansk 2013. The third woman in the world. We didn't have access to 0-degree ice during training, so I spent three months working on my mindset to accept the journey. It was all about driving into the pain and staying strong. The next Irish swimmer to complete 1,000m at 0 degrees was in 2015.

Tyumen 2015, Russian Winter Swimming Competition. I loved the pomp and ceremony of competition and I was so excited to finish strong and be happy rather than beat anyone. I learned to love racing at my own standards!

His head jolted backwards.

'Quite unconscious and close to dead,' was the reply. Even that information excited me.

In exchange for their medical assistance, we agreed to the medical teams taking whatever information and tests they needed, given that 30 minutes at 6 degrees is a very long immersion. Rescue teams also get great training from handling swimmers who have been immersed in cold water. Our bodies were fragile to handle and yet controlled. It was an interesting experience for everyone.

This was by far the longest and coldest voluntary immersion by any swimmer in Ireland. I can still remember the feeling of stinging pain in my fingers and toes as my body circulated the cold blood back around my body. The rewarming was as challenging as the swim itself.

After 45 minutes of blood-pressure cuffs, pulse oxygen clips and thermometers, being pricked for blood sugars and prodded for information, our core temperatures, measured internally, read 35 degrees. Dr Stewart was happy to leave his 'mother hen' position and step away from us. We had taken the best part of an hour to get back up to that level, but it had been a good, solid recovery.

It fascinated me when I read the sheets with all of our statistics. Ice swimming required so much management of the swimmer, and that piqued my interest – it was like starting diving again. I was also fascinated by the impact of cold water on the heart and the body, especially the need to recover slowly. The scuba-diving world is very much about the risks associated with ascending from the dive. This was so interesting – the greatest risk in the ice appeared to be in the recovery.

'The more movement of the body, the more movement of the blood. If you have cold blood moving too quickly back to the heart, this can cause problems. We like to see people calm and seated in rewarming,' Dr Stewart warned us. I was euphoric immediately after the swim and not focused on my recovery, but time was crucial with the wind and cold when I first got out of the water. I took that on board. I would have to learn to stay calm and controlled. The heart is fragile when it is cold – that was the statement I kept in my mind. I was interested in the physiology of cold-water swimming. I had trained a lot with the Irish Coast Guard on casualty management in hypothermic situations, but monitoring ourselves was different because we could answer the questions.

We had proven our ability to stay committed and focused, to endure pain and to accept challenges and risk. It was a mixture of madness and adventure, extreme swims in this new, extreme world. It was about looking beyond our limits. I was hooked, and ice swims in Russia beckoned. Anne Marie and I were invited onto the first international team to swim the Bering Strait.

At home, the balance had shifted in my personal life. My father needed an even greater caring role from me now. That meant I needed to spend more time at home. Marathon swimming required such a huge time commitment – all those hours in the water – and not being able to commit that time caused a difficult shift in my emotions. I struggled to deal with the sacrifice. But ice swimming was about short distances, intense pain and pushing to the limits. It would give me lots of free time to sit by the fire, to be there for my father, to recover and thaw out. It seemed a match.

When the student is ready the master will arrive. That was a quote given to me a few months ago. I was the student; the master was the ice. I was ready.

All in all, the pain of swimming and pushing limits in cold water was a tiny cost. I was willing to work hard to achieve at the extremes. I was not afraid of discomfort, nor was I afraid of failure. I was comfortable in my world of learning. I was not frightened of being exposed to my weaknesses, of stumbling along, nor of beginning again. I was more concerned about losing the standards I had developed – the image I had of myself, the reflection of what I looked like when I was achieving and felt I should be. I was afraid of becoming irrelevant to the sport and becoming invisible to my dreams. I was so happy having to be strong.

I was addicted to extremes and that feeling of being on the edge. At 18 metres I wanted to dive to 30 metres; at 30 metres I wanted to try mixed gas. I wanted to teach; I wanted to learn. I had worked my way up the professional ranks of scuba diving and was teaching instructors to teach. The ice was a new opportunity. The fact that so few in the world did it excited me. I gave a commitment to Ram that we would grow the IISA and be among the first women to compete.

By accepting the challenge of ice swimming and not showing fear, nor being dissuaded when so many swimmers felt we were crazy, by following our own path and creating a way forward, I was now entering a sport from the bottom rung of the ladder, with passion and confidence. There was something exciting about being new to something. Ice swimming required patience, humility, courage and understanding, skills life had given me in abundance, and skills I would need to keep sharp for my future.

In the autumn evenings of 2012, I found myself defending the cold water regularly. Our experiences allowed us to view outcomes differently. It did not surprise me to hear swimmers saying that ice swimming was dangerous, that cold-water swimming was too risky. Extreme sports often create this response. But the cold water bears no risk until we get into it. What distance and time we decide to do as swimmers is up to our experience and our team. Listening to the fear in their words was something I struggled with. Surely the danger lay in the failure to understand and prepare, not in the experience itself? Life is a risk. For me, there were greater dangers sitting at home and doing nothing. There were dangers in that darkness.

Staring into the fire at night, waiting for my father to get out of bed, I often broke out into random bursts of laughter at the craziness of it all. We had only dreamed of ice swimming. Now Anne Marie and I were invited by the winter swimming federation of the Tyumen Region to compete in 0-degree ice in the far east of Russia, with air temperatures of up to −30 degrees.

There, we would be swimming in just our togs, about to embrace our greatest personal achievement, about to find out how much of ourselves we were willing to sacrifice in physical pain and humility, baring our souls to risk and failure. Stepping up to true ice and being a team member carries huge responsibility. I was so excited about being invited to compete in Siberia. I had no idea what that challenge entailed, but I was saying yes to everything. 'Yes' was my new word.

I just knew that control of some part of my life was going to be the most important thing in the coming months and years. I was becoming a carer, working full time and trying to manage my life. So much was now moving beyond my control. If the pain of swimming in 0-degree ice, the pain of potential failure, the pain of exhaustion and the pain of pushing into the unknown were the price of adventure and fun in a world that was becoming more and more time constrained, then they were a small price to pay. The alternative was losing myself in a world that scared me. It scared me having to sit patiently night after night, waiting for my father to get up, waiting to tend to him. This was my new path in life and, however painful, however risky, it held no fears compared to the challenges of doing nothing and waiting for the days of my life to pass. Being in control of one single outcome allowed me enough of a chink of light to smile. My reflection showed tiredness, but there was an excitement behind those eyes, which could see into a secret world. I would face my reflection and follow the light.

10

BREAKING THE ICE: TYUMEN

'My dreams were all my own; I accounted for them to nobody; they were my refuge when annoyed – my dearest pleasure when free.'
Mary Shelley

When I woke up, I felt as if I'd been hit by a bus. I tried to open my eyes, but my eyelids seemed stuck together. My body ached. I was exhausted. Yet all I had done the previous day was swim 50 metres – just 1 minute – and then 100 metres – just 2 minutes. What had happened to me? Where was the athlete? Why did I not expect this pain?

Draped over the curtain rail in front of me was our washing from the day before: towels, swimming togs, thermal underwear, survival suit. As we were in Siberia, the rooms were heated like furnaces; everything would be dried from yesterday's swims.

Anne Marie lifted her head from the bed across the room.

'Why couldn't we have gone to Vienna with our friends and had a nice, luxury weekend away? Why are we in south-east Russia with swimming togs hanging off the curtain rails?'

We burst out laughing. A few deep breaths and, mechanically, we moved our bodies. Regardless of how we felt, we were in the game. I jumped out of bed.

Swimming in the ice had been an extreme experience, but one I'd loved. I didn't know if I'd enjoyed the swimming – in fact, I was pretty sure I hadn't – but yesterday had been complete madness. My emotions were all over the place – a mixture of excitement, anxiety, stress, adrenaline and fear. But I smiled. I was proud. I was so proud of us. We had been slowly peeling back the layers of the ice over the last year, slowly uncovering its secrets, moving in baby steps. Today would be a giant leap: my first real test at 0 degrees.

We had 4 hours before the marathon races – that is, distances over 500 metres – began at 11.00 a.m. As we walked into the breakfast room, I could sense the nervousness, the anticipation. I was comfortable with my decision to take on the 1,000 metres, based on nothing other than confidence in my own ability. I felt I had enough emotional and mental strength to make it happen. Over the years I'd developed the ability to block out all the things I couldn't control and just focus on what I could. I knew I could rotate my arms; I felt I could swim though immense pain. There was no reason for me not to take on this challenge.

Cristian Vergara from Chile looked up and said, 'You do know that the only other woman in the world, that we know of, to ever have swum 1,000 metres at 0 degrees is the American swimmer Lynne Cox?'

Only a few months ago, Lynne Cox, the world's most experienced extreme swimmer, had reached out to me online after our ice miles. I was blown away and we chatted many times since 2010. I was quite overwhelmed. She was also a carer, for her parents, and loved dogs. She gave me great pointers, but mostly told me to enjoy the experience.

'I only have to stay alive for 20 minutes,' I replied.

It was a contradiction to have such a sense of confidence when I had no experience of swimming distance in ice water, or any water under 3 degrees. My belief and trust were in myself. Maybe it was naivety, but my logic was this: if I can swim for 50 metres or 100 metres, then swimming for 1,000 metres, with my skills and understanding, should be possible.

At 8.00 a.m., a bright orange circle of light in the sky threw a golden orange across the lake. Once outside the bus the wind-chill temperature of –30 degrees took any feeling of heat away. Walking over to the clubhouse to register, I struggled to control my coughing.

The sound of chainsaws filled the air, sluggish and slow, as they cut their way through the 15 centimetres of ice that had formed overnight. Large logs were dragged in to break the remaining ice so we could swim in the pool. Whatever romantic notions I had of swimming 1,000 metres in 0-degree water were quickly draining away. Standing against the railing, frozen solid, was my towel, left behind the night before. We laughed.

My hands cramped in the few moments that I tried to hold my camera. In that split second I thought, *How am I going to breathe, let alone kick my legs to swim?*

One of the men with chainsaws turned to my camera and said, 'You swim? You swim today?'

I nodded and smiled. 'Yes, 1,000 metres.'

He rolled his eyes. 'Crazy, crazy Irish.'

Maybe I was.

I walked towards Ryan Stramrood and Kieron Palframan, two other South African ice milers, who were also videoing their pool.

'What are your thoughts about the 1,000 metres?' I asked them. 'I want to take on the distance.'

Ryan replied, 'Delighted we are not trying the mile.'

There were honest and understandable concerns for the swim

and it felt great to hear their open and respectful opinions. This was also their first 1,000 metres in 0-degree water.

After some chat, I walked to the side of the ice and followed the length of the pool, up and down. My swims yesterday had confirmed that the touch turns in the pool would be my enemy. I had not swum in a pool in a few years and there was a big difference in mental approach between swimming in open water and pool swimming – in the giving over of trust. I am not a pool swimmer.

I visualised the distance. I counted the turns and pinpointed when I could get out. *Why would I want to opt out? Why did I think that?* It was such a strange feeling for me to be creating a plan to give up rather than to finish. My eyes travelled up and down the ice-filled lanes and my mind created the pathway. *I can come out at 150, 300, 500 or 800 metres, or stay for the 1,000 metres.* It was a good insurance policy to have an opt-out strategy, I supposed, even if I didn't like that option. For me, each time you touch a wall to turn, your mind has the choice to stop because the pool actually stops you. You have to actively choose to turn and start again. I respond better to commitment than choice.

I ran to the tents to get out of the cold. Inside, the swim teams from all over Russia were gathering in their groups to read the entrant lists. The marathon-distance women were first up. There were only four in total, and my name was on the list.

I took some deep breaths but my heart was racing as I stood in line for the pre-race medical. I tried to focus on the calm. If I did not pass the cardiac and medical check, I would not be allowed to swim. A thermometer was directed at my forehead to measure my core temperature: 36.1 degrees. They placed clips connected to wires and a computer onto my ankles and wrists.

'Close eyes and breathe,' Dr Irina Zhidova, the head medic, said matter-of-factly, using her hands to indicate slow breathing.

With my hands facing palm upwards, and despite breathing slowly, my heart seemed to be racing. The tracing started on the rhythm of my heart.

Dr Irina called the translator and she explained to me that my heart was beating very quickly. I needed to calm down. I thought I was calm.

The third test was the blood-pressure monitor. It displayed 150/90. This was very high. I was quite dismayed, but not surprised. I had been running around, not to mention the two cups of coffee for breakfast. The doctor explained to the translator that it was not possible for me to swim with my blood pressure at this level.

I presented my Irish medical form. I explained that my normal blood pressure was 120/80, while my pulse was normally much lower. I showed her the tracing of my ECG. The translator explained that they would only allow me to swim when they felt I was calm and medically fit to take on the pressure of the ice.

'You go for 30 minutes to a very quiet place. Drink water, close your eyes and see if you can change your blood pressure. If you can, then you can swim. If not, then you must do a shorter distance – 500 metres,' she said. Then she whispered to me, 'There are already four other swimmers in the quiet place.' I grabbed my bottle of water and off I went. This was the first time I took in the gravity of the challenge of swimming 1,000 metres in 0-degree water.

Thirty minutes later, feeling confident, I presented at the medical tent. Dr Irina smiled at me as she confirmed that my blood pressure had reduced to 130/85. This was acceptable.

If you are going to challenge your limits, it is important to have trust in the eyes that are watching you and to draw from their strength. That is what I had learned. But today, Anne Marie would be swimming immediately ahead of me, so I would not be there for her and she would not be there for me. We had always worked as a team, so I felt nervous. Anne Marie and I had watched each other for years. I was glad to have Noel Brennan with us.

'Everyone at home, they will all think we are heroes,' Anne Marie said. 'We have nothing to prove. We are ice swimmers.' We had to remind ourselves we were pushing the boundaries of the human body.

We laughed and I rolled my eyes at the absolute insanity of our situation: sitting under a tricolour flag, representing our country in far-eastern Siberia, dressed in our dressing gowns.

I heard Anne Marie's name being announced over the loudspeaker. She was swimming the 300 metres. With a hug, she left for the changing room.

'Good luck,' I said. I was so excited.

She turned back and said, 'Remember, they will all think we're amazing when we go home, whether we swim 50 metres or 1,000 metres. So just enjoy the swim. See you in the sauna.'

We moved to the warm-up tent.

I started to think again about all the things that could stop me. How would I breathe? How could I breathe in −33-degree air? Would I know when to stop? My mind went back to a conversation I'd once had with Mike O'Shea at home in Dingle. Mike is an adventurer and was part of the K2 West Ridge expedition team. We had discussed breathing in ice-laden air and he explained to me that it was best to breathe shallowly, to start slowly, taking air into the mouth, and breathe into the back of the throat, not deep into the lungs.

I closed my eyes for one last moment and tried to relax. I focused on the task: 40 lengths of a 25-metre pool; that was 20 doubles. I counted up and down and visualised every turn. The loudspeaker blew and it was my turn to move. With one final inhalation, I stepped out and braced against the biting Siberian winds, white snow and ice as far as the eye could see. I began greeting and responding to people I did not know in a language I did not understand.

I walked to the poolside in my teddy-bear dressing gown and my Crocs, a mixture of excitement and fun, fear and anxiety, stress and expectation all bundled into this moment.

The wind was cutting through me as I stood on the ice in my swimming togs. Once I put my feet on the first rung of the ladder, searing cold shot up my legs. I grasped the handles tightly as I took the first step down into the dark ice water.

Focus, focus, breathe, I said to myself. My breathing started to race. *Breathe in through the nose, out through the mouth. Just focus with everything you have. Stay alive and swim in here for 20 minutes. Twenty times up and twenty times down. That's it. No more, no less. You can do this. You are built for this. Breathe.*

I took the next step into the ice. My response was to gasp air and my heart felt as if it would burst out of my chest. I put ice water on my face and my neck, put my face in the water in a standing position and breathed all the air out of my lungs, as I had been told to do. This was cold shock, an expected response to cold-water immersion. I followed all the directions.

There was a Russian lady standing in the lane beside me and she shook my hand. She was all smiles and wearing a woolly hat to top off her togs. She gave me a thumbs-up. I turned to Noel and Mariia Yrjö-Koskinen from Finland, the president of the International Winter Swimming Association (IWSA). Thumbs-up. Then, the starter sound: *beep, beep, beep*. I pushed off from the side of the pool and embraced the darkness of the ice water, dark from the silty bottom of the lake.

For the first 50 metres I rotated my arms and spent the time focusing purely on breathing in and out. I went really slowly. The swimmer in the lane beside me, the lady with the woolly hat, was,

I later discovered, Natalia Seraya from Moscow. She was swimming breaststroke, head up, with no goggles, staring at the horizon, focused. She looked mechanical and very comfortable as I passed her. With each stroke I repeated to myself: *There is no pressure*. I pushed long into the water. My hands were paralysed with pins and needles. My face felt as if a thousand nails were being forced through the skin; there was searing pain through my teeth. A few times, I forgot to exhale under the water and then had to exhale and inhale when I raised my head.

At the 100-metre mark I touched the ice wall and turned to push off the timber wall block with my feet. But I had turned too deep and my feet went under the board. For a brief moment, I sank under the water and went backwards under the block into the pitch-black lake. This resulted in my body sinking under, into the dark, silty, brown water.

I opened my mouth to take a breath, but there was no air. I surfaced but my rhythm was gone. I gagged as my mouth filled with water. *Follow your fingers*, I screamed to myself. *Reach into the darkness and find yourself.* I was gasping for air and could not control my breath. It was the strangest sensation.

Four lengths done, thirty-six to go, my mind suddenly became very dark, as dark and murky as the water I was swimming through. The pain in my fingers had by now started to cramp them into a claw. My breathing cut to very short, laboured gasps, getting caught in my throat. I was unable to get enough air. I started to panic. The monsters were now in control.

Normally, when I'm swimming, I think of the stretch ahead. Now I couldn't visualise the next 100 metres. I couldn't remember whether I had counted four lengths or five lengths. I couldn't figure out how to breathe in and out in a rhythm that was in sync with my arm stroke.

I looked to my left. Everybody was giving me the okay signal, but I wasn't okay. I said to myself, *Get to 300 metres and see how you feel,* but I couldn't remember if I was at 100 metres or 250 metres. I wasn't able to count. I just couldn't see the way ahead. I was stuck. I was stuck because I couldn't figure out how to breathe. Every stroke was intense, the pain in my face now like 15 ice-cream headaches. My feet started to spasm from pushing off the boards at each end. My brain started to scream at me: *What if you are not okay? How do you know if you are not okay? You don't.*

My breathing became so ragged I thought I was going to drown. My mind exploded with thoughts: *I have to get out of here. I am going to die.* My stroke got short and panicky until I reached for the end wall. Immediately my feet went under me, and I stood up. Through my goggles, I could see Natalia. I thought I could see some ice on her face, but still she was swimming breaststroke as if on a Sunday-afternoon dip. I grabbed the wall and put my feet under me.

I lifted my goggles off my head and, step after step, got to the top of the ladder. When I put my feet on the surface, I looked to Noel and Mariia with a huge smile. I was done. Noel was coming over to me with my teddy-bear dressing gown. I went to step towards him, then realised that my feet were frozen to the icy ground and my hands stuck to the ladder. They had to pour water over them to release me.

I wasn't tired. I was free. It was the strangest feeling of euphoria. I looked over to Natalia. She was still swimming. I could see that her eyelashes were now frozen and there were ice drops crystallising on her hair, which was now white under her hat as she swam forward. I was not cold at all. And I could not remember the pain.

With Noel holding my arm, we walked through the snow to the sauna. Outside, there was a room for swimmers entering initially and here we left our clothes. This space was warm but not too hot, so as not to shock the circulatory system. A few minutes here, and then we entered the sauna and I was greeted by Russian men singing a song. Through the steam, I recognised Anne Marie staring at me, smiling, her two frozen hands tucked in under one of the men's armpits. Another Russian man grabbed my frozen, clawed hands and pushed them under his armpits, too, heating them up using his body. I stared at Anne Marie. Here we were, standing with our hands under the armpits of men we had never met, singing songs in Russian. I just went with it. The singing continued and one by one people filed into the sauna as the heat crept back into our bones. This was such madness.

The atmosphere changed with a sudden bang as the sounds of shouting and urgency filled the room. The door bust open and, in a few short seconds, the singing men exited the steam-filled sauna room.

Ten seconds later, the burly bodies of two other Russian men forced open the small door. They were faces I recognised from the poolside, carrying what appeared to be a lifeless body, arms limp. We pushed ourselves into the corner, trying to be invisible. The woman was placed in a foetal position on the lower bench, knees to her chest, and the two sauna attendants immediately began removing her frozen clothing. Her woolly hat was replaced with a special felt hat. Her face was as white as any I had ever seen. Even through the steam and lights I could make out her eyes, frozen, pupils fixed in a stare that showed no signs of life, ice hanging from her hair and eyelashes. Her head, unable to support itself, bobbed from side to side. Her fingers curled inwards to form claws. Buckets of water, cold water, were placed at her feet and the sauna attendants placed her feet and hands in this cold water. I was fascinated and transfixed. What were they doing?

The two bikini-clad sauna attendants spoke in words that I did not understand but in a tone that I very much understood. This was a serious situation. Towels soaked in warm water were draped around the woman's body, under the armpits and around the thighs. Minutes later they were replaced with fresh, warm towels. The towels acted as a poultice, to drive out the cold. The woman's eyelids fell down and closed for the first time since I had been watching her. She tried to speak, but the words that came from her mouth sounded like a robot from a *Star Wars* movie – slow and laboured. The sauna attendants continued to draw out the cold from her core and, with each towel change, life seem to be returning. Her hands and feet, no longer in the cold water, were now wrapped in warm towels.

Natalia slowly began to move under her own control, like a person who'd had too much to drink. My eyes darted to Anne Marie and I whispered, 'That's the lady who was swimming in the lane beside me.'

'How long did she swim?' I asked.

The sauna attendants said, 'An hour, plus 1,000 metres.'

Were we here in the sauna for that long? How could we have not thought about the woman who was still swimming?

'Is that what 1,000 metres at 0 degrees looks like? She's in bad shape.' I stared at Anne Marie.

'No wonder we got out of the water,' said Jackie Cobell, a UK ice and marathon swimmer and amazing lady, as we tried to understand the impact of swimming in ice water. 'We did great, girls.'

One last look back at Natalia, who was now thawing out and looking better. We opened the door and were immediately ambushed by the searing winds and Siberian snow.

Walking through the snow came Ram Barkai, a towel wrapped around his waist, smiling with confidence. He was followed by Ryan Stramrood and Kieron Palframan.

The stunning Peddler's Lake in the Conor Pass, 20 January 2013. I made the decision with my team to swim 1,800m for my ice mile. Since so few people in the world were pushing distances sub 5 degrees, I didn't have a training programme, just me, training by feel and pushing into my own boundaries using my own theories. Sometimes it is just us and our own limits – it's only by going too far that we learn how far we can go. © *Mossy Donegan.*

Once I was dressed after my 38-minute immersion in Peddler's Lake at 2–3 degrees, the wind lifted and the air dropped to –6 degrees with a stiff wind chill. It was only 100m down to my jeep. I became weak. My team decided to call for assistance. My transfer to Rescue 115, airlift and transfer from swimmer to casualty was one of the most humbling experiences of my life. © *Ciara Lynch.*

Broadhaven Bay – RIS 2006. Anne Marie and I, the tiredness starting to show. Having completed 1000km of swimming, we continued to battle tides and conflicting waters in the bays and inlets of north Mayo. There was little or no tidal assistance in these areas so swim times were slow as the wild Atlantic Ocean battered us day by day. © *Kathleen King*.

The Original Bond Girls – Anne Marie Ward, me, Melissa O'Reilly (USA) and Jackie Cobell (UK) in Murmansk at the Russian Winter Swimming Championships in 2013, preparing for our Bering Strait Relay. We inspired each other. Each individual's strength helped to push boundaries despite the risks, creating amazing adventures and memories.

Christmas Day Swim – Beenbawn beach. There was always a 'Mary way' of doing things. Most people come to the Christmas Day Swim with flasks of warm drinks but Mary always arrived with more than five of the biggest pots of mulled wine, mulled gin, hot chocolate and homemade soup.

Wales, Alaska, 2013. Five days after we started our relay swim at Cape Dezchev, the last point of the Russian Federation, we swam onto the coast of Wales, Alaska. Swimming with our flags in the air for the last 500m was very difficult. Teamwork, resilience and willingness to adapt was the recipe for success.

The Bering Strait Relay handover between Anne Marie Ward and Paolo Chiarino (Italy), water temperature at 3 degrees, 80 knot winds from the Arctic. Despite the cold after my swim, I loved to lie on the bow of the RIB and just revel in the adventure. © *Jack Bright.*

Toothed walrus – Bering Strait Relay 2013. The swim route had to be pushed south of the Diomede Islands due to the lines of toothed walruses protecting their colony on the islands. Their size, tusks, 2,000kg power and threatening presence was something to behold, knowing they could be curious and hungry. © *Viktorv Torbin.*

Bering Strait 2013 – Anne Marie, our Russian teammate and me leaving the command ship to transfer to our swim start in freezing temperatures. We would recover in these open RIBs. Our immersion suits were lifesavers for us, as we were exposed to the freezing winds and water of the Bering Strait. © *Vladislav Vasilievich Bykov.*

'The most dangerous swim in open water history' – Bering Strait Relay. The RIBs were swallowed by 4-metre waves. In this photo, there are two boats and a swimmer in the water. Progress was metre by metre, but each swimmer had to keep fighting hard. In one and a half hours, nine fast swimmers completed a total of 50 metres. We battled over five days but, inch by inch, arm over arm, we swam from Russia to America.

Staying warm after 2km in ice – Italy Glacier 2018. Preparation for transfers is part of the swim. This was taken post 2 km swim at the Beagle Channel, water temperature of 2–3 degrees, during the transfer back to the *Fortuna*, where I was warmed up for our journey south to Cape Horn. © *Catherine Buckland.*

Tyumen Siberia. We were invited to take part in the Russian Winter Swimming Championships by Aleksey Salmin, coordinator of the winter swimming federation of the Tyumen Region. It was our first swim at 0 degree ice. The air was −33 degrees. Ice swimming opened a portal to a wonderful world of fun and friendships.

Perito Moreno Glacier, Patagonia, Argentina 2014 with Swim Argentina and Matías Ola. The Perito Moreno glacier waters were so soft and gentle. It was surreal to hear the crushing sound of the ice caving and breaking off. Despite it being a 'race', I always found time to stop and smile for the camera.

Trust and let go. No Land East or West – The Drake Passage, 2018. Water temperature 7 degrees and strong winds. The reality of this moment was terrifying. As the pilot boat steamed away, I knew that I might be pushed backwards. At this location there is no land east or west. The oceans meet in one of the most dangerous bodies of water in the world, in frustrated seas. But I did let go and trusted myself and my team – Chris, Catherine, Julieta Nunez, Cristain Vergara, Roni and Olivier on *Fortuna*. © *Catherine Buckland*.

Proud to leave the first Irish tricolour at the lighthouse at the remote Island of Cape Horn. I was the first swimmer in the world to complete the 'Meeting of the Oceans' Pacific Ocean to Atlantic Ocean, south of the southern tip and observed by Adan Otaiza Caro, commanding officer of the lighthouse of Cape Horn, 2018.

So proud to stand at the monument of the Albatross facing the southern oceans at Cape Horn. I dreamed of this moment for many years, and was so proud of my courage in taking this risk. 2018. © *Catherine Buckland.*

Mary and I, Beenbawn, under the lighthouse, Dingle. 2020.
One day, one world, one love, one thought, one gift, one passion, one life.
Live in the moment. Smile often! Dream big.
May you have an angel on your shoulder.
Remember you are loved and never, never give up.

I shared little with these men as regards our swimming backgrounds, but there was a common streak of madness in us. That is what made us all tick – a sense of belief, a sense of courage, a sense of 'nothing is impossible' – and it gave each of us a casual acceptance of the other's thinking, something that made us want to be in their company. It was an excitement I had not experienced around swimmers since the Round Ireland Swim. Once you break into that part of your being, you can only find support in like-minded people.

The decision by Ram, Kieron and Ryan to take on the 1,000 metres at 0 degrees looked a lot more bothersome than it was for us. Anne Marie and I were unknown in the world of ice swimming, but they carried the weight of expectation. I stayed to watch because I wanted to see the physical shape of Ram exiting the water – to see how he would manage the distance. I could never learn whether it was possible until I saw it happen. I heard them discussing their genuine fears of the outcome of this swim. It was an attitude that I appreciated: we all have questions, but fear does not frame our decision to do it. Training and pure courage do.

The daylight was beginning to disappear. Both Ryan and Kieron, arms folded under their armpits for protection, faces tucked deep into their chests as they walked the 40 lengths up and down, maintained eye contact with Ram as he swam. I was more focused on the dynamics of the swim than the swimmer himself. Ryan and Kieron stood at the ladder to help Ram out when he finished.

I had just witnessed someone swimming 1,000 metres at 0 degrees and he was still moving and functioning. It was possible. My mind was trying to work out if I could push myself that far. Could I go there? Could I lose control? This was the thin line. I had not been willing to let go – was that why I had got out?

The sounds of screams, clapping and music announced the arrival poolside of Ryan and Kieron for their attempt at 1,000 metres. The music poolside seemed such a contradiction to the activity in the ice.

As Kieron was getting ready to swim, I stepped forward and said, 'I'll watch you poolside.' He nodded. Mainly, I wanted to remain poolside. I wanted to see his eyes through their goggles. I wanted to be up close, not behind the barrier. I needed to watch each length and understand how to swim. I needed to be part of the team.

Like synchronised swimmers, Ryan and Kieron flew high through the foggy air and broke the ice water at exactly the same moment. It was beautiful. Their stroke rotated at exactly the same pace, indicating that they had been swimming together for years. I took photos, despite my freezing hands.

Their arms pulled hard to glide forward. It was rhythmic, synchronistic, neither man being left behind. I met Ryan's eyes through his goggles. It was so strange how a pair of eyes could connect, his pupils piercing and straining for contact, despite the fog, the spray of water and the darkness of the day. Both swimmers' eyes fascinated me.

This was bringing me back to the Round Ireland Swim, when, despite all the physical and emotional exhaustion, we sat and stared at each other – not because we had to, but because we understood what meeting a pair of eyes meant to a swimmer searching for answers. Watching Kieron moving so fluidly, I wondered why I had not been able to swim through the emotions.

The daylight was dropping away and the air was now thick with freezing fog as we watched the two bodies moving with such wonderful umbilical support running between them. Kieron's hands and feet were clawed, frozen. His fingers were unable to hold the towel and he could not dress himself, but he was able to communicate. I immediately reached down to put his feet in flip-flops, and I wrapped a towel around Kieron.

It was the strangest vision – two Russian men, heavily dressed to withstand the freezing air of Siberia, holding the arms of a man wearing nothing but a pair of swimming trunks, wrapped in a towel, his feet unable to grip his flip-flops, barely moving his legs as they disappeared into shadows of fog, through the snow to a timber hut.

There were no high-fives, there was no elation. It was straight to phase two: get the two boys to the sauna. Up close I could see the impact of swimming in the ice. There was a vacancy in their eyes, a need to be held owing to the unsteadiness of their feet, a sense of void in their comprehension. This was a different level of commitment.

I was replaying my own swim in my head. *Why did I get out of the water? Why could I not let go? What stopped me? I could do this.*

The sky was now a deep orange and the lights poolside were the only assistance. I was truly freezing, but two Russian swimmers were now beginning their swim. Stumbling through the soft snow, I took out my camera and started to focus on their faces. Two swimmers swimming breaststroke. The pain of the searing wind was making standing outside very difficult. The air temperature was now −40 degrees in a strong wind, but I had to stay to understand.

'How long is this swim?' I innocently asked Aleksandr Jakovlev, chairman of the IWSA.

'They are swimming until one of them stops,' he replied.

I stared at him, then at the swimmers, then replied, 'What if no one stops?'

'Someone will stop swimming, at some point,' he said calmly.

My anxiety levels started to rise again. *What does that mean, until one of them stops? Stops how?*

'They are attempting the world record, for the longest time spent swimming in 0 degrees.'

I could not get my head past 'until one of them stops'.

The atmosphere poolside had become very tense. Forty minutes had passed and both men, Alexander Brylin and Andrei Stoyev, were still breaststroking up and down the pool. Alexander looked the stronger of the two, but this was not about strength, this was about survival – who could keep going, or rather, who would stop. What were we watching?

Ice had formed on Andrei's goggles and his clawed hand lifted them high off his face, despite the protests of his supporters.

I was now walking up and down the side, stroke for stroke with Andrei. Alexander was moving more slowly but much more strongly than Andrei. There were loud groans and grunts with each breath, as if their bodies were screaming for help. Hands in frozen claws and eyes frozen open. Icicles forming on their eyelids from the water splashing back on their faces. The tension was now clear. A woman started to scream. I ran to my bag and brought back a tinfoil blanket, as if to help in some way. Russian men started to shout at Alexander, who was responding. Fifty minutes had passed and Andrei Stoyev, despite moving his arms, was making little progress. I started to cry. How would this be stopped? I started to walk up and down the poolside, seeking someone to help. In that instant, Alexander Brylin grasped the ladder and removed himself from the pool. He was strong enough to manage his own movements. Andrei Stoyev's team decided to allow him two more lengths, to win by 50 metres. They were a difficult 50 metres to watch.

But he did it. At the ladder, Andrei was lifted from the water and held in a horizontal position, face down. He was frozen. His feet were inserted into large boots made from reindeer skin. He was wrapped in two blankets and carried like a log headfirst at speed to the sauna. I was enthralled and, despite the sense of panic, I ran after the team.

Andrei Stoyev had completed 2,100 metres in 56 minutes at 0 degrees, breaking the world record.

The air was now so cold that it was becoming more difficult to breathe. A tall, athletic figure was walking towards the pool. It was Estonian swimmer Henri Kaarma. We had shared a taxi this morning, with Anne Marie. I ran back to the poolside. The hair that was exposed from under my hat was firmly frozen and white, but I was not able to draw myself away.

At the sound of the whistle, Henri flew through the air. He dived high and was briefly suspended before his body broke through the thin sheet of ice that had formed on the pool. The air was still −40 degrees with the wind chill. Henri pushed his arms at speed and with such power, never wavering. Aleksandr from Latvia shouted out each length. I tried to take some photographs, but my camera refused to operate at this temperature.

It was beautiful and surreal watching Henri rotate his arms. It was effortless. His turns, his leg kick, his push off the wall. It was difficult to even think this was anything other than a regular swim for Henri. I had a new hero.

At 32 minutes, with 1,650m completed, Henri Kaarma climbed up the ladder, smiled and waved. He walked to the timber sauna. I was euphoric. I had just witnessed the three longest swims in the world of ice swimming. I was certain I was strong enough. I was captivated by the sport.

All of the other women at the medal-presentation ceremony were dressed so glamorously, but the only clothes Anne Marie and I had with us were our thermals. All the same, we enjoyed the party atmosphere alongside the Chilean swimmer Cristian Vergara, who lived in New York. The theme tune from *Dallas* was blasting through the speakers. It was ironic – here we were in Siberian oil country, clapping to the theme tune of *Dallas*.

Despite not understanding the process or speaking Russian, we cheered and applauded every winner. A sense of elation filled my heart when Alexander Brylin, Andrei Stoyev and Henri Kaarma stood to receive their medals. They were my newfound teammates and a medical miracle in my eyes. The medals had little value – we all recognised a sense of possibility in each other. A sense that we were on the cusp of great adventures, that we were forming a team.

Suddenly I was being ushered to the podium. I had won bronze in the 150 metres. Rather than elation, I felt embarrassed receiving my medal dressed only in thermals.

At 10.00 p.m. we sat down to dinner hosted by Alexei Salmin, a businessman who was passionate about the sport. We were torn between eating and sleeping, but decided we had better fuel our bodies. At 11.30 p.m. we got into our taxi and headed for our hotel, leaving the party behind us.

Three hours later, the alarm on my phone abruptly pulled me from sleep. I felt every muscle in my body aching.

I woke Anne Marie, then had a shower. Despite the warm water, I felt a cold sweat come over me. I felt dizzy and lightheaded. My breathing started to get ragged. I turned the hot water to cold and back to hot in an attempt to focus, but the sweat kept coming. My leg developed cramps; then the arch of my foot to the inside of my knee and all the way to my groin suddenly went into spasm. Unable to stand or stretch, I fell to the floor, contorted in agony.

I curled into a foetal position, feeling as if someone had pulled the veins from the instep of my foot right up to my groin. I noticed a line of bruises, like dots along my inner thighs. Using my hands, I pulled myself upright. The spasm had passed, but it took every ounce of my strength to prevent myself from fainting as the cold sweat poured from my skin.

It passed. Between the heat of the room, the heat of the sauna, the heat of the indoors and frequent peeing, my body was totally dehydrated. Now I had to get to the airport. My mind immediately went to the risk of flying without adequate hydration. I had three flights from Russia and I understood the danger. I drank 3 litres of water in Moscow airport.

My sister Mary picked me up at Cork Airport at 11.00 p.m. with sugary drinks, electrolyte powders and a Tupperware dish of chopped pineapple. My feet were swollen. I had a lot to think about. I knew it was very important to stay awake for the journey home to Dingle, a 3-hour drive.

'Now so, how was the 1,000 metres?' Mary asked.

I explained how I had stopped at 150 metres, that I could not figure out how to swim, that my breathing had gone and that I had panicked.

'That is so not like you! Why did you stop swimming? What do you mean you panicked?' Mary asked. She was not impressed. We were from a family of strong women and panic was not an acceptable response to life.

We chatted about the fact that I had been tired from being up through the nights with Dad, but feeling weak wasn't really what I was struggling with.

'You never panic, Nuala. You will figure that out. When can you try again?' she asked when we stopped for coffee and cake.

I spoke about the experience of eating with the Russians and how they toasted everything with vodka. Mary had just started her new job as general manager of the Dingle Distillery. At the mention of vodka, she was off on her marketing plan. Mary was a marketing genius at any hour of the day.

'When are you going again? Do you think we could get a few bottles of Dingle Vodka to Russia?'

A huge smile spread across my face in the darkness of the car. I had been given the go-ahead to travel and try again. I was so excited at the possibility.

'Of course – that would be easy,' I replied. Mary seemed to have completely missed the concept that I had immersed my body in ice.

She dropped me home with her usual parting words: 'Now so, if you need anything just give me a call. And 11 o'clock is time enough to be opening your shop.'

It was 2.00 a.m. when I turned the key in my door, dropped in my bags and was greeted by two bounding dogs, Hally and Beethoven.

A voice came from the back room. 'Is that you?'

My father was delighted to have me home, even though it had only been four days.

'Put the kettle on. Is there anything on the telly? I'll get up for an hour. Turn on the telly,' he shouted from his bed. 'Did you bring a tab nab?' My father always called sweet cakes 'tab nabs'.

In the dark of the hallway, I closed my eyes and smiled. Back to normal life.

'Yeah, it's me. I'll make you a cup of tea.'

An hour later, Dad was organised. His tea and tab nab were delivered, a small fire had been set so that he could watch the news on TV, the dogs had been walked and we'd had a long chat about Siberia and the ice. I climbed the stairs and fell into bed at 3.30 a.m., setting the clock for half past nine, for work. Propped up with pillows, laughing to myself, I sipped my cup of tea. I had slept little in the last few days, but my mind was still running at warp speed with excitement. I had learned to love the silent moment I took to debrief before I lay down, a sort of rewinding of the day's activities so that my head could rest.

Where do I go from here?

I was disappointed with myself – not in a downcast way, but I knew that I was capable of a better distance. What I had learned over the previous decade was that we need the freedom to succeed. These last few days, I had not been free to succeed. There were barriers in my mind – obstacles of emotions, the panic of the unknown. Feelings and blockades I had managed to create internally.

The pool of ice, the feeling of weakness and panic, the sense of my shortcomings, the need to get out of the water after a few minutes … these were new experiences for me.

Why had I panicked and grasped the ladder? Was I tired? Was I losing my sharpness? Was becoming a carer, with the new shift in my life balance it brought, a new challenge? Was it to do with the pressure of my new role? I could not pinpoint the exact moment in the ice that the panic and fear became the dominant emotions. Panic and fear are not normal responses for me. Failure was not a problem, but being unable to commit to the swim bothered me. I had become sniper-like in my attention to my emotions. I examined every weakness.

My mind flashed back to 2007, when my world had fallen apart after the Round Ireland Swim. I had learned so much about myself in the following years. I had worked hard to be strong again, so why was I so fragile in the ice? Why was I not able to find that strength when it was only pain I faced? Pain had never frightened me. What was it that had stopped me, then, from swimming? How did I go from 10,000 metres being comfortable to 150 meters being my maximum?

I closed my eyes and replayed the swim. Arm over arm. I could see myself finishing 1,000 metres, so now all I needed to do was do it. It was a gap I needed to fill.

A sentence fell from my lips: 'If you think something will stop you, you may as well let it.' Henry Ford, I thought. I smiled. I would keep pushing. I would train for what had stopped me.

But I don't know what that is, I thought. *Okay. My first task is finding out what stopped me. I knew I was better than this.*

A few long breaths, in and out, to focus on my calm. My eyes felt heavy. I turned the room to darkness and my head started to think of what was possible. I could see myself finishing the swim. I could see myself climbing out of the pool. I just needed to figure out how to get there in real life.

11

MAKING THE CALL

'The mountains have rules. They are harsh rules, but they are there, and if you keep them you are safe. A mountain is not like men. A mountain is sincere. The weapons to conquer it exist inside you, inside your soul.'
Walter Bonatti

The soles of my feet were numb as I eased my frozen body out over the rocks, now greasy from the previous night's frost and rain. I used my hands to stabilise myself while my beautiful collie sheepdog, LJ, licked my face in excitement. His brown eyes and his barking were the things I searched for as he ran the swim course over and back, as if to protect me. I rolled onto my bum and eased my way backwards, hand over hand. The fog rolled around the colossal backdrop of the cliff face, making it seem like a rough-hewn amphitheatre awaiting a dramatic act. There was no graceful way out of Peddler's Lake, at least none that I could manage.

The lake is a corrie on the stunning Conor Pass, 6.5 kilometres away from Dingle town.

Once I reached my mats and towels, my routine was to sit a while and flex my feet. Despite it being only 9.30 a.m., the winter darkness gave an eerie and foreboding feeling to the lake. The only sound was the occasional bleating of rambling sheep. There were times that being up here alone caused me to feel nervous and then other moments, like this, when I was immersed in the privilege of being here. I was a tiny person, surrounded by the vastness of Mother Nature, a 360-degree view of magnificence. As I sat there, sipping my hot chocolate, I pictured my goal: to spend 40 minutes in this freezing lake water, to train for my ice mile. Anne Marie had completed her ice mile last year and now it was my turn. It was only by being here, at the centre, that I could truly assess the risks and prepare for the challenge.

LJ, now content that his mommy was safe, started running the length of the lake, barking at the water and his reflection. The echoes magnified the eerie sound of silence. I loved that feeling, of being so small. It reduced even further my personal challenges on the grand scale of life. My eyes scanned the cliffs; I tilted my head as I picked up the sheep standing, grazing calmly, in what seemed like an impossible position, defying gravity. I smiled at the limits we place on ourselves. Sheep are not exactly designed to be streamlined, but they hang in there. We find inspiration everywhere.

As bizarre and painful as swimming in the ice water felt, I constantly reminded myself of the excitement of pushing the boundaries of human limits. Precious few people in the world had achieved what I was training to do. I would be joining an elite club: Lynne Cox, one of my role models, and a small but growing international group. I felt I was forging a path that would allow others to believe in what was possible for the human body and mind. I was spending a lot of time mentoring swimmers and was confident they would follow me into the ice in the coming months. These mornings sitting on rocks, surrounded by gigantic mountain backdrops, allowed me to appreciate the silence, the 'me time', where life stood still, frozen by the cold. Having to stop my swim in Tyumen still intrigued me. I had never before had that feeling of being mentally frazzled or uncertain after 150 metres.

The phone rang. It was Mary.

'Just me. Where are you? I want to run something by you.'

'I'm up at Peddler's Lake, heading down now,' I replied, standing up and gathering myself.

'I'll meet you at the car park in 15 minutes. I'll bring coffee and something sticky,' she said.

I was delighted, but I knew there were emails to write.

When I stood up, there was an extra chill, as if the cold blood was running around my body, and that sense of cleansing the mental clutter. My pulse oximeter and my blood-pressure monitor both read within the normal range. I gathered my bags and started my walk down, heading to the car park.

Today I had spent 16 minutes swimming in 3-degree water. The air was pure winter mountain morning air, and I felt in control, sharp and cold. I was disciplining myself to stay inside the plan. I was using the same theory as for diving – that I would have to develop the skills to stay longer, to understand each step forward before taking it. Today's focus was not to stay in the water for a long time, it was to have an excellent recovery. So far, so good, notwithstanding my frozen feet and hands.

The physiological impact of swimming in freezing water has its own requirement for patience attached. It is a challenge not to swim beyond the goal. Swim for 10 minutes, recover strong. As soon as your recovery is under control, increase the swim time. Few other swimmers were swimming these temperatures – there were no blueprints or anyone to follow – so all I could do was swim to stay in control. The last few weeks of training had shown me that it was essential to understand all components of the swim, to be able to piece it together to succeed. It takes so much patience to stick to the plan when you might allow the ego to take over. Humility is key. Ten minutes at icy temperatures is a long swim.

Over the last few months, I felt I'd been forced to defend my decisions and my choices more and more. So many people asked me why I wanted to push myself beyond the limits that others thought possible. The only answer I could give was that it excited me. Also, training was a place where I could be alone and be entirely myself. My father had started to sleep longer into the evenings and then get up at 8.00 p.m. or later. Unfortunately, this meant I was sometimes up with him from midnight until 2.00 a.m. So much of my time was not my own. I was on a shop-owner's schedule and a carer's schedule at the same time. But in the water, in the dream of the achievement, I came alive. It gave my life a whole new purpose. It gave me control.

Now it was 20 January 2013, five weeks since Siberia. Standing in the car park at Peddler's Lake, the air was still and heavy, with that feeling of snow about to fall. I was anxious, waiting for my team to arrive, but I was also content that I could not have trained harder or prepared better for my ice mile. I was emotionally drained, but I decided that I was still willing to try, as long as my team were happy.

Today was a year in the making: since 2011 I had worked really hard to be able to complete 2 kilometres strong at 7 degrees in the sea. I had completed over 20 individual miles in water colder than 8 degrees, training to be strong afterwards in recovery. There was a solid difference between a mile at 6 degrees and a mile at 3 degrees. The lower the temperatures, the greater the impact of the cold water. It was the same theory as depth and pressure in scuba diving.

The waterfall sprayed as the powerful river flowed down the side of the mountain. The cutting and biting north-east wind was getting stronger. Once we climbed up into the maw of the lake, there would be some shelter. We were a team of five today and our safety plan covered all potential outcomes. Every morning for the last two weeks I had come up to this location and walked the same path, up and down, memorising every rock, counting the steps and giving myself directions to follow so I could remember the route. The distance was short, 100 metres, but it was a tough descent with unsteady footing, requiring me to use my hands and sometimes sit on my bum.

Maryann jumped out of the car and immediately gave me a huge hug. We both started to cry. During the night, my beautiful 12-year-old Labrador Hally had finally passed away after a long fight with diabetes. I had known the day was coming, but how I had wished it hadn't been last night, with my ice mile planned. Her loss was traumatic.

'Frances and Ciara are on the way. We may as well give it a go,' I said to her. 'I'm 10 minutes from home, so it's easy to come out of the water. And, if things don't work out, the cold water will do my head good anyway.'

Frances Lynch and her daughter Ciara had been friends of mine for over a decade through triathlon and swimming. Garry Kavanagh, another good friend, was there too, along with his friend Paul. They were both rescue service members. All together, these people were my rescue unit. I had assembled a great team.

The lake was at 366 metres above sea level, 43 metres up through rocks with an air temperature of −5. Fog had gathered on the top of the huge backdrop, moving in a slow advance-retreat dance. There was no sun and the lake looked dark, but so beautiful. Garry and Paul talked us through the safety plan. Peddler's Lake is not the official name for that location, so for rescue purposes Garry requested that we key our GPS coordinates into the plan. We had some flares and a VHF radio. Despite the cars being only

150 metres away, there was never room for complacency with a remote location. It was vital the team understood the process and we all agreed our roles. Everyone was very experienced in the management of hypothermia. The wind was due to increase but we agreed to move as fast as possible.

Maryann went through her checklist, discussing the rewarming and the measurement of the route. Next, we had to test the water temperature. The probes arrived back after 10 minutes in water 0.6m below the surface with three readings: 2.6 degrees, 2.8 degrees and 3.5 degrees. Realistically, the lake would be colder in parts, especially at the back, where the freezing water pours off the mountain.

'We're marking a 1,800-metre route by going over and back. We will not fall short,' Maryann pointed out.

She had her clipboard with the timings, my stroke rates and the distances to be recorded.

We sorted the signals and emergency signs and I returned to my space to relax. Behind me, Frances and Ciara ensured that my clothes went into my large drybag in the right order. I placed a list of the clothes on the outside of the bag and the sequence they were folded in, so my team could find any item of clothing quickly. In remote settings, these small details are important, all roles are understood.

I stripped to my swimming togs, and immediately there was a small giggle at the sight of my arms. They were covered in writing. I looked like an exam student trying to cheat.

On my right hand I had written my blood pressure, taken just 30 minutes ago (125/85), my pulse oxygen (99 per cent) and other medical details. On my left hand was my sister Mary's phone number. On my left arm, from above my elbow on the inside to my forearm, I had drawn the pathway of my vein. In extreme cold veins can drop and become invisible. It might have looked odd, but I felt it would be an effective way of communication if I should become unable to speak or think.

'I'm going to be the best casualty possible,' I told them. We laughed at the medical storyboard I had made of my body. 'If anything happens and I can't talk, my life is on my arms.'

A final thumbs-up and I made my way slowly over the greasy rocks and into the water. The cold was piercing and the water was shadowy as the clouds gathered and jostled above. I splashed my face and neck and under my armpits with the ice water, spending more minutes doing so than usual. I repeated my mantra for today: *Everything is sweetened by risk. Take the pain. This is why you are here. Life has trained you for this moment.*

I scanned the measured route, rock to rock, as I acclimatised and allowed the water to envelop my body. I visualised left to right and right to left, picked up landmarks, spotted the sheep I could focus on.

I stretched my arms and fought to keep control of my breathing as my body broke the surface of the lake. I had learned so much about the impact of cold shock and its automatic response, that moment of gasping. That was what had stopped me in Tyumen. I now approached the process of cold immersion methodically, allowing it to work its way through my body. I worked to keep control with my out-breaths. *If you can't breathe, you can't swim. One function at a time.*

I had put some toothpaste on one tooth that I was worried about. One nerve that might bother me. I initially breathed with my mouth slightly ajar, not allowing the cold water in, using my tongue as a splashguard. After a few loops, my hand trailed the copper-toned water under my body.

I closed my eyes. The pain had taken over. All I had to do

now was endure. There was a tightness to my breathing that I had become comfortable with. It was short, it was measured. I opened my eyes to confirm that I was swimming in a straight line. I felt comfortable giving in to the ice and enduring it for the moments I was here. It was a very strange comfort – to control the pain, to roll freezing from side to side, reaching into the darkness, knowing that I was pushing the limits of my own possibility. Nothing else mattered, just this moment of control.

Breathing to one side, I counted the faces of my crew. A tiny character came into my sight – Ciara Lynch – sitting tucked into her jacket on the rock, visibly freezing and uncomfortable, eyes strained on me, a bright-pink patch amidst the brown rocks of the winter mountain. Ciara was a fully qualified lifeguard and strong swimmer. I smiled to myself. Frances had told her a few hours ago to come to the mountain lake, to take a break from her studies and help with my ice swim – she would have a great day. I could imagine her face, sleepy, as she was hauled out of bed on a Sunday morning in January to sit on the side of a mountain in the freezing wind and cold. I wasn't sure how much fun she was having.

My fingers were freezing and white against the clear water. I could see the shiny, shimmering coins on the stony bottom. I wondered just how much money visitors had thrown into the lake. Would it be bad karma to take some?

Faces appeared – Frances, Garry, Maryann and Paul. Paul was my marker: after Paul, about 20 strokes, touch the rock and turn. The water temperature at the northern corner of the lake was bitter and hurt my face. That was where the water poured down from the mountaintop. The absence of sunlight and the fog made this section very eerie.

The pins and needles tightened my fingers. This was a different piercing sensation from the salty, 6-degree water of Mulroy Bay. The mountain air was cutting and the wind was whirling around the lake. I seemed to be swimming into rough water for both lengths. I was determined to stay focused.

I could see my crew coming closer to the lake edge. Did I look okay? I'd best communicate with them. In fresh water, without a leg kick on the surface, the body can appear lower, and I must have looked to be sinking a little. It's a buoyancy thing. Frances did an exaggerated wave dance for me with outstretched arms. It was something that Ger McDonnell, our wonderful Kingdom Masters Swimming Club coach, would do to remind us to kick. I tried.

The wind was now gusting. The challenge in the mountain lakes, where the wind bounces off the amphitheatre walls and swirls, is that the lake water turns and twists. I battled the short, sharp waves that slapped me on the face. I felt I had passed Maryann six times over and back. I normally don't seek to know the distance, but with this level of pain the temptation was great. I glanced at my watch as my hand trailed underneath my body: 1,400 metres completed. I was feeling great.

The wind had driven me out into the centre of the lake. I had to adjust my route a few times. My stroke was very balanced – I didn't deviate – but I was veering towards the back wall because of the swirling power. My ankles were cramping, losing their flexibility, and each leg kick was forcing my calf muscles to spasm. I could now only drag my legs. I was delighted to see Frances and Ciara pulling my bags together. That meant I was nearly finished. Another quick glance at my watch. I was at 1,900 metres. I had completed the mile. A huge sigh of relief as I eased my way through the final stretch.

I tried to say that I was done – but Maryann's hand signals were determined.

'You must finish another 20 metres!' she shouted.

I should never have looked at my watch. I should have trusted my team. I had given in to that sense of letting go before it was over.

I put my face under again. My breath was now ragged. There was such a contrast between the calm of the underwater world, the stillness, and the swirling and angry wind that was now building above my head. I was frozen.

Finish strong, I repeated. *This is why you are here.*

The fog was tumbling down the back wall. Finally, their arms waved me in. I glanced at my watch: 40 minutes. I pressed the stop button with my frozen fingers.

'That was over 2 kilometres,' I said, my tongue frozen. I was speaking as if I was at the dentist again. Maryann reached out to my hands.

'You were weaving all over the place. We agreed the distance was point to point. Come on, come on!' Her voice was urgent.

I put my feet under me. The rocks were greasy and I slipped a few times. I decided it was safer to exit on my hands and knees. I crawled out of the ice water. The wind was gusting, earlier than forecast.

'I'm okay, Maryann. I'm okay.'

Maryann put out her hand and stared at me. She turned her head to the team and all I heard was, 'She's in trouble. Hurry up.'

It was the worst cold I had ever experienced. My arms were shaking and my eyeballs were freezing. I wanted to close them. I could feel the cold in the back of my head and my tongue was freezing.

Frances and Ciara worked as fast as they could to get my swimming togs off my frozen body, then pulled thermal inner layers over my head. Maryann pulled socks and thermals over my lower body. I was sitting on the towels on the rocks as the freezing wind bit through me. All the time I was repeating to myself, *Halfway there – hang on tight.* The wind was now swirling with immense power in the cauldron. I envied those sitting in saunas and it definitely crossed my mind that a lake in a mountain was not a great idea. But we were here now.

'The snow is coming,' Maryann said.

'How long was I in?'

There was no answer. I could sense the urgency of getting me moving. Three pairs of hands worked as fast as they could to get me dry and covered. Frances was trying to get my arms into my fleece, but in my mind I was already walking down to the jeep.

'Help me, Nuala, help me!' she said sternly as my arm was pulled backwards into my immersion suit.

Was I not helping?

The feeling of being tucked up in my huge survival suit was precious. I smiled as Maryann pushed two tinfoil blankets down the front of my suit and one down the back, to protect my core. The ninth woman in the world, the second Irish swimmer. I knew I could do it and I had done it. I was so proud that I had finished strong, and so glad that it was over.

We were beginning our journey 100 metres down to the car park. My feet felt numb. I was uncertain about where to place my weight when I could not balance. *Will I have a drink?* I thought. *Would sugar help?*

I could hear LJ barking and, though I wanted to walk, I wanted to sleep more. I kept thinking, *Hold on and keep it together.* I knew we were in difficulty. I closed my eyes and decided I had better formulate a plan as quickly as I could. How bad was I? Mentally, I felt exhausted. It was like that feeling of driving home at 3.00 a.m., when your eyes are struggling to stay open and your head keeps shaking to wake you up. I remember closing my eyes and someone saying, 'We need to go down – the snow is coming.' I wasn't recovered and I wasn't home.

'Can I have something to drink?' I asked.

However I sounded when I asked that question, the sense of urgency changed around me. I decided to sit down again. When I sat down on the rocks, the air temperature was −6 degrees.

'She's in trouble. We must get her down to the car park,' was all I heard.

'What are you doing with lemon and ginger tea? Where is your hot chocolate? Where are your jellies?' Frances shouted at me as she scrambled through her own bag, looking for her flask.

I kept my eyes slammed shut, as you do when you need focus. Once I reached the top of the rocks, starting the descent, the jeep in view, the wind nearly took the feet from under me. I needed everything to stop.

It is very difficult to describe the feeling to those who haven't experienced it, or who haven't seen what we look like after prolonged immersion in ice water. I felt like a compass unable to set the needle, unable to find a heading. This was life in survival mode. My eyes were freezing. I pictured the faces of the South Africans in their recovery tent, those bodies frozen and shaking. I was certain I looked just as bad, except that I was walking down a mountain.

I wanted people to move slower. I smiled inside, picturing people on their way out of pub doors, full of drink, uncertain whether they can fit through the space but determined to try. I felt drunk. I took deep breaths and kept trying to focus, but I did not have the energy to keep my eyes open. My head was light each time I stood up. My voice sounded like a 45RPM record being played on a 33RPM setting. The words come slower. My tongue was frozen and my speech slurred.

The mind works at its own pace, and it really only focuses on the necessary, or so I thought at that time. Things were happening so fast that I could not organise my thoughts.

I had memorised the route down and I would depend on my memory. I stood up and took a few steps, allowing Frances and Garry to help me. But my mind went fuzzy. I felt dizzy and weak. I asked to sit down again.

'Come on, Nuala, we have to go,' Frances said.

A voice inside whispered slowly and calmly: *You're actually in trouble, Nuala. How can you get up and out of here?*

It was a challenge to balance. I felt I did not have any power or control. I had not factored in the strength needed for the walk. The pain in my hands and feet was horrendous.

All I could think of was the word 'no'. I said no to everything as the wind whipped around me. I was now facing the full force of the weather, in the middle of the harsh, swirling wind, exposed to the elements. I struggled to focus my squinted eyes.

I won't make it. I can't do this.

I had finished the swim; I was dressed and walking, but I was not in control. I was saying no again. There was so much fog in my brain, no clear thinking. I could not see how I could finish this.

I stared at the jeep about 75 metres away, so close. Standing on uneven rocks, a wind-chill temperature of −10 degrees searing through me, just out of 40 minutes in a 3-degree glacial lake on the side of a mountain, I was losing heat fast and the shivering was becoming violent. Thirty minutes had passed since I'd got out of the water.

If I slipped and fell now, one of the team would be injured along with me. A slight jittery fear was creeping in, a realisation of the situation I had placed myself in. I became aware that Frances was asking me to come on, to take the next step forward, saying, 'Look at me, Nuala.' I refocused my eyes on her. I looked ahead at Maryann and Ciara. Like a house of cards, the plan that I had spent weeks formulating was starting to tumble down around me.

I was frozen in time. I could hear their voices, but I was not listening. I stared at the horizon, trying to muster up the courage to quit again. That word 'quit'.

I am compromising my team, I told myself. *If I slip now, I'll bring Frances down with me. They have to go to work tomorrow. My team are my priority.*

The greatest lesson I ever learned is that, once a swimmer puts their face in the water, they give themselves over to their team. The team must make the next call, because the swimmer is too involved in the process. Swimmers should never compromise or endanger the team and right now, for the first time in my life I felt unsafe.

This was another Siberia moment. I was afraid to cross the line. I was afraid to take that risk.

I'm dressed and I'm out of the lake. We are all safe.

I was emotionally and physically empty. I needed every ounce of energy to recover. The shivering was still getting worse.

'I can't. I can't.'

Whether I meant that I couldn't go on personally or that I couldn't create any more trouble for my team, I didn't know. *I can't* was all I could think. I sat down and tucked my face away from the wind, into my immersion suit.

But we had planned for this moment. Maryann pulled out the phone.

'We need hands, Nuala, to get you down. The weather is getting worse. I'm calling Frank.'

I slammed my eyes shut. Frank was head of the Irish Coast Guard Dingle Unit and a friend. I had served some years on the rescue unit and knew all the members very well. This phone call would mobilise the rescue service. I had trained for situations like this as a rescuer; now I was the reason for the callout. I felt guilty.

'The team are coming up to help.'

A huge exhalation. They would be here in 10–15 minutes. My team was safe.

I felt better now that I was sitting down. I could hear and see the activity around me: Maryann discussing the plan, Frances throwing my lemon and ginger teabags on the ground and feeding me jelly babies instead. I looked over at Mount Brandon. Snow was falling and the fog covered the summit. I remember trying to shake my head a few times, as if to get control again.

Did I react too quickly? Could I struggle down? It's only dizziness. Maybe I'll be okay in a few minutes.

I had achieved what I set out to achieve and had spent longer in the ice water than many thought possible. Now I had to hold on tight and focus on staying strong.

The switch from being a rescuer to being a casualty is a very strange one – what a battle inside! To the rescue unit, I would be a casualty. I had never been a casualty before, so my thinking landscape needed to change.

I tried to visualise the next phase: once the team arrived, they would package me, secure me and make me safe, get me down the mountain, then transfer me to an ambulance and hospital. That was the procedure and it had to be. There would be no more discussion.

Ciara sat behind me to keep my lower back warm and to protect my lungs, which in turn would help my breathing. My feet and hands were still cold, but I could feel my belly warming, despite the wind. The activity around me became less important as my brain went into rescue mode.

I'm trained for this moment. What information is important right now?

I might have forgotten chocolate, but I had marked my veins. Check. I was not on any medication and my normal pulse was on the palm of my hand. Check. I had written Mary's phone number on the palm of my left hand. I could not see if it was still there with the gloves, but I closed my eyes and tried to remember it. Check. In what seemed like a second, a smiling face, that of Carol Leahy from the Irish Coast Guard, was beside me.

'Thank you, Carol. I'm sorry,' I said.

'What else would we be doing on a Sunday, Nuala?' Her smile and her eyes were just as gentle as in normal life. 'You're fine,' she said, grabbing my hands.

I closed my eyes again, to focus, and tucked my head deep into my chest, even though I knew my eyes would offer a lot of evidence about my hypothermic state. I decided to try to centre inside and only open to the team when necessary.

The wind stopped and the air changed. There were lots of sounds and movements very close to me. I opened my eyes and there were three or four people very nearby. I was in a tent. How had that happened? Had I fallen asleep?

A survival tent had been placed around me. I was emotionally secure now. I felt safe and surrounded by familiar faces. Arms came from behind and wrapped me in a bear hug. I turned my head inside my hood and could make out the rugged handsome face of Fergal Slattery. In different circumstances this would have been a beautiful moment. I closed my eyes and tried not to laugh.

I began to heat up. There were many questions being asked about my swim, but I decided not to answer and just to stay focused instead.

Don't fall asleep. Stay strong. Keep breathing that cold air out of your lungs.

Carol leaned in and said, 'I'm just going to find your pulse,' as she pressed her fingers to my neck.

'You won't find it – it will be very low,' I said quietly. 'But I am alive.'

There were a lot of people packed tightly around me and, even though I would have liked more space and some air coming in, I knew that the cold was now the greatest risk.

Mark Greely, my best friend Claire's husband, unzipped the opening and stared at me.

'Claire says hi. She told me to get up here quickly to help.' He smiled. I've known Mark for 20 years and the reality of the worry I had caused hit me.

'Can I take a photo for Claire to prove that you're okay?'

Claire always made sure that I was okay. She is one of those friends. Since we started school together at four years of age, Claire always made her presence felt in my life. She and I were often mistaken for sisters.

'Tell her I'm fine,' I said. 'Mark, can you take some videos as well? They will be good to look back on.' I really wanted to see what was going on from an outside perspective. I knew Frances would be taking photos. Photos would be valuable to me, to debrief and learn. I wanted to see my face.

I closed my eyes again; there were too many people, moving too fast. Inside my head, I repeated my information and blocked out the movement.

My name is Nuala Moore. I was swimming 1,800 metres at 3 degrees. I was in the water for 40 minutes. I have taken one painkiller tablet. My normal blood pressure is 120/80. My sister's name is Mary and her phone number is … My brother's name is Edward and his number is …

I smiled, realising that both Ed and Mary's numbers had 999 in them.

I lifted my head, realising I was in trouble.

'Can someone ring Mary and Ed?'

What was taking so long?

'Where am I?' I asked. I wanted to know where I was in the plan. Were we heading down the mountain?

The energy shifted in the tent. I could hear the wind starting to lift again outside and see the sides of the tent moving. Our weight was the only thing keeping it on the mountain.

'What's your name and where are you?' one voice asked me, the face close to mine.

I thought it was a silly question, so I did not answer and focused on keeping my eyes closed. I remember feeling agitated. I knew my name and what I was doing up here, but once in the tent I could not see where exactly I was. My plan had failed, so now I wanted to know *their* plan. My eyes would be in a stare and my voice slow. If I were them, I would be worried about me. So why were we not moving?

The zip opened. The tiny gap exposed a gale of wind, a day that was fading fast. Maryann's head and upper body crawled inside the survival tent and a pair of hands wrapped the tent around her to keep the cold wind out. That tiny second created a shiver. I was now warming up. I felt stronger.

She knew the keys for my jeep and my phone were in my pocket of my immersion suit. I nodded as she took them from me.

'Frances is calling Mary now,' she said.

I nodded again.

'Don't tell her about the helicopter,' she said to Carol in a low voice as she reversed out of the tent. I jolted upwards.

'No, no, no, not the helicopter!' I mumbled. *Not the helicopter, not an airlift.* That would change the game again.

'My jeep! Who will drive my jeep? LJ has to be brought down the mountain. Maryann?' I could not see her with the faces so close to me.

'Elevate her legs,' a voice said.

I don't need my legs warmed. They are all wrapped up. Please don't elevate them.

I really wanted to speak but, before I could, Maryann was there, instructing the others to leave my legs lower than my core, that I was in a good position. I was quite warm at this stage – I just felt weak and tired. There was too much happening, too many decisions I could not control.

I closed my eyes again to focus on the next hurdle.

Where exactly have I ended up? Where did I sit down? What should be done with me now? Do I need to be airlifted up or carried down?

Frances reached into the covering, shoved a handful of jelly sweets into my mouth and handed me a cup of hot chocolate. I stared at her, to apologise.

She smiled.

'We love a drama, Nuala, but what were you doing with bloody lemon and ginger tea? I threw it away. I've just rung Mary.'

'Tell Ciara to take some photos,' I said.

'She's already down at the car park, on it.' She disappeared.

The voices on the radios in the tent were helicopter crew deciding their approach. I focused and listened intently. The thunderous sound of Rescue 115 approaching Peddler's Lake was like something from a movie. We held on tight – the downdraught would move us.

'Rescue 115 is 3 minutes out,' Carol whispered in my ear. 'You're fine. It's freezing out there now. You're going to be lifted, so we have to move you.'

I tucked my head into my survival suit.

Be the best casualty you can be. Be the best casualty you can be. You have 3 minutes to gather yourself. Focus and be strong.

A deep breath and I started to repeat my statements to myself.

My name is Nuala Moore. I am at Peddler's Lake, swimming an ice mile. The water temperature is 3 degrees. My sister's name is …

I closed my eyes and waited for the voice of the winchman to come.

I could tell there were many feet running around outside and I focused on the noise of the helicopter blades. I had one responsibility at this point – to ensure that my recovery was strong, to hold on to this concentration.

There was a lot more space in my small tent and, with a zip down, into my vision came the huge, round helmet and visor of a rescue winchman in an orange suit. He leaned in and said his name was Philip.

'I just want to check a few things.' A calm, smiling voice. 'How are you doing?'

'My name is Nuala Moore. I just swam 2,000 metres in 3-degree water. I can't remember how long I was in the water. I had little sleep, no food, a pint of warm water with some maple syrup. I have marked my veins and my blood pressure and heart rate are marked on my palms. I have foil blankets against my core. I had one painkiller tablet last night. I have been in communication with your fellow winchman Adrian O'Hara on hypothermia.' Exactly as I practised in my mind, and all said staring straight at him. I focused strong on his face, as if I'd saved all my energy for this moment. I was proud of how strong I was, I held on.

'She's lucid,' is all I heard as he turned away.

I tucked back into my own world. Being an official casualty was very tough for me, but I felt I did well. As an ex-Coast Guard member, I was embarrassed.

'I'm going to take off your blankets and transfer you to our stretcher,' Philip said as he checked some stats.

He had to check my blood pressure and my stats before putting me onto the stretcher. I pulled down my immersion-suit top and exposed my bare arm, to a fit of silent laughter. Both my arms were covered with writing. I looked down, not remembering which arm had which information. I held them both out to be read.

'That's all my medical information and my veins marked, in case I couldn't speak.' Philip's head and helmet were shaking and my team were all smiling, not one bit surprised at my attention to detail. 'I just wanted to be a good casualty,' I said. I was so embarrassed.

'Did you prepare to fail?' a voice said. More laughter.

My body was packaged into a tight bag, so warm and so tight. My head was surrounded with heated padding and I was strapped tightly into a cradle.

Surrounded by the team, I was shuffled up the mountain to higher, flatter rocks so that the winch could happen. A rope attached to the helicopter was thrown down and held by two members of the team. This was to steady the stretcher as it reached the underside of the helicopter. I looked around me. A blanket of white now covered the entire tip of Mount Brandon, as the wind swirled down the side of the mountain. The snow was here.

The sound of the helicopter above my head was thunderous. It looked so animated suspended against the cliff. A winch operator strained his body over the side as I faced him upwards. It seemed a long way up. The final okays came and the lift began. The mountains came closer.

Two men worked the winch. The winchman, Philip, would come down to help me, while another man, the winch operator, would pull us both up. Philip was in a seated position. My eyes focused upwards on his goggles. The lift took no more than a few minutes, but the final approach to the underside of the helicopter was daunting – scary, even. My eyes spanned the amazing cliffs on the side of the Conor Pass.

As we approached the side door, the large figure of the winch operator leaned out the side of the helicopter. The downdraught forced my cradle to start spinning, but Philip stabilised it using his legs and, in a split second grabbed by the winch operator, the two of us were inside.

I became totally alert, as if I had held on for this moment. I listened to the voices. Headphones were placed over my ears and suddenly I could hear the crew. I noticed a mouthpiece, so I spoke. I wanted to tell them about my swim.

'What are my stats?' I asked. I wanted to explain why I was swimming, but thought it best to stay silent about that for now.

'140/95 BP, HR 75.'

They were high for me. I wanted to ask more questions, but I didn't.

'You're warm and you're fine,' Philip said with a gentle nod.

That was perfect. I closed my eyes. I had done well. I wondered who was driving my jeep home.

Over the radio, the comms announced my arrival at Kerry General Hospital. I heard the sentence, 'She is warm – her core was protected by a survival suit.' I heard talk about a possible 'circum-rescue collapse' and hypothermia. I was uncertain as to why I'd got into trouble, but I knew my team had done well. *What was circum-rescue collapse?*

I could see why swimmers were walked directly to a sauna in Siberia and not onto the side of a mountain. Few swimmers in the world had completed 2,000 metres at such low temperatures, so there was little known about the effects. I was at my limit. If I had eaten and slept, would I have been able to stay standing?

As the hospital came into view, the comms became much more interactive. Two minutes to landing. Thumbs-up to the paramedic ensuring my packaging for transfer. I closed my eyes to prepare for the next group of questions and procedures. I wanted to protect my achievement. I did not want the adjudication to be about the immersion and my decision to do it. Even though I felt much better, I was still nervous at the next judgement facing me. I repeated to myself the information the hospital medical teams would need.

The helicopter landed.

'Thank you all so very much,' I smiled at the pilots of Rescue 115.

We can never predict every outcome. Things happen and we have to adapt. My safety plan was solid – and I did get out safely. It worked.

I was determined to try and explain the reasons I had collapsed. My friends and family would be nervous about what had happened. I would have to defend my decision to be there. I was upset – I could have compromised my team.

The doctor put it bluntly: 'You can't put your body into 3-degree water up a mountain for 40 minutes and not expect an outcome like this.' One hour later, my ECG and medical stats cleared, I was sitting in the hall of the hospital with a chicken sandwich.

The phone rang at 4.30 p.m. as I sat in Maryann's car on the way home. It was Mary. I had forgotten to text to tell her I'd been released.

'Just me, just checking in. Are you defrosted? What ward are you in? Did you get your jeep down?' Her voice trailed off.

'I'm en route home. I'm with Maryann. I was only kept in for a few hours and reheated. I'm fine now. Yes, the jeep is at home, along with LJ.'

'The Conor Pass is closed with the snow. Glad your jeep is home.'

Mary loved a drama and sounded almost despondent that I was on the way home and not in the ICU. But she was happy I got the ice mile completed. I smiled to myself. I often wondered what it would take to frighten my family.

There was a lot to think about. The greatest challenge would be to convince others that this was the right journey to be on.

Sitting beside the fire that evening, thinking about the airlift, I knew there were uncertainties I had missed. I explained to my father what had happened. We watched the report on the nine o'clock news.

'These things happen,' he replied. 'Sure, that is why the helicopter and the lifeboat are there. You know well that many's the time we have to make that call.' He was happy I was home and not fazed at all by my airlift or my collapse. He was right. It's not how many times you fall down that matters, it's how you get up.

The term 'circum-rescue collapse' interested me. Could I have avoided it? I had a lot of debriefing to do – some memories were not quite adding up – but I was delighted our safety plan had worked.

We decided to submit the 1,800 metres at 3 degrees, point to point, on our affidavits to the IISA, despite my watch showing 2,100 metres. I had a feeling that that would be less of a battle to explain. Saying that I'd passed the 2,000 metres would cause some commentary and judgement.

In the following weeks I felt content that the 1,000 metres at 0 degrees was now within my grasp. I could see myself becoming the first Irish swimmer to succeed at 0 degrees. It was just a mindset issue. I turned the pages on Lynne Cox's *Swimming to Antarctica*. She and Natalia Seraya were the only two women in the world who had completed 1,000 metres at that temperature. As the words fell off the page, I felt her emotion; I felt her pain as she immersed herself in the icy water.

Lynne messaged me online after my airlift. I read her inspiring words, telling me not to quit – that understanding the ice was a long battle. Since 2007, I had been adamant that I would keep working on any weakness I found. I loved feeling controlled and strong.

This was personal now. I had to train my mind and figure out how to move into the pain. I had discovered how to let go and give in to the ice at the same time as holding tightly on to myself. I just needed that extra moment of control. These extremes made for a complex game, but I felt I could win it. Strangely, the pain itself was never a factor. I felt there was an honesty in the ice – a sense of excitement that lit a fire in my belly, a giddiness, a secret world. Being able to do something others felt impossible was something I had missed since finishing the Round Ireland Swim. I was determined to keep trying, to keep pushing my limits.

It was in the darkness that I found the greatest control.

12

DIGGING DEEPER: MURMANSK

'Risk! Risk anything! Care no more for the opinions of others, for those voices. Do the hardest thing on earth for you. Act for yourself. Face the truth.'
Katherine Mansfield

Reading online comments that my airlift had 'pulled essential coastal services away from other areas' and that my safety planning was 'reckless' was very upsetting for me and my team. I had completed one of the longest distances in 3-degree water in the world and this malicious online commentary blindsided me. Not one person commenting had any idea about the safety plan, nor had they made contact with me or my team to find out. They had no information.

We had created a solid safety plan and brief. I had followed it. The fact that I was airlifted showed that my safety plan had worked. Every swim is individual, as are the factors that determine the outcome. The outcome might be different on any given day. An ambulance and medical teams are required at any major sports events. It's not uncommon to need assistance. We all have witnessed instances where athletes have received treatment after finishing. This social-media commentary took the focus away from the amazing swim I had achieved by setting fires. It was designed to do so. It felt impossible to celebrate my ice achievements or post on social media without being attacked.

It was that dramatic word, 'reckless', that hurt the most. People who knew me knew that this was so upsetting. These responses were based purely on people's inability to understand swims outside their own fears. The catastrophe that I was faced with had layers to it. I had to ensure my family and team were shielded from judgement, manage my own emotional responses to being airlifted and deal with my own personal questions. On top of that, day after day, I had to protect the integrity of 'making the call'. I was an ex-Coast Guard member and had trained for these moments – so I knew it was important to promote the culture of 'no judgement' in making the decision to call for help. Promoting a culture online of fear around making that call, on the other hand – *that* was reckless.

My mindset was completely shattered. My family were comfortable with my progress into the distance at 0 degrees and I continued to train at Peddler's Lake. The sensational element of the story was ramped up online to create drama. I was fighting fires on all fronts, whilst trying to focus on my training. I was ill-equipped to deal with this. I wanted to celebrate the amazing achievement of my ice mile. I could not.

I had an official invitation from Dmitry Blokhin to travel to Murmansk, Russia, to represent Ireland in the International Winter Swimming Competition in four weeks' time, in March. It was a chance to become the first Irish swimmer to achieve 1,000 metres at 0 degrees and only the third woman in the world to do so. I was continuing to push my boundaries in ice water and I was determined not to allow people so unconnected with my life to dictate my outcomes.

As a swimmer, the greatest impact from the online commentary was the emotional pressure it placed on me – the mental difficulty of reading about myself online and still trying to stay focused, and the ongoing insistence that swimming distance in the ice was dangerous. The ice is a personal journey. No one takes on this level of pain just for fun.

Maryann and Frances were delighted to help me train for the 1,000 metres, to start to focus again on the positives and on my breathing. I felt I could go deeper into the cold and that I could be stronger, even if I didn't know what going deeper and being stronger would mean. I knew that I was so close to understanding the secrets to staying in control – that it was about letting go and trusting myself, knowing the right supports were in place. There was something about the ice that excited me.

'Let's start jogging uphill,' Maryann suggested. 'When we feel like quitting, we won't quit. We will just keep moving slowly without stopping. Control the breathing.'

This was going to be mindset. The 1,000-metre distance was so short. I had learned a lot from Tyumen and my ice mile. I was training for whatever took my breath away. I was training to focus on my breathing and be strong.

One morning, wrapped in my thermals, I was behind the counter after spending 15 minutes at 2 degrees and going straight to work to recover. My computer was open on the counter.

'Now so.' Mary came into the shop. 'What's happening? Has that online stuff stopped?'

She knew the answer by looking at my face. She handed me a coffee and a bun. It really upset Mary that we had to waste so much energy fighting people who chose to hide when confronted. Both of us knew that if we could just meet these people face to face, there would be no argument. We were both fighters and disliked injustice.

'The emails and posts have drifted. They're saying the airlift was a media stunt and ego driven.' I read the comments to her. Between us we were so angry. We were helpless to stop this landslide of judgement, when there was no truth in it.

'I don't want those around me to worry that I am risking too much. I know what I'm doing.'

'You have to listen to thunder, Nuala,' she replied, looking at me over her glasses. We both smiled. 'Success is the best revenge.'

Mary didn't even blink at the idea that I was going to immerse my body in freezing waters again, for a period many people thought impossible. She did not ask what could happen to my body or my brain. If I was happy to try, she would support me all the way.

Mary was a born leader in her field of business. She loved a battle and being told it was not possible fuelled her, like it fuelled us all. Each 'no' in her life had simply forced her to push in a different direction, or from a different angle, without fear of failure. The fact that no Irish swimmer had ever contemplated this distance and temperature before meant little to her. She was a pioneer.

Mary stood up to leave.

'Be the best. Don't let them take your swagger or your success.' She smiled, and with that her phone rang and she left. We were our own fan club. We were so proud of the strong women we had become.

As I ate the sticky bun, a text came through from Mary.

'Keep your powder dry.' It was finished with a winking face. (Mary had just discovered emojis.)

Like the rest of my family, we all viewed risk in life as a condition of the reward. My brother would sometimes steam out to sea in his fishing boat in weather others would not, but he saw the path through the waves, watched the timing of the winds, steadied his ship and took the risk. For some, life's decisions come back to what they fear. For many, the risks are a step too far – the chance of failure or rejection, being exposed to their own weaknesses and the results of their own decisions. There was a family pride in the fact that I had the courage to try, that I had belief and commitment.

Three weeks later, Mary and I were sitting in the car on the road home from the Russian Embassy in Dublin, my passport visa stamped, my journey to Murmansk booked. I was going to become the first Irish swimmer in history to take on and complete 1,000 metres at 0 degrees. My goal.

Each day, I trained hard to recover. I treated each weakness like a hole in a fishing net: I mended it and moved on. In those final swims in the lake and sea, I closed off my head to all outside clutter. I focused only on myself. I had found my balance again. I stayed away from the internet. I tuned out the noise. I became calm. My life was so different from the lives of others. My evenings were spent by the fire with my father. Family had become my priority and I was happy for it to be. My reasons for swimming in the ice were about internal success. I hated being less than I was capable of. I just wanted to be the best version of myself, while also calming the chaos of the other parts of my life. It was about finding a sense of adventure in a world that was becoming more and more restrictive of my time.

In my training swims, I had moved happily to 25 minutes at 2 degrees and had been recovering strongly. I was totally in control of the pain, in fact, I enjoyed it. I was the happiest I'd ever been, because I could feel I was on the cusp of greatness. The 1,000 metres would take me 20 minutes minimum. I had mastered the turns in the Skellig Hotel pool and counting the lengths to 40 was now something I could visualise.

Lack of sleep from caring for Dad, working and the genuine fear of change in my life circumstances may have made me fragile, but the ice gave me strength. There was something in the pain that sharpened my focus. Something happened in the freezing waters that allowed me to stay calm and happy. It was like jump-starting my body each day. The pain was nothing to the excitement I could see in invitations to the extreme. It was creating an honesty in myself, a sense of control. I had felt I had to let go to achieve, when in fact I had to hold on tighter. I had learned the secrets of the ice.

In the water, the chaos disappeared. All the screaming voices of doubt in my head were silenced by the cold, as if squashed by a mallet, in an instant. The calm of the lake, the echo of the mountains, the silence of the water, the reflection of my life, balanced. Spending time at the temperatures close to 0 degrees forced me to focus and survive, to decide what I needed from my life and, even more, to find out what I was capable of. I got to control the chaos. That is what the ice gave me. It gave me a place to be calm, where I could hear my breathing and see my face reflected in the water in front of me.

As I handed my father a cup of tea, I told him about my plans to swim in the ice again – in Russia, the following weekend.

'A man could live for three days in that water,' he said with a customary shake of his head. Unimpressed. 'I've fished out of the North Sea and I've been to Murmansk.' I had no doubt he had. He'd spent many years fishing from north Scotland.

The sea was his place; he had no real interest in the ice. And maybe he was right. Maybe a man could live for three days, but I doubted he could swim for three days. I handed him his tab nab and his tea and went upstairs. There was no point in discussing it.

The one quality my father was sharpening in me was patience! No member of my family had ever given me reason to believe that swimming in the ice was not possible. It was in our DNA.

'Call every hand,' Dad would say. As I closed my eyes at night, I would giggle at the fact that not one member of my family ever asked about the dangers.

My life's path had taught me that each success and failure is a building block of the next challenge. There is never an end – it's all a journey. I knew it was possible to complete this distance – I had watched it being accomplished – and now the idea of having another opportunity possessed me. I could only control so many things, but this was one of them. I felt so strong and determined.

Anne Marie and I landed in Murmansk on 22 March 2013. A man, standing over 2 metres tall, stood at the airport with two huge bunches of flowers to welcome us inside the Arctic Circle. This was Dmitry Blokhin, here to welcome the Irish team.

The next day we were in the breakfast room with the South Africans, Cristian Vergara from Chile and Melissa O'Reilly, who had landed from the US, Henri Kaarma from Estonia and Jackie Cobell from the UK. We were joined by Alexander Brylin, who in Tyumen had completed 2,200 metres at 0 degrees with an air temperature of –30. Aleksandr Jakovlev from Latvia and Mariia Yrjö-Koskinen from Finland completed the group. It was so exciting. All of them were on our Bering Strait Relay and the conversation moved to the planned upcoming swim from Russia to the USA. Suddenly the reason to succeed was morphing in my mind: it was to be a member of this group, to prove my position. Strength was the only option. I had to be one of these swimmers. Extremes required us to be the best version of ourselves. The energy in the group was electric.

Melissa, a tall, athletic American swimmer, had decided to take on the 1,000 metres, even though she was new to the ice. I loved her commitment and professionalism.

The questions flowed between us about what today would bring. It was the first event hosting a competition of distances over 500 metres. I was excited to trust the others if I became unresponsive. It was the challenge of pushing beyond control. That is what it would take to swim 20 minutes at 0 degrees. I was ready.

The air outside at −6 degrees, the ice was being lifted from the six-lane swimming pool. The 30 minutes before the swim were surreal. My heart was beating at an intense pace as I took my place next to the only other 3 women in the world ever to have taken on a 1,000 metres at 0 degrees competition event: Melissa, Jackie and Natalia Seraya, who had swum in Tyumen. Melissa was in cowboy boots and her bikini, Jackie was in a zebra dressing gown, I was in my teddy-bear dressing gown and Natalia was in a jacket. We were the only four women in the world to take on this swim in 2013 and the Irish flag flew high. The atmosphere was thrilling.

Out of the corner of my eye I saw Anne Marie, in her dressing gown, being hurried along to the sauna past us, after her 500 metres with Mariia. Her face smiled and her eyes shone with laughter.

Silently, the four of us stood and followed the marshal to the ice pool. I counted my steps to the frozen lakeside. Despite all the festivities, music, clapping and waving, I was so focused. I had walked up and down the pool several times, I had counted the steps and memorised the route. I visualised the route now.

This is why you are here, I kept repeating to myself. *This is what you are built for. This is your moment. You've seen it done, now let go. The work is done. Be the best.*

The head of the sports department, Andrey Avsyankin, and the head referee, Vitaly Poborchiy, gave us the final signal to get in the water. I put my feet on the steps of the ladder as the whipping wind stripped my body of heat. There was something so hilarious and so insane about stepping into the ice. The feeling is so hard to describe. Everything in my body tightened, as if my insides were pulling away – a sense of survival. My hands grasped the ladder but I soon let go, in case they froze to the metal. The ladder was very straight along the wall and the water was deep, so we were immediately immersed. *This is why you are here,* I repeated.

I took a second to breathe. The cold-shock response was immediate. My breath was ripped away, as if someone had put their hand down my throat and torn the air out. That familiar gasp.

I dipped my face in the water to prepare for the swim, to create some calm and take my heart rate back down again, breathing out, releasing the air trapped by the gasp.

Within a minute the starting beep sounded. I let go and pushed off from the wall with my feet. I made a conscious decision not to focus on any other swimmer, not to compare my progress with theirs. I was swimming my own swim.

For the first few strokes, turning my head to breathe, I thought that my chest was going to burst open, that I was going to gasp and not be able to breathe out. I focused on releasing the air in a hum, bubble by bubble. The need to gasp can be overwhelming, but in scuba diving we learn how to do a full 10-metre ascent to the surface with one breath, exhaling continuously. I needed control, so I went back to my training. *Stop, breathe, think and act,* I kept repeating until I got control. *If you can't breathe, you can't swim.* The rest is only pain.

I felt an incredible urge to gulp in some air. Arm over arm, slow it down to get the sequence of breathing right. After about 10 strokes, nice and relaxed, I took a breath. The moment had passed. Calm came over me. I had control.

The burn, the tingling, was building in my hands. My fingers felt so painful. I found that I was clenching my hands into fists as

I pulled underneath my body. My teeth started to feel the freeze. I used my tongue to block the water. I tried to focus on the positive. I had a solution for every problem. The snow was glimmering, the scenery was stunning, the crowd was amazing. I had decided to swim five times four lengths twice. That was 1,000 metres. I found the lane count hard to see, but I loved the maths. Finally, I spotted the card: 23 lengths left.

Melissa was powering up and down and every two lengths I could see her eyes. She was so focused; her stroke looked beautiful. Natalia was working methodically with her woolly hat on, still using the same approach without googles. Jackie was easing herself along. I was halfway through, at 20 lengths, when I suddenly became aware that Melissa was not in the pool. I became quite anxious, worrying if everything was okay. Could she be finished? Was I that slow? The other two swimmers were still there. Now the darkness was creating some anxiety for me. My mind went into a heightened sense of awareness; my arm walloped the lane rope. I was weaving. Instantly, I felt anxious. I thought of Peddler's Lake. Was I at a fragile stage?

Do a body check. Start at the head, breathe and focus.

I asked myself some random questions, tried to remember song words. Once I was on the final 10 lengths, my mental state became excited. I had given my camera to Cristian to take photos and I searched for him. I smiled for the camera as he snapped away poolside. I was totally focused ahead now, tunnel vision.

My mind was very strong. I was so proud of the level of control I felt, even though it was like walking home after a few glasses of wine. I touched the wall with four lengths to go and lifted my head. Anne Marie was leaning over and looking down. I was never so relieved – she was fine after her swim, and all smiles. Anne Marie would know what to do with me if I needed help.

With 100 metres left, my leg kick started to increase automatically in an effort to get to the end quickly. *This is survival, not a race*, I reminded myself. *You are on the cusp of your greatness. Relax and breathe. You have won.*

My hands were at an end-stage burn and my fingers were so sore as I reached for the ladder, but I had the strength to lift myself up. Hands grabbed me. 23 minutes at 0 degrees – I was so proud.

The crowds, the music, the sounds that had brought me through the first 20 lengths were now replaced by a complete eerie silence. There were no sounds, no people. I could not understand what was being said to me. Peddler's Lake was fresh in my head. I focused completely on Anne Marie and Mariia. I was moved so quickly that a sea of people opened up to reveal the tent.

The heated timber of the sauna immediately softened the pain. Hot, wet towels were wrapped around my core. My hands and feet were held in buckets of cold water. Vicki Brylin and Irina Makarova, the recovery attendants in the sauna, worked so hard. I closed my mind and for a few minutes I focused on the heat filling my core, as I put myself back into the tent on the Conor Pass. I was that drunk person navigating that doorway. I held on tight.

I followed direction, even through a language barrier. I followed their instructions to force-exhale the cold air from my lungs, and inhale deeply the warm air from the room. Keeping my hands and feet in basins of cold water prevented the cold blood from returning to my core. It was important to heat the blood around my heart and other organs first and keep my brain warm. I watched the women and what they were doing. Slowly, I regained focus outside my own space.

Anne Marie and Mariia arrived behind me. Melissa stood beside me in her stars-and-stripes bikini. Then Jackie arrived in, wearing her zebra dressing gown.

'All right, girls,' she said in her cockney accent.

Melissa had stopped at 500 metres, mainly as it was her first time ever swimming at 0 degrees. She was doing this to challenge herself before undertaking the Bering Strait Relay, which we had listened with interest to the others discussing. I was carrying the pride of the Irish. I was the third woman in the world to have swum 1,000 metres at 0 degrees. Jackie Cobell from the UK was the fourth.

Words started to become fuzzy and sounds were muted as I tried to engage, but I was concentrating so much on reheating that I needed to disengage. Irina and Vicki continued with the hot towels. I could feel my body function returning. Every few moments I felt waves of weakness and tiredness, but I snapped out of them quickly.

I managed to break through another barrier, working my way to a new level of extreme. What I had learned about myself in Siberia and on the Conor Pass had allowed me to succeed today. I had taken off my training wheels; I was now an elite ice swimmer.

The medical team arrived several times. My blood pressure had reduced to 130/90 from 140/100, but they required me to stay another 10 minutes as my ECG had not settled.

'There will be six men coming now. Can you help? They will come together.' Irina said.

My mind jolted. The men swimming a mile and 1,000 metres would soon be coming in to recover. Recovery beds were prepared from the benches in the changing room. I was so excited that I was going to witness the recovery procedure first-hand.

Then came the sound of humans banging off walls, like a group of drunk men hammering their way into a narrow space, trying to manoeuvre themselves, frozen after their swims. There were only three attendants working in the area, but Melissa and I grabbed hot towels to make five helpers.

I followed direction and did exactly what Irina and Vicki asked me to do, soaking the towels in hot water and immediately wrapping them over the core, the chest and the thighs. Within minutes the towels became frozen. I was an apprentice in the recovery station, dressed in my teddy-bear dressing gown, standing over the frozen bodies with clawed hands. Their pupils pierced through me, searching for communication, but at the same time unable to communicate. Each swimmer was trying so hard to come back to life, to regain focus. Now I was able to watch the transition from freezing-cold ice swimmer to functional person. The ice was truly the master. The more I studied, the more I understood.

Recovery was different for each swimmer. Henri was stoic and calm, but in a difficult physical state with a challenging recovery after completing 2,150 metres. His face and his eyes were something I will never forget – that piercing focus and determination to survive. The sweat was now dripping off me, still in my dressing gown, moving quickly, replacing towels as they froze from the cold being drawn out from the core. I remember their facial expressions when their hands began to reheat. I was captivated, not so much by their ability to swim the distance, but by how they were still functioning after that level of freezing exposure.

The attendants were moving at a fast pace, changing the heated towels on different parts of the body. The men's eyes became less searching as the heat seeped back into their bones. Their skin colour changed from white to red and black patches appeared on their bodies – possibly blood dispersing. One by one the men became stable enough to move into the sauna.

I did a quick tally and noticed that Kieron had not come in. Then I heard urgent voices outside and, even though I didn't understand the language, I sensed there was a challenge coming. Four men burst open the door to the changing room, carrying a large stretcher, and the head visible at the top was Kieron. His eyes were closed, and the rest of his body was covered up. He looked cold, genuinely frozen.

My eyes were wide open. I turned to look at Irina, searching for an answer.

'He swam more than the mile – two lengths more, I think. Can you help him?' It was matter of fact.

It was like an adrenaline rush. I had my own swimmer to manage. I was in charge. I smiled down at Kieron, wondering if I should start by introducing myself.

He stared directly at me in a searching way. Doing exactly as I was told, I repeatedly placed hot towels around his body, paying attention to all areas, watching the blood refill into certain places, like a blue train-track disappearing into his skin. Keeping the hands and feet cold was vital, working from the core outwards, focusing on the lungs and other organs, shoulders, back, neck and thighs. I could see the heat creeping back into his body. His skin was so thin that his blood tracks were visible as black lines on his back and neck. Replacing hot towels as the others froze on his body and repeating this over a period of 10–15 minutes made such a difference. His pupils relaxed a little – the searching had stopped – and his eyelids started to close naturally. I could see his body coming back to a state of calm. The survival fight was over. He was back. It was one of the best experiences I had had and one that shaped my need to understand more. There was so much to learn.

Those moments in the recovery area in Murmansk, with Vicki and Irina, moving between the recoveries, were some of the most defining moments of my journey in the ice. I had not only experienced the extremes of the ice, I had also witnessed first-hand the return journey – the visible risk and, more importantly, the vital role of the survival mechanism.

Despite the capacity of the human body being phenomenal, these were delicate moments when human error could creep in. They were the most fascinating. The recovery process was essential. Left to our own devices, without the team we would not survive an ice mile or a kilometre at 0 degrees. I had now started to understand more about my collapse in the Conor Pass. I could see how it happened. The work of Vicki and Irina and the medical teams was a crucial part of the swimmers' ability to succeed. I realised that distance swims at 0 degrees were truly a team sport, from preparation to recovery, and these teams were preparing to bring us to the Bering Strait. I was hooked – by the honesty that was necessary within both ourselves and our team; by the humility. There was a lot to learn about the insidious nature of cold water, the impact of the ice.

A swimmer exiting the water after 1,000 metres or a mile could not just walk away. Trust was crucial and so was communication. An outsider would never understand this. This was truly a world of extremes.

Five hours later, all smiles, the excitement was surreal. Exhausted, we were sitting down to dinner in a restaurant, receiving applause for our world firsts, standing in front of the IISA flag in our red jackets, preparing for the Bering Strait Relay with the most accomplished ice swimmers in the world. I was bursting with pride and adrenaline. Anne Marie and I had worked our way into the most elite ice-swimming group in the world. Under my chair were two boxes of Dingle Vodka and my Irish flag. We were being hosted by the mayor of Murmansk, Alexey Veller, and the chief municipal officers of the region, including Dmitry Blokhin.

After the meal, the toasts began – shots of vodka toasting our health, toasting our adventures, toasting our new friendships, toasting the Bering Strait Relay. Bottles of vodka were delivered to the table to fill the toasts in the group of 20 people. There were speeches. I introduced the group to a magnificent, solid, square purple bottle with the words 'Dingle Vodka' on it. I proudly handed it over to the Russians and we toasted the team, extreme adventures ahead and the Bering Strait.

Six hours later, head spinning, wishing I had not taken so many shots, I was running around the halls of the hotel, gathering the group to ensure we were all on the bus to the airport at 4.00 a.m. to begin our long journey home. Murmansk to St Petersburg, then onwards to Amsterdam, Dublin and Kerry.

Sixteen hours later, I turned the key in my front door and walked back into my life. I switched the kettle on and made Dad his cup of tea. There was a huge smile on my face. I had silenced the voices; I had frozen the rants. I had faced my reflection; I had proven my worth as a member of the Bering Strait Relay. I was strong and this was my path. I was the first and only Irish swimmer to ever swim 1,000 metres at 0 degrees. Along with Jackie Cobell, we were the third and fourth women in the world. I would go back to work and smile at my secret world, in which those coming and going would never know what it took to succeed. The patience, the appreciation of failure and weakness. Those moments where I was one-on-one with nature. If I told people I swam 1,000 metres at 0 degrees it would mean little to them. But having the strength to hold on meant the world to me.

13

UNIFYING NATIONS: SWIMMING FROM RUSSIA TO THE USA

'Adversity has the effect of eliciting talents which in prosperous circumstances would have lain dormant.'
Horace

The Bering Strait is a 56-mile channel lying between the Pacific and Arctic Oceans. It separates the Chukchi Peninsula in the Russian far east from the Seward Peninsula in Alaska.

The Bering Strait International Relay Swim was many years in the making. The plan was to relay swim from Cape Dezhnev, Russia to Wales, Alaska. A group of international swimmers from 16 countries and many Russian federations was selected – some of the best cold-water swimmers in the world. There had been multiple attempts to start the swim in 2011 and 2012, but various difficulties, including permits, had got in the way.

Finally, the cooperation of multiple governments and agencies was secured. Visa and customs support were offered and, at long last, the swim was cleared to take place. The navy of the Eastern Military District supplied a hospital ship with full staff, including Dr Nataliya Fatyanova, head of the medical team, and Dr Irina

Zhidkova, whom we had worked with for the previous two years at ice-swimming events in Russia.

Still, the greatest challenges lay ahead. Quite apart from immersing our bodies in the most dangerous body of water in the world, how could a group who had never met come together, with language and cultural barriers, wide-ranging personalities and experiences, and work to meet a common objective? How could we put aside all of our personal objectives and sacrifice everything to complete this swim? The uncertainties were truly exciting; the risks were unknown. This was the most dangerous open-water swim in the world. But we were a group of experienced extreme swimmers committed to doing it.

On 29 July 2013, the group met in Yakutsk, far-eastern Russia. Yakutsk is the coldest city in the world, with winter air temperatures of –64 degrees and the world's largest diamond mine. When we met the organising committee, their opening statements were honest: 'Safety is everything. We would like the record, but not at the expense of the project.' From the first moment, they showed a complete commitment to our welfare.

At 8.00 p.m. on 1 August 2013, swimmers from all over the world lined up on the deck of the *Irtysh* in front of the commander of the expedition, Victor Torbin. Our friend Irina Makarova translated his words: 'I am in charge of this ship. Your life will depend on how well we do things. You must follow the captain's commands and mine. Thank you for being here.'

He followed with directions regarding the expedition – the rules of the ship, how we had to flush the toilets for 15 seconds continuously, not 16, how safety on board would work and, most importantly, how we should operate a buddy system when coming through the ship and never enter an open deck alone. This was a military-style operation, to be sure, but it was the silence when he spoke that set the tone. It lined up with my ethos.

'I hope we will all come back here, in 10 or 15 days, in good health. I will do my best. Thank you,' the commander finished.

Anne Marie and I were allocated a cabin together. We hauled all our stuff inside the tiny space and hung up our Irish tricolour. We had a mountain of stuff, from dried food and recovery snacks to Barry's teabags, coffee and full personal medical kits. Once we had stowed everything, my immediate and sole focus was on getting myself into the kitchen to secure a kettle for our cabin. We could not operate without cups of tea, as we had learned on our Round Ireland Swim. I made my way through the narrow hallway and, in the kitchen, I found two lovely ladies preparing supper for us. I greeted everyone and spoke in gestures with my hands. I saw some electric kettles on the top shelf and asked if I could take one, along with two cups. They shrugged and said yes. I was so excited, running down the hall, my precious kettle tucked into my jacket. Anne Marie burst out laughing when she saw me. We had cups and a kettle: life was as normal as it could be. I could rest.

'What day is it?' Anne Marie asked, shaking her head.

'I don't know. I think it's four days since we left home. We've had three sleeps – one in Dusseldorf and two in Yakutsk.'

'What time is it at home? We should really try and ring to make sure everything is okay and to tell them we're fine.'

She was right. We would lose signal as we headed north. For now, our texts were still landing, but speaking to home before we lost contact was important. They would be worried otherwise.

'Did I tell you we're swimming to America?' The words fell from my mouth.

My bunk was beside the door and I held the door ajar with a book, so I could peek out and see who was passing by. Our cabin was directly opposite the showers. I giggled as I told Anne Marie we had the perfect viewing spot. The ship's engines rumbled and we began to move, suddenly aware that we were now steaming north to the Arctic Circle.

Anne Marie woke up at 6.30 a.m. after our first night onboard and consulted our ship schedule, reading it out in the tone used by the commander.

'Wake up 7.00 a.m. Breakfast 7.30 a.m. Training/cleaning the room 11.00 a.m. Lunch 12 p.m. Dinner 5.00 p.m. Evening tea 7.30 p.m. Sleep 11.00 p.m. Another fine mess we got ourselves into,' she said, shaking her head. She looked at me. 'It's only 6.45 a.m. We should get back into bed in case we are breaking the rules!' As the ship bounced through the waves, we laughed and put our kettle on.

Later, at breakfast, I was told that the women serving us and working in the kitchen were the medical teams from the hospital downstairs. The chef was the cardiologist and the woman washing the dishes was the nurse. That was the way the ship worked. I immediately started clearing the tables and resetting for the next service. I did not speak Russian, but they were grateful for the help.

The ship tore through the Bering Sea, waves cold and strong. It felt so strange to contemplate the expedition ahead. This was the first time the entire team had been together. There were so many faces from the winter swimming competitions, the difference being the majority were individual competitors, now meeting for the first time as an international team. Could we work together as a team to achieve a common goal? How could the team work with language barriers? How would panic manifest itself with the challenges of the raging seas?

So many concerns and yet, here we were, about to put our lives into the hands of strangers.

Both Anne Marie and I had great experience in allowing our personal needs to fall second to the objective of the team. During the Round Ireland Swim, I felt that would be one of the greatest challenges.

That afternoon, we began our medicals at the hospital. It was a floating hospital that travelled the length of Russia down as far as the Sea of Japan. Down two levels, into the belly of the ship for the first time, we navigated the hallways filled with cabins.

Irina Makarova, who was acting as translator, introduced us to the hospital chief, the surgeon, the traumatologist, the dermatologist and the stomatologist, Svetlana. Irina gave us the guided tour. Diagnostics, a clinical laboratory, a dentist. Denis, whom I'd met in the restaurant earlier, was the anaesthetist. Others I'd met earlier, working in the kitchen, turned out to be the neurosurgeon, the pharmacist and the radiologist. The smiling Igor, a man I would meet again the following day, was the ophthalmologist. Many spoke good English and were very interested in our expedition.

Drs Irina Zhidkova and Nataliya Fatyanova were our medical team. They were engaged in a study on the effects of exposure to hypothermia and cold-related injuries on cardiac function. We were their guinea pigs. I was so excited. One by one the swimmers were moved from primary blood-pressure check-up to ECG. We moved from room to room. I was trying to gather as much information as possible. I was nosy.

My blood pressure read 120/80 and my pulse oxygen was 99 per cent. Next, I was hooked up with wires at my wrists and ankles for my cardio tests. I waited patiently.

'Close your eyes and breathe, Nuala,' Dr Irina said.

I did, and her smile when I opened them said it all. I was cleared and given the stamp of approval to swim.

'Your heart looks much stronger than in 2012, in Tyumen.' Dr Irina smiled as she showed me the cardiology tests taken nine months ago. I was very proud as she pointed out the different areas of stress. I had become stronger and fitter.

Not everyone passed their medical, but there were a few days to retest, after we'd recovered from the flights and relaxed.

Our mornings now began with aerobic bootcamp on the helipad at 6.30 a.m. I was willing to try anything and enjoyed being part of the team as I lunged, squatted and jogged around a helipad on a moving ship with the group.

The ship was ploughing its way through the cold, dark waters off the east coast of Russia, steaming its way to the Arctic Circle. The winds had lifted to 18 metres per second from the north-east, Arctic winds blasting directly into the path of the ship. That is close to gale force 9 – horrendous conditions. The darkness of the water showed its intent and the power that we associate with remote waters. We would be steaming north for six days in total. In so many places around the world people can only swim in rivers or lakes, or go ice swimming in confined spaces. Many of the swimmers had never seen the sea before. During our lifeboat drills, it was the first time using a lifejacket for many of the swimmers, let alone being on a ship. They were looking at these conditions with different eyes. Their fears at the vastness of the seas around us were real; they exuded stress from every pore. The level of respect I felt for them increased so much.

The team began a discussion about how most of our swimmers would swim 3 kilometres per hour. If the crossing was about 120 kilometres, that meant the finish time would be 40 hours.

Anne Marie and I exchanged glances that they expected anyone to complete 3 kilometres in an hour in frustrated seas. The tides were running north–south, and eddies and currents were vying for position as the Pacific Ocean tried to fill and empty itself into the Arctic Ocean through the tiny mouth of the Bering Strait, and as the Arctic Ocean filled south and returned along the coast of Alaska. We would be tossed around like corks in a bathtub. The Round Ireland Swim had been supposed to take us 28 days, but it took 56. This was the Bering Strait. What would happen when we did not make progress? Many swimmers were so competitive and certain – how would they feel when a mile took an hour? Or when they were pushed backwards?

However, I wanted to be a valuable team member and there were already a lot of voices involved, so we kept our opinions to ourselves. I had studied my charts prior to leaving and I had chatted a lot with my father about the currents along the Alaskan coast. Dad had fished out of Dutch Harbour and he warned me of huge currents that would stop us. I felt that, as the days went by, experience would be the only teacher. I could hear Mary's words of wisdom about life: 'Keep your powder dry.' I nodded: time would tell.

'The swim will be over when it's over,' Anne Marie said, and we smiled.

After six days steaming north to the most easterly point in the Russian Federation, the gateway to the Arctic, it was decided to take a recce trip to the start point to see if the water was swimmable. As we watched the Zodiac pull away from the side of the ship, the reality of our task became clear. The Zodiac was bounced around like a plaything, until it disappeared from view into the raging waters.

Oleg Dokuchaev, the chief organiser, made the call: the relay swim would commence in an hour. The announcement blindsided us as the plan became a reality. A sense of anxiety filled the gym as the list of pods – the groups of three in which we would swim – was placed on the gym wall. Anne Marie and I were together, along with Toks from South Africa. There would be orange buoys issued and used for all swims. They were tied around swimmers' waists for visibility and could be grabbed hold of in the event of an incident. The wearing of these was non-negotiable, even in waves.

The chief safety officer made it clear that each swimmer would have to be medically cleared to swim. For the duration of the swim there would be no unnecessary movement outside our cabins – we were to remain resting. There would be no activity on the deck after 9.00 p.m. There would be random breath tests by the medical teams for the duration of the swim to ensure no alcohol was consumed. Safety was the priority. The communication style was clear, each sentence was translated and each group sat and listened while the briefings were delivered, followed by discussion and questions. Feedback was entertained and welcomed, but the leadership was clear, from the top down. Each meeting finished with a medical briefing from Dr Nataliya Fatyanova.

A telex was read out: the US government confirmed that our visa for American waters would expire at 9.00 a.m. on 8 August. By that time we would have to be in Wales, Alaska. The time allocated for the swim was approximately 40 hours. The wind was not due to lessen and the waves would continue to be high. It was deemed swimmable. Looking out from the ship, that was a subjective opinion. We all smiled.

It was time to swim the 56 miles across the Bering Strait..

The emotions were overwhelming as we stood on the bow, leaning over the side, watching the first team load into the RIBs. The weather would be our chief competitor. There was very much a sense that this was not water anyone should be swimming in at all, let alone for days on end. The waves were thundering at 4 metres high, banging against the sides of this huge ship.

Within an hour, American swimmer Melissa 'Mo' O'Reilly, in her trademark bikini, was lowering her body into the rough, freezing waters of the Bering Strait. She rotated her arms with such ease, her physical strength and conditioning visible as she headed to the stony shoreline. But it was her courage and fearlessness that were most clearly on display. Her arms, so tiny, rotated like a birds' wings on the waves; then she disappeared, swallowed up in the mountains of sea. But, within seconds, she was standing tall on the shoreline of the last frontier of the Russian Federation. She was the only swimmer in the world to start a swim on the most easterly point of Asia: a gravel patch on Cape Dezhnev, the nose of Chukotka, near the monument to Semyon Dezhnev, who in 1648 became the first European to sail through the Bering Strait. A final wave in the air to the crew and Melissa burst through the waves. The first international relay across the Bering Strait had begun. Silence fell on the ship and candles were lit in the gym with religious images, as a place to meditate.

Anne Marie and I were the third group, so we gathered the waterproof bags, swim hats and goggles, and gave thanks that we had our sponsored Sioen suits. These were huge sea-survival immersion suits with thermal properties – two pieces – and thermal underwear, which we would step directly into over our swimming togs after our swims. They had been tried, tested and proven during the Round Ireland Swim. Windproof and waterproof, they would be lifesaving for us when exposed to Arctic conditions.

Each swim would be 10 minutes – a time based on the water temperature and recovery time. There would be risks attached to swimming any longer. The best chance of recovery, medically, was to keep the swim times short. Human error was always going to be the greatest enemy here. Recovery would happen on the boat, meaning that swimmer one would be cold and wet on a RIB, in roaring Arctic winds, waiting for swimmer three to finish. But we each had a choice: to swim or to opt out. The conditions looked incredibly challenging, but no one had travelled this far to be a passenger.

Looking over the railings, the water was dark and foreboding, winds gusting from force 6 to gale force 8 from the north-east. How would the coxswains keep the RIBs close to us? That was my biggest question – but I reminded myself that that was not my job. I would have to keep my mouth shut – to be invisible but strong, to be confident but humble, and to be respectful of the sea.

At 5.30 p.m., wind swirling around us, we stood on the metal platform of a box about 60 centimetres square, which held 50 steps attached to the side of this huge ship. The magnitude of the water from this vantage point, as it rose high and dropped large under my feet, made my heart beat fit to burst with exhilaration. We had to time our jump onto the 7-metre RIB, which was secured by rope and rose and fell by about 3 metres with each wave.

I threw my bags into the front, held on and, on the count of the crew and the word of the coxswain, leapt into the front of the RIB, landing and grabbing the rails. I was in.

We tucked in to the seats behind the coxswain. Melissa was returning with her Russian teammates, cold but wrapped up well, and she looked brilliant, her face beaming. It was possible. We were swimming to the USA.

Within 5 minutes, the RIB had battled its way through the waves to come alongside Ryan, who was swimming strong. The wind and the waves made it difficult to hold the RIB steady. Our eyes scanned the conditions, watching how Ryan's arms were rotating and how he would get himself onto the boat. This was the first time actually visualising the relay.

Our group would be Toks first. I would be the middle swimmer and Anne Marie the finisher, meaning we would be exposed to these conditions for an hour at a time.

'Water is 4 degrees,' Aleksandr Jakovlev, who was acting boat crew and also a main swimmer, said to us.

A nod of our heads: the game was on.

We watched with intent as Toks pushed through the waves. As expected, the remote recovery of the swimmers would be the most challenging aspect. We would be losing body heat in the freezing wind. Ten minutes at four degrees was acceptable, it was the other variables of transfers and waiting on the RIB that were cause for concern.

I started to get undressed, my hat and goggles on my head. I stared and focused on the waves, trying to find a pattern. The waves were coming from different angles.

'Three minutes to swim.' Vladimir Nefatov, one of the team's referees, gave me my time warning. I was ready to get going.

'One minute.'

I stripped the immersion suit from my body. I felt that force-6 Arctic wind, blowing in from the north-east and freezing my body in an instant. A few deep breaths and I lowered my body from the tubing of the RIB into the dark, icy waves of the Bering Strait, careful not to sink too deep. I reached forward, touched Toks's hand and smiled. My breath was immediately taken away by the icy waters pressing on my chest. The challenge was the wave pattern and finding an air pocket to breathe when I rotated my head. I eased my arms forward, exhaled and took a few light strokes until my face was numb. I was free to count down the 10 minutes.

I decided to focus on the power of the waves, the greatness of our strength, the courage it took – and breathing. *Who gets to swim in the Bering Strait?*

Within minutes, the strap of the orange buoy was pushed forward by the wind and caught in my arm. I was getting tangled with each stroke as the orange buoy danced around in the wind, but I was determined not to stop for the remaining few minutes. I found a rhythm by moving my arm more slowly. It was something we would sort out for the next swim.

In what seemed like a short moment, Anne Marie was getting ready. I could see her drop her jacket. Aleksandr held up his hand. *Three minutes.* I felt amazing – frozen, but incredible. It was swimmable.

One minute.

I watched as Anne Marie eased herself into the dark waters and the waves surrounded her. A huge smile and a big laugh between us.

'Feck's sake,' was all I said as we tapped hands, and then she was off, swimming into the Bering Strait. I had to pinch myself in disbelief. I had just swum in the most treacherous waters in the world.

Getting back onto the RIB was difficult with cold hands. As I watched Anne Marie's arms disappear into the Bering Strait, I felt an urgency. I reached the rungs of the floating ladder and pulled myself onto the rear of the RIB. I had the sudden realisation that, unlike the Round Ireland Swim, the engines did not have engine guards. One false move and my reach could end up on the propeller. I stood at the front of the boat in my togs, wet and cold, but taking a few moments in the wind, determined to relax and steady my breathing. Steadying my own ship was more important. The doubts were over. I could gather myself, ease the manic speed my mind had been racing at over the last month, ease the emotions arising from having to react speedily to our new reality. For now, we were only swimmers, rotating our arms as part of a team.

My eyes opened wide in disbelief as I took a 360-degree view of this moment – the Russian coastline behind, the iconic Diomede islands ahead, with a blanket of fog sitting on them. *Smile and be calm.* I wiped the water from my body and pulled on my immersion suit. The sense of power was palpable. How proud I was for us to have accepted the challenges! I trusted the ability of the crews and teams. Deep inside myself, I felt at peace out here.

Turning back to check with the coxswains and referees, I laid my body over the front bow on the tubing, eyes lower than that point where the boat leans into the wind. This had been my position for the entire Round Ireland Swim. My legs steady on the ground, but my face closer to the water than ever, I pulled out my camera and took photos of Anne Marie and the command ship. *Take it all in. Look at where you are. Look at who you are. Look at us.* Just in case it would all end suddenly, I wanted to savour each moment.

Another group alongside, Paolo Chiarino dropped into the dark waters, reached to tap Anne Marie's hand and then powered away, legs kicking and living up to his nickname, the 'Italian Ferrari'. Ten minutes at 4 degrees was technically not a big swim for us. Rotation one complete.

A thumbs-up from Anne Marie to say she was happy to sit at the stern of the boat for the spin back to the ship, without pulling on her immersion suit. It was not easy to balance and get dressed as the RIB danced in the waves. The boat sped through the waves, freezing spray from the Bering Strait drenching us for the 15-minute spin to the steps on the side of the ship. Then the transfer, which was dangerous. Anne Marie was still in her togs, with a blanket around her. Standing on the bow of the RIB which was bouncing in the waves, resting against the metal hull of colossal ship, we had to hurl our bodies forward so that arms could grab us and pull us up onto a small metal platform.

I could not make eye contact with the men positioned to grab us for fear of laughing. For many, there would be panic, but our default was always to laugh. There was nothing we could change now, as Anne Marie, in her swimming togs, reached upwards to be lifted by two Russian men in a 30-metre-per-second Arctic wind, soaked and frozen.

The insanity of it all made us laugh out loud.

'How could you explain this to anyone?' I said as my body was hauled up onto the metal platform.

Each swimmer was immediately ushered to the medical unit, where Drs Irina and Nataliya were waiting for us. Our cold bodies were put under warm showers and into the sauna, after being connected to wires to monitor our cardiac responses to the cold immersion. The shivering began and the heat of the metal ship was a life saver. All results were documented for the medical research project. My blood pressure was relaxed at 120/80 and my pulse oxygen was 99 per cent. Anne Marie was shivering uncontrollably after swim one, but then again, she had had her feet dangling off the back of the boat in freezing waters for 15 minutes, exposed to the Arctic winds.

Our saturated immersion suits and blankets would dry so quickly with this heat in the belly of the ship. Once we were inside, the safety and calm were an absolute contrast to the mayhem and the insanity of the water.

It was now 7.30 p.m. We checked the rotation list on the wall, as each swim was being updated.

Swim 2 – Group 9 – 2.30 a.m. – meeting at 1.30 a.m.

'We're back in the water in 6.5 hours' time? No way.' I turned to face Anne Marie, who was muttering under her breath.

I don't remember closing my eyes, but my diary was still in my hand when the alarm woke us. I felt like I'd been hit on the head with a hammer. It was 12.30 a.m. We put the kettle on. We looked at the bruises on our bodies from being grabbed and lifted and falling on metal. Paolo Chiarino knocked on the door with a cup in his hand, looking for some coffee. He had his own cappuccinos, like every Italian. He was followed by Aleksandr Jakovlev, reminding us to bring the glow-sticks for our hats.

Darkness had fallen and the wind felt sinister. The sound of the boats banging against the side of the ship was scary in the blackness of night. We jumped onto our black RIB, illuminated only with spotlights, unable to identify the crew, as all had hoods pulled tight to protect their faces from the sheeting rain. The safety briefing had exposed the nature of the risk.

Swim two was a different beast – a real test, the dark of the Bering Strait hiding its malicious intent. The wind had increased, holding on tight, our boat bounced our way to our swim start, rocking at the mercy of the sea. The moment we came alongside the other boat, the extent of the challenge became real. Huge spotlights were shining on the swimmer who was disappearing into the waves, trying to highlight their location. The darkness complicated the swim further, mostly at a psychological level. Where were we swimming to? What were we following? How could we be taken out? Swimmers were tossed and turned like plastic toys.

There was shouting and klaxons screamed as the pilots tried to alert the swimmer to a need to change direction. Language barriers were more obvious now, making communicating even more difficult. Hand signals were useless to swimmers blinded by spotlights. A silence dropped over our boat, to the point where even our breathing went quiet. Our coxswain tried to communicate by radio, his hand inside his jacket, shoulders hunched to block out the wind and rain. We sat motionless, as if frozen. The water had now picked up the icy flow from the Arctic. The temperature had dropped to 2 degrees, with a freezing wind. This was now survival.

Out in the darkness, the screams realised that a swimmer had to be rescued from the water. He had begun to sink under the waves and was in a risky condition. The tone of the rescue and the underlying feeling of panic crossed all language boundaries. We understood.

Personal responsibility was now a priority, especially as the crews were approaching their physical limits. Ten minutes at two degrees is a completely different immersion. Added to this was the anxiety of the darkness, of having no idea where you are going, the stress of not being seen in these waves and the intense fear of being lost. What if we were separated? Our screams would not be heard.

'We need to go slow, forget the speed,' I whispered to Anne Marie. She nodded.

I knew the cold shock – that sense when the breathing increases and panic rises high in the chest – would be a bigger issue now with the wind and waves. I closed my eyes.

Focus on the darkness; focus on the now. Don't be a problem for yourself and your team. It's arm over arm.

As I got ready, there came another set of screams from the water. The swimmer ahead was in difficulty. The searching spotlights showed the monster of a sea and its intent towards us. We needed to be passengers on its path. *Keep your mouth shut*, I reminded myself as anxiety rose around me. Your job is to swim.

'Slyne Head,' I whispered to Anne Marie. I was thinking of the moment when a wave had separated Anne Marie from the vessel off the west coast of Galway. Derek had had to manage the RIB, get away from the rogue wave, locate Anne Marie and come around again to pick her up. Anne Marie had had to stay calm and focused on the boat so that they could find her.

'Slyne Head in the dark,' she whispered back. 'We'll stick to the side of this boat.'

The difference between fast and slow speed could be life threatening.

The boat crews were now 12 hours out in these conditions. Exhausted and visibly nervous, they were tasked with keeping us safe, yet how could they tell if a swimmer was having issues? They would see a light and then the swimmer would disappear again in the huge waves. Was that swimmer okay? Who knew? It was just a light attached to a body.

I had 10 minutes to get ready. I pulled my body inside my suit and closed my eyes. I swam my swim, over and over again. I counted the strokes.

Around us, winds gusted to a force 6–8, at 12 metres per second. Walls of dark water hurled us about. So much for the bright nights of the Arctic. This was solid darkness. I whispered to Anne Marie, 'Some of these swimmers have never been on a boat, let alone swum in the darkness. Can you imagine their fears? We've been here before. They have not.' Who would choose to lower their body into this kind of risk? I focused on the dream of pushing my body so close to the edge and having a team willing to risk everything to save me. This was the edge. This was privilege, to spend 10 minutes at the very limit.

Three minutes.

The blind darkness and rain focused my mind acutely. The wind was icy Arctic gusts. I closed my eyes and numbed every emotion. I decided to tie the orange buoy very close to my back so that it wouldn't blow around. There was a flashing light on the back of my goggles. I lowered my body into the water, dark and menacing. Careful not to sink too deep under the freezing water, I glanced up. The waves were as high as 2 metres, Anne Marie was sitting behind the coxswain, leaning over the tubing. I could see her face in the spotlights. I kept her focus.

I pushed out into the darkness.

I was lucky that I was breathing to the side of the vessel, each stroke connecting me to the sight of Anne Marie. The coxswain was able to hold the RIB close to my body. Their skills were unbelievable. *This is the edge*, I kept reminding myself, as the reality of the 2-degree water caught me. *Find the beauty in the darkness*.

The faces on board were ghostlike, illuminated by the light bearing down, each stroke forward, fingers frozen.

Arm over arm. Breathe.

The 10 minutes passed very quickly for me; then Anne Marie was lowering herself in to take my place. Anne Marie went slow until I was onboard as decided. Swimmers were at the mercy of the waves. How could anyone know whether we were heading back to Russia or towards America? We were just swimming and staying alive. This was the most dangerous situation I had ever experienced, I focused on Anne Marie.

Three minutes to finish.

One minute to finish.

There was an elevated sense of urgency to get back to the ship. Once on board, we were ushered down a side corridor, freezing but moving, medical teams acting quickly around us. Through an open door I saw a Russian swimmer lying unconscious on a stretcher and several other swimmers wrapped in blankets and looking very unwell in the next room. I wondered how many would call time on their swim after their first experience. The first casualties of the Bering Strait Relay.

Anne Marie and I headed to the medical testing area. Our immersion suits were saving us from the exposure, but many were just in normal clothing. Our bodies now descended into extensive shivering, a mixture of tiredness, freezing temperatures and being exposed for so long on the transfers and back-to-back immersions. Dr Irina keep her hands pressed hard on our legs trying to minimise the shaking for our ECGs. There was a marked increase in blood pressure and cardiac responses.

It was 4.00 a.m. We checked our next swim: six hours away. That meant we could sleep and have breakfast at 7.30 a.m. There was a silence falling on the swimmers, people moving from boat to medical to bunk and repeat. Paolo Chiarino was standing, waiting to transfer to the boat. The jacket he was wearing was light for the wind and rain. I dropped my immersion suit from my body and handed it to him. I did not need it on the ship. Keeping swimmers like Paolo warm would be important for the speed. The smile, the silent nod, all actions geared towards the common objective, and to survival.

At breakfast, Oleg called a meeting for available swimmers at 9.30 a.m. Our swim was at 10.30 a.m., we readied ourselves, bodies bruised and tired. With all the meetings, medical checks and reheating, we'd only slept for about 4 hours out of the last 24. Even when I could rest, I wanted to be out on deck. For me this was the most exciting moment of my life since the Round Ireland Swim. I wanted to be on every swim, on every boat.

Despite all the voices up on the bridge of the ship – different languages, many expressing fears – Oleg asked how we felt and wanted our opinions on how the swim could be improved. Feedback was important to the leaders, as each swim rotation was presenting different challenges. We discussed using the tugboat as a guide vessel for us to follow, for our focus.

I decided to risk asking Vladimir Nefatov for the GPS requirements of the next swims, so I could keep our swim on track by focusing on the GPS. We had monitored our own swims during the Round Ireland Swim. He scribbled them on my hand.

There was a sigh of relief as we were told that the swimmer who was unconscious was now well but had decided to retire from the event. So had others.

'We need three strong swims today in daylight. Then we push into the night before our visa expires.' This was translated for us by Irina. Oleg looked exhausted – he was swimming and leading at the same time. The pressure of the risks to personal safety and dealing with the visa requirements was showing. But his communication style was perfect for the expedition.

We were 16 hours into our 40-hour window and close to the halfway point, with over 20 kilometres covered. The plan would see us soon crossing the International Date Line into American waters.

The sunlight cast shadows high over the islands of Diomede, Big and Little, in full view. The waves had become more challenging, so the rise and fall of the RIB side of the ship made it a bigger jump now, but we had learned to accept the risk and just hurl our bodies forward. It was wonderful to see a piece of carpet now tied onto the metal. My leg was bruised and my arms cut from a few bad landings onto the metal platform, but my limbs were numb from the cold, preventing me from feeling the pain. A layer of fog lifted like a circle of light around Fairway Rock, like a scene from a movie.

In the distance the coxswain pointed out two toothed walruses, their gigantic heads popping up over the waves. They were huge animals, weighing over 2,000 kilograms each. My eyes lit up at the size of their tusks, visible in the sunlight. In the distance, on the islands, was their colony. Then the idea of us sharing the water with them filled my mind with a moment of fear, until I realised my swim was 20 minutes away. Anyway, if they were hungry, there was a swimmer already handy in the water. A brief giggle to myself and my survival mode reasserted itself. There was nothing we could do; our swim route was pushed a few miles south to create distance from the Walrus colony.

Our third and fourth swims were mechanical, the exhaustion was clearly visible in the team, sleep was a luxury and food was eaten in silence. We were swimming around the islands in daylight hours. The cold water still between 4 and 6 degrees, but it was a welcome distraction to look up at the iconic islands of Diomedes, 2.4 kilometres apart, with inhabitants on both, separating the USA and Russia.

The waves were reduced in height thanks to the protection of the island, Big Diomede, the last piece of Russian territory before entering international waters. The silence among swimmers was our calm acceptance of the crazy journey. We had done well. Our medicals cleared by 11.00 p.m., we crawled into our bunks, day two completed.

There was a knock on our cabin door at 1.00 a.m. that startled me. Vladimir and Aleksandr were standing there, wet. The rain was sheeting down and wind had increased, visibility was low. Could they have a cup of tea as the kitchen was closed? Anne Marie and I jumped up and put the kettle on.

'The fog is going to cause a problem,' Aleksandr said. We hadn't thought about fog.

We looked out the porthole as the waves smashed the side of the ship. Zero visibility and yet we could make out the light of the boats and swimmers in the storm.

I pulled out my copybook and, with pen and paper, I asked

about distance covered. I was delighted to have their drawings on my diary. I could study the route. I really wanted to go to the bridge to engage with the leadership, but felt there were enough voices.

When they left, we rolled back into the bunks. At 4.00 a.m., another knock at the door came. It was Ryan and Melissa looking for hot coffee, shattered from their swims. They were the swimmers in the darkness. The weather had changed and there was a lot of anxiety rising again. Back on went the kettle.

'The crews are struggling managing the swimmers,' Melissa said. 'It's been a bad night.' They left and we rolled into our bunks again.

'It would have been nice if people called in during daylight hours,' Anne Marie said, laughing.

Our teammates laughed at us Irish, with our welcome mat at the door and the kettle plugged in, always on the boil. (Although, since water was rationed, we were now asking people to bring their own.) I was delighted that information was coming to us over cups of tea.

Sleep is not something that comes easy, you are always in a heightened state of alert. Over the following hours the team was now reduced by 20 swimmers, who, for medical or personal reasons, had decided they were not able to continue so the time between swims was reducing.

At 9.00 p.m. Anne Marie and I prepared to swim again. Fog surrounded the ship; a storm-force-9 wind was causing the ladder to bang against the side of the ship as we held the railings; visibility ahead was zero. We waited, swim bags and lights in hand. It felt bizarre to be immune to the conditions, to be emotionally vacant, arms for hire. We had both been here before on the west coast of Ireland. We present, we prepare, we swim, we recover, and we do not comment. The atmosphere on deck as swimmers left and returned was so encouraging. The crews looked exhausted, working 12-hour shifts, lifting and pulling swimmers, knowing if one of them fell or did not make contact, the outcome could be fatal. There was a ring of steel around the swimmers.

Word filtered down that there was an incident ongoing: two boats returning with swimmers and were trying to locate the ship in the fog. They were not far from us, but the crews, experienced as they were, were unable to see the ship. All of us went out on deck, spotting. The horns sounded, the sirens sounded, but the RIBs could not find their way, the whiteness of the fog was so dense. The lights rotated and, after a period of calling on radios and GPS, the RIBs approached to huge applause. The relief! The swimmers were frozen and shaking uncontrollably. After an extra 40 minutes exposed to the wind and rain, they needed to be transferred immediately.

The decision was to suspend the relay to assess the risks and present dangers and to fit radar reflectors on all the RIBs.

'How do you explain this to the open-water community?' I asked Anne Marie as we watched the boats being hoisted onto the ship. We were past questions, simply waiting for direction. If we had to swim, swim we would, but we were delighted when the decision was announced to hoist the boats out of the water. It was now storm-force 10 with 4-metre waves and low visibility. There was a real risk to life.

The excitement of a full night's sleep was contrasted with the emotions that we had only completed a total of 59 kilometres. Thirty hours had passed and the swimmers had been pushed very far south of the islands. Less than 2 kilometres per hour.

I laughed as we discussed Mary's suggestion that we should submit our route, leave the details of our ship with Russian military and government officials, and get the name of the Irish ambassador to Russia in case we needed to have an emergency extraction.

'Is it time to make the call for an extraction?' I said as we laughed at our situation, sitting with our cappuccinos.

We were sitting on the International Date Line, with America just 2 kilometres away, still in Russian waters. It was our first real night's sleep in three days. We collapsed into a deep slumber.

The morning brought the news that calls had been made through the night between the governments of both the US and Russia. Our visa expired at 9.00 a.m. that day – 40 hours had passed. But we had secured an extension to allow us to finish our relay. When that would be, became a huge source of anxiety.

The decision was made to push the swim another 5 kilometres south of the islands, which would push us into deeper and more turbulent water and add more distance, but would also give us a line of defence against the walrus army. Jellyfish suddenly seemed easy. Now we were worried about being eaten by a hungry walrus with tusks half a metre long – and the walrus, in turn, was worried about being eaten by the orcas patrolling outside. But we had to pass them to move onwards. Although big, walruses are fast swimmers, and the males would defend their females and calves.

The International Date Line is the boundary from which each calendar day starts. Areas to the west of the line are one calendar day ahead of areas to the east of it. The date line runs from the North Pole to the South Pole through the Pacific Ocean. It is not a straight line, however. It curves around several landmasses. For example, it curves around the islands that make up the nation of Kiribati, to ensure all regions of the country remain on the same day. The date line makes a big detour between Asia and North America in the Bering Strait. Cape Dezhnev in Russia is always a day ahead of Cape Prince of Wales in Alaska, even though the landmasses are less than 80 kilometres apart.

Later that day, the swim resumed. Our group, swimming after Henri Kaarma, Cristian Vergara and Craig Lenning, a strong American cold-water swimmer, crossed the International Date Line. It was difficult to get my head around the fact that, in a few strokes or a few waves, we would swim into yesterday.

The rain beat down as Anne Marie and I sat in front of the steering, hiding our bodies from the searing winds. We watched the commanding figure of our friend Cristian Vergara driving through the water, a fast, strong stroke, but it now looked like he was swimming uphill. The waves were now 4 metres of slow uphill and slow downhill. We would lose sight of the boat and the swimmer until we climbed the waves and tilted downwards in cartoonish fashion.

Looking at the GPS on the boat, I could tell we were moving south-east, with a north-east wind now gusting to force 7, which was driving us wide of our destination. It's so hard to describe the conditions: rolling waves, erratic and excited, backed by huge winds. When the tides turned these waves were angry and mostly broke mid-water, causing swimmers to be separated from the vessels. So much effort, and the islands still standing in front of us. We had not yet progressed into American waters.

The anxiety was twofold: the pressure to finish, coupled with worry about what continuing would mean, physically and emotionally. The stop for shelter inside the islands had broken the momentum and each swimmer who returned was talking about how they were achieving nothing more than 100 or 200 metres in their 10-minute swim. Water temperatures were still low, at 6 degrees, and with so many immersions it was not possible to extend each swimmer's time in the water. Anne Marie and I kept silent. We just slept and swam and left our door open for tea and coffee – a cabin to debrief in.

Even though it was 2.00 a.m., it was bright as we sat low on the floor of the RIB, in front of the transom, to protect ourselves from the wind and cold. The boats were being turned and twisted and I was thinking, *How is this coxswain even staying on course?* This was a much more aggressive sea than earlier. There was no pattern – waves were turning from all angles. I had the GPS coordinates written on my hand. I was determined to figure out if we were being pushed back or pushed off course. We had seen it all before.

The Arctic brightness had made its way through. Fairway Rock stood eerie, just south of us. It was very similar to Skellig Michael, off the south-west coast of Ireland – circular and jagged with fog wreathed about and its summit sticking up high in the sky. We were on the oceanic meridian separating east and west.

Standing up to ready myself to go in next, I focused on the illuminated GPS screen. I showed the coordinates to Vladimir, the referee. A smile and a wink as I lowered my googles. Mindful of the fog, I said to Anne Marie, 'When we change over, stay close to the boat until I get back on board.' I eased myself into the turbulent waters.

We were making our own rules for the low light condition: we were now a team inside a team. We had personally decided to forfeit some speed for the sake of safety.

I completed my stint and, once back on board, took my now familiar position, leaning over the bow, staring down at Anne Marie as her arms rotated through the freezing waters. The coxswains had become comfortable with our experience and with my questioning them and staring at their screens.

The physical costs and the emotional costs were now consuming energy. The warmth of the ship was the saving grace as our bodies were constantly rewarmed.

'What day is it?' I asked as I wrote in my diary. Anne Marie responded by pulling the blanket over her head. The cabin filled with laughter.

At 3.30 a.m., arms and legs bruised from the jumping and being hauled into and out of boats, we fell asleep. I was jolted awake by a tap on the door. Bleary eyed, I opened it. It was Aleksandr Jakovlev. His face was tired and anxious. I knew he needed some space.

'Come in, come in. We'll put the kettle on.'

We had now been swimming for three days and, as a swim starter, assisting with the organising group up on the bridge, and a swimmer, Aleksandr had probably only slept a few hours in that time.

It was 6.00 a.m. The three previous groups of swimmers had hit a countercurrent south of the islands and, despite being fast, strong swimmers, had managed only 150 metres. That was a terrible outcome – to have boats out and crews battling horrendous conditions for 1.5 hours only to achieve 150 metres was soul destroying. I was truly shocked, to the point of being emotional, mainly for the crews and the team. We accepted we were not making fast progress, but to hear it in such simple terms was soul destroying. My eyes darted to Anne Marie. The islands would have water swirling around them. My mind went into overdrive.

Oleg and the organisation on the bridge had not slept, their days spent plotting and planning, but many people had now stepped in, applying pressure to go home. We needed to be finished – the swim was not advancing. They were absorbing risk after risk, and now this wall of water, this countercurrent, was pushing us backwards. But the constant communications and briefings allowed us all to keep pushing. Our minds went to the west coast of Ireland. The patience that was needed.

I handed Aleksandr my copybook and a pen, so I could see and process the information. The scribblings on the copybook as Aleksandr drew some maps of the currents showed me how the ship had rotated on its moorings through the night.

The tides, I thought, surely. Anne Marie raised her eyebrows as if to say, 'Been there, seen that.' How could they think that the tides would not affect the swim?

There were two oceans moving north and south daily, squeezing huge volumes of water up onto a shallow ledge of 30 metres in the Bering Strait and squeezing through a tiny gap. We were trying to swim across that gap. The west coast of America has currents and flows racing up and down its complicated coastline. The relay was due to be finished and we were expected home in a few days. But here we were, somewhere in the belly of the Bering Strait, with no sight of the finish line.

The unknown was when or if we could get there. How much risk would the organisers accept? When might the swim be called off? My eyes drifted to Anne Marie, that silent exchange of words. *How can we stop this?*

We explained that we had aimed to swim around Ireland in 28 days, but it had taken 56. That was the nature of the ocean. How does a team of this size and cost quit?

We were now joined by Vladimir, who was also anxious to discuss the relay and its chances of succeeding. Just debriefing really.

'It is possible,' I said. 'It's about patience and will and time. We've done amazingly.'

Achieving only 150 metres was terrible, but it was progress. It was all about speed and power now. The faster swimmers could drive harder against the resistance of the tide and break its rhythm.

We described Anne Marie's North Channel swim and how the team planned for her to swim for two hours, training in the middle of Beaufort's Dyke, trying to understand which part of the tides she would need to swim with so as not to go backwards. They were excited to have her swim for two hours and not advance, because the goal was that she would not be pushed backwards. We shared all our stories, trying to show this was not uncommon. Progress and patience.

We were now joined by Paolo Chiarino, here for his cappuccino, and Melissa O'Reilly, both swimmers who excelled at speed. Jackie Cobell and Mariia Yrjö-Koskinen joined us too and our cabin was full.

The discussion would eventually have to take in which swimmers would be strongest and fastest, who would be able to push us onwards and achieve the distance. Progress could not be lost. We might stand still between swims, but we could not afford to lose distance. We had to continue to push forward, and egos would have to step away now. This was not about the swimmers; this was about the swim.

'The tides have their own ways of working and we're just passengers in the water,' I told them. 'The six hours north and south of each tide have their weak moments.' I was stunned to hear so many had not heard this theory, but then reminded myself that many swim in pools or other confined waters, and many swim for speed. Many do not fight to finish.

There was a mental exhaustion in the room and the question of whether to stop was hanging over us. We hoped everyone could be patient, but the costs were also mounting.

The Bering Strait was giving us a glimpse of possibility, allowing us to have a few centimetres at a time. It was giving us passage, albeit slowly, and we had already come so far. To my mind, the only way out now was through. We needed to have patience and to respect our opponent. But it was difficult to try to convince people that 150 metres in 90 minutes was progress.

'This rising ocean has negotiated its way around the islands,' I explained, 'eddying and running when it's hit land, then trying to squeeze through the tiny space of the Bering Strait on its journey north. The water that doesn't manage to get through, because there's no time or space, must eddy backwards. Imagine a splash bucket hitting a gap in the wall. The water hits the islands and splashes outwards; then it circles around the islands and comes back through the gap, which is the countercurrent. And the swimmers are affected by everything.'

I tried to explain as best as I could using pen and paper. I drew maps and circles around the islands.

'"Study form," as my father used to say. Choose the right time to go and it will let us through. Watch the water, see what it's doing. Look at where we need to go. Do we need to go north-east and counter the wind and flow, rather than east? Do we need to make some calculations and put the faster swimmers in different time slots? We can't change the tides, but we can change the swim rotations. Alaska is only 20 kilometres away.'

Anne Marie nodded.

'To break the current, just put in the fast swimmers. It is possible. We will break free. Short, fast sprints.' We recognised that some swimmers were breaststroking and this was too slow. It needed to be fast sprints.

We had to believe it was possible.

'There is pressure to finish,' Vladimir said. 'A million dollars pumped into this swim, with the vessels and crews.'

'Throw in the fast boys. That's why they're here,' Anne Marie said, and we both laughed.

Aleksandr and Vladimir had to go back to the bridge.

With this level of fatigue, human error and ego were now the biggest challenges we faced. That included our own decision-making. As the door closed and they headed off to the command centre, I looked across at Anne Marie. I was thinking about how exciting it was to be part of the solution-finding, how badly I wanted to go to the bridge, to look at the maps and the charts, to explain everything I knew. I was like a child ready to bolt, eyes darting to the door.

'No,' she said. She knew exactly what I was thinking. 'Sit down there now,' she laughed.

Thirty minutes later we were all summoned to a meeting in the gym.

Oleg began to explain, assisted by the translators. His face was now drained of energy.

'The last 3 boats of 3 swimmers completed 50 metres in 1.5 hours. We gained, and then we went backwards. We are stuck in this countercurrent south of Diomede Island. The tides are running north, and the wind is coming from the north-east, so everything is driving the swimmers south. Nine swimmers and fifty metres total.' The shock was visible.

The room filled with sounds of muttering. There was a sense of nervousness. People were obviously wondering if this was the end, if Oleg was about to announce that the expedition was over.

'So, we will now make a team of the fastest 27 swimmers – those who can complete 3 or 4 kilometres an hour. These swimmers will push hard for the next 10 hours, changing and swimming and resting and moving again. We will need a full commitment. We will need you to focus only on swimming and sleeping. There will not be a long time between swims. The time will be 15 minutes per swim, increased from 10 minutes. Is everyone okay to swim?'

That was a question we were asked every morning during the round Ireland swim. 'Are you okay to swim?' The answer was always yes. Once we were in the game, every emotion was boxed and sealed, to be exposed again only when the objective was achieved.

So that was it. One team and no discussion. Anne Marie and I shared a little smile, quite proud that our information had been taken on board.

Anne Marie and I would be happy to swim, but also happy if we were not selected. We knew we had the physical and mental strength, if only to swim to stand still and allow the stronger swimmers some rest and extra time to recover. This was not our first battle. We may not have been fast, but we were strong.

The list went up on the wall. Our names were on it.

Two hours later, we eased our way behind the RIB, the waves climbing high. There was nothing swimmable about this water. These conditions were storm force. The risks were mounting. This was about holding on tight.

I asked Vladimir for the GPS coordinates. I would manage our GPS screens while the crew were busy with each swimmer. I was not going to allow our boat off course. The water temperature was now 10 degrees, considerably warmer than our previous swims, but the RIB was being bounced about like a toy boat in a bathtub, bashed from the side by multiple waves.

Ryan was in the water, his stroke recognisable, long and strong, driving into the waves. We were about 300 metres from their boat. I was looking at the GPS on the console but my coordinates were not lining up. I watched and waited. I showed the numbers on my hand to our coxswain. He stared at his screen and stared at my hand. No language needed. He picked up his VHF to radio his comrade.

'You're swimming to Russia! Swimming the wrong way! You're swimming backwards!' I shouted as loudly as I could at Ryan, indicating with my hand that they should turn him around and swim in the opposite direction.

I stood up from my seat and kept directing the boats to stay in line with the GPS coordinates, my arm outstretched to direct them. I didn't speak Russian, but I could point. I was past caring.

The crews were so focused on safety, on keeping us alive, that they were not focusing on the direction.

My efforts worked. The swimmer was redirected. I smiled at my Russian coxswain, who smiled back broadly. I stood tall. If I could have driven the boat, I would have. I spotted Jack Bright in the boat alongside, a big smile on his face at my antics. Jack was a UK swimmer and someone who had been involved in the planning of the Bering Strait Relay since 2011. This was a special time for Jack. I was loving every moment too, despite the fears.

My last words to Anne Marie as I slid into the freezing, mountainous waves: 'Don't let him move off the route. Keep turning me straight. I'll keep watching you.'

I rotated my arms close to the tubing. At times I had to pull away as the wind hurled the boat close to my head, but the risks of being further away were greater in my mind than the risks of being closer. Concussion was a lesser ill than being lost. Anne Marie slid into the water, a high five and she was gone. I was past emotion at this stage. We were in survival mode.

The boat lurched into huge troughs and the Diomede Islands disappeared north of us as we were swallowed up. Every now and then we reminded ourselves that south of us were the coasts of Japan and America, roughly 4,000 kilometres apart, that it was all water as far as the Antarctic Ocean. We were in a storm of wind and waves, engaged in a mighty human struggle as each swimmer lowered themselves into life-threatening conditions, risking their own safety to fight for their position in the game of life. This was as dangerous as it got, and we were still fighting, without sleep or food.

The coxswain held the vessel tight to the side of the 150-metre metal hulk and the ship rocked in response to the wind and waves. The RIB was lifted 3 to 4 metres high by the waves, sometimes higher than the platform and the faces of the men, and then dropped with a bang into the vacuum left by the dark waves. We held fast to the ropes on board. It was hard on our backs and knees. A fall here, a mistimed jump resulting in a slip into these waters at the side of the ship, would be a disaster, most probably life threatening.

I bent my knees, ready to grab and jump. I was milliseconds away when the nose of the boat was hurled forward by the waves and my skull crashed under the metal platform. I shouted an automatic, 'I'm okay!' Even if my head was split open, I was getting on board a hospital ship.

I had to time my jump between the next waves. I readied myself, my bag in hand, pulling up the crotch of my huge suit to get the biggest stride. I leapt into the darkness and two arms reached forward from the men tied to the 60-cm-square platform. My legs and arms were bruised, but I made it. I had a huge lump on my head, but I wasn't bleeding.

The adrenaline rush was colossal. As children, when we had to jump to the next boat, it was all about timing, too. I had spent my childhood years crossing boats at the Dingle Pier and this was a similar experience – loving the risk, but knowing in the back of your mind that, if you fell or slipped, your life would change forever.

As we walked up the gangway, we met Paolo heading out with Craig, Henri and Toomas Haggi, Henri's Estonian teammate. Immediately, I noticed Paolo's light jacket was wet from the previous swim, so again I took off my huge immersion-suit jacket and handed it to him. A wink of gratitude and he was gone. His speed was vital to the team. *Protect the speed, protect the team* was all I thought. There was no need for medicals with 10 degree water, the cold as we knew it was gone.

Passing the gym, we saw that we were listed for another slot in only two hours' time. There were only nine teams of three swimmers now, so it was straight into bed with some snacks to write in my diary.

The wind was now gusting to force 7 and there was a sound to the wind that spoke of malicious intent, as if it was showing its power. The atmosphere was a heightened sense of anxiety and the waves had a 6-metre drop. After less than an hour's sleep, we disengaged from the ship and navigated to meet the other vessels. High lifts as the bow of the RIB rose 3 metres in the air, the engines stalling as the boat dropped again. Swimmers and boats were now being gobbled up into the troughs, mountains of water rolling over us.

Suddenly, all I could see were the tops of heads – the entire boat was swallowed into the belly of each wave. It was truly terrifying. In the distance I could make out an orange buoy. Glancing at each other, it was beyond our understanding how any of this swim could work. This next swim would be all about staying alive and getting back to the ship.

One minute.

I stared at Anne Marie, a look that shouted, *Keep your eyes on me!* A sharp outbreath. Time signal given. I lowered my body into the water, now 8 degrees. The boat was going from horizontal to vertical, like riding a bull at a rodeo.

That 15-minute swim was the most frightening I had ever experienced. I was swimming up the side of a mountain and sliding down again. The boat was being bounced around, thudding down 3 metres, within inches of my head. The insanity of it all. The waves broke over my head on two occasions, white water rolling with bubbles. Each time, I turned to find the boat and give an okay signal. There was genuine fear. I would surface, delighted that my tow float was secure to my back and that it would always come back up. The boat was being lifted and dropped by the thunderous waves. I swam away from the RIB, choosing to expose myself to the surf, but then I was terrified that I would get caught in an undertow and pulled down as a wave turned on itself. My mind was racing. The RIB was at a 45-degree angle and we both worked to climb each wave, wondering what would meet us at the top of the crest. Anne Marie readied herself. I kept focused. She tapped my hand and, with a shake of her head, went forward into the maw of the ocean.

I swam for the rear of the RIB but, each time I made a lunge forward, the RIB moved away. *Retreat, breathe, try again.* This was the most dangerous moment. I was mindful that the engines did not have engine guards and an ill-timed leg kick could result in my hand or arm getting tangled in the propellers. I did everything in my power to stay calm. *Try again, try better.* Finally, as I kicked to the rear, a hand dropped down and grabbed the back of my swimming togs, my arms and legs still rotating in the air, as if I was nothing more than a luggage bag on a conveyer belt at an airport. I was on board, I was safe, and the RIB took off after Anne Marie.

This was the most alert and alive I had felt in years. This was the edge that awoke every single fibre of my being.

I was so proud of how so many swimmers were willing to enter this storm, to give so much of themselves in order to find a way through. Their bravery was being met with unknowns –

exhaustion, emotions, fear. This was the moment when fears could become monsters in the mind, as bodies and spirits weakened. Then the moment came. It was 8.00 p.m. and we gathered in the gym for a meeting.

'The teams of 27 swimmers over the last 6 hours completed 2 kilometres' distance,' Oleg told us.

Just 2,000 metres in 6 hours? In normal terms, that was a horrendous achievement, something the open-water swimming community would mock and see as a waste of time. To us, though, it showed the might of our opponent and the patience it would take to overcome it. Some of the fastest swimmers in the world of cold-water swimming, working together over six hours, had only swum 330 metres an hour between them. How would this affect the team dynamic? We stood back, wanting to say, 'That's brilliant!' Some wanted to know which group was the fastest and which was the slowest, not quite understanding that in the six hours the tides had weakened. The opponent and the sea have their own rules. I tried to not engage. It was about understanding that this 2,000 metres may release us. This was one team progressing, not each swimmer.

Once the shock of the speed was forgotten, people began to understand that we had broken the back of the current and the countercurrent. With patience and perseverance, we could complete another few kilometres. With that came the next realisation: the calculations of the time required if it were to continue for hours. At this rate, we would have many more days ahead of us.

Silence.

Oleg continued: 'The permit to be in American waters has now expired for the second time. With the storm, we are going to retreat into the shelter of Big Diomede – back over the International Date Line, back into Russian waters.'

We were going backwards into tomorrow. The ship had been over and back the International Date Line so many times by now. How many days had we gained and lost? And yet, we would be glad of another night's sleep.

We had been swimming for four days in 80-knot winds and mountainous waves. Now the US government had agreed an extension, until 13 August, to allow us to finish. Our faces buckled; emotions took over. Another week's swimming? What about flights home? How was that going to work? The stress in the room was clear, but silence was the response.

It was 2.00 a.m. and, in the brightness of the Arctic morning, a storm team of 27 swimmers was selected. The time pressure forced a real focus on us: so many needed to get home, not to miss flights. The entire team dug deep and, over the next few hours, the coastline of Wales, Alaska, came into view. Patience was rewarded.

By 8.00 a.m., after 6 hours of continuous relay rotations of 15 minutes each, another two swim rotations without rest rewarded the team with a distance of 3,500 metres and a water temperature of 10 degrees, allowing for a better recovery. That was an increase to 580 metres per hour. What swimmers would battle these conditions for hours on end to swim 500 metres – the impact of getting into the water, fighting for every metre, knowing how much it counted? Few swimmers in the world would ever risk this swim. This redefined success. Nine fast swimmers had completed 580 metres in an hour between them. Considering our previous hour's progress was much slower, that was success. That is bruising to the ego but the counter currents of the Diomede Islands were now exchanged for the current running south to the Pacific. This was a different beast, this was purely a fast-running river, a turbulent battle which was honest. This required speed and power.

Once again, the fast swimmers rotated their arms, pushed their legs and drove deep. Water temperatures were rising to 10 degrees, now the only challenge was sleep and exhaustion. Human error was still our enemy, but the end was in sight.

After another 16 hours of swimming, Wales, Alaska itself became visible. It was a tiny settlement close to the beach, on the edge of the world, 2,000 metres away. The last frontier in American territory. The RIBs were filled with swimmers and flags from each country. The final 500-metre swim was to be completed by all teams together.

We all jumped into the water 500 metres off Wales, Alaska, as the indigenous community appeared on the beach. It was almost over. We began our swim, breaststroking our way forward, holding our flags high in the air. It was a tough swim, as we sank beneath the waves, but this time we laughed and wondered if our forefathers would be proud of us, landing on the shores of America with our Irish flag.

A final few metres and then our feet reached down to touch land. We stood and walked through the waves. It was over. We were safe. We had weathered the storms.

It was the strangest feeling to think that we had successfully crossed the Bering Strait. It had truly been a team event. The leadership and the integration of the entire team had made the difference, especially the management of all the voices. We had completed the crossing. It had been a pure battle, and I had loved every moment. Disembarking the ship was the strangest goodbye. As quickly as we had walked on, we left. Hugs for many, waves to others, knowing that despite having held the lives of each other in our hands, there were many we would never see again. The intensity of the parting emotion was visible on all faces. A silent relief that all had survived. Not unlike finishing the Round

Ireland Swim, the finish was bittersweet. We were delighted to have succeeded, but sad to be leaving the eye of the storm. That silent place inside all of us where the battle is so honest. Where each swimmer had to present as the best version of themselves. Lives depended on it. Language had not proven a barrier, courageous swimmers risked lives for the team, crews sacrificed everything for the swimmers, leadership was honest and focused, problems were addressed and rectified, but mostly it was through persistence and perseverance that we moved stroke by stroke. It was the resilience of the group, mainly as we all shared the common goal. Those who could not continue to swim supported, but never became the focus. Failure was never once discussed. Challenges were dealt with and pushed to one side. The main objective, to be the first international team to swim from Russia to the USA in the most dangerous body of water in the world had been achieved.

As the international team flew to Anchorage, the concept of what we had just achieved was almost too big to carry. The Russian team returned by ship. It took us 24 hours to fly home and we had not slept properly in days. Being off grid for 16 days had been difficult for us all.

Mary had suggested coming to get me from Dublin Airport and now her van pulled up, ready to drive the 4-hour journey home. I said a final goodbye to Anne Marie, with the promise that we would now try to live a normal life. How could we process the previous few weeks?

'Now so, get in the back. We can chat on the way,' Mary said.

A huge mattress and duvets were squashed in the back, with about four pillows. I crawled into the middle of the large makeshift bed, lay down surrounded by the pillows and threw the duvet over me. I spoke a few sentences and fell unconscious. My last memory was how Mary used to carry her daughter Bridget in the car when she was very young. She loved driving and decided to take a mahogany drawer from the chest of drawers, layer it with blankets and place baby Bridget into the drawer. Mary would then wedge the drawer in on the floor of the back seat and head for Donegal. There was always a 'Mary' way of doing things, and it always worked. Family was everything to her and it showed in everything she did.

We pulled up outside my house in Dingle. This was the longest time I'd been away for years, and I was anxious to see if there had been a change in my father over the 16 days. I so loved my adventures, but there was always a nervousness about coming home.

'Now so, if you need anything, give me a call,' Mary said. 'I'll drop in a bowl of stew later. Open the shop for a few hours. I know you're wrecked but sit there and you can sleep well tonight.'

I nodded. I knew it would be better to get to work for the afternoon.

Dad was up, TV blaring, waiting with the fire on.

'Is that you? Put the kettle on. Did you cross it?'

'It's me and we did it. You were right about the flow. The run of water off Alaska was horrendous – but we made it to Wales!' I shouted in.

I prepared tea, tab nabs and cake and went to join him.

'Well, that's good now, you're home.'

A few nods of the head as I told a few stories. He gave a smile that I caught out of the corner of my eye. He was proud of me.

One hour later, I walked up Green Street and opened up the shop, anxious to get back to work.

'It's been a busy weekend, hasn't it? The town is busy,' a customer remarked as they milled in and out of the shop.

'It certainly has been a busy few weeks,' I said, smiling.

I was grinning at that secret I held inside. Just 60 hours earlier I had been battling monstrous waves, huge emotions and the perfect storm of life. Imagine if I said that to that lady: 'Well, actually, I've just swum from Russia to the USA.' It would have been lost on her. It was almost lost on me.

I was determined to do as much publicity as I could. The swim deserved respect. Determined to get the swim acknowledged by the International Marathon Swimming Hall of Fame (IMSHF), I spent time securing and organising certificates for the entire team, not just the swimmers. I purchased and printed close to a hundred official certificates from the IMSHF and posted them around the world. In December 2014 I travelled to Tyumen Siberia to compete in the ice once again, but this time I carried with me a presentation for the organisers of the Bering Strait (a bundle of certificates for the crew and team on the ship). Each member of the team needed to be acknowledged and recognised. I was filled with pride. This was not about the swim; this was about the team.

It was labelled the most dangerous swim ever undertaken in the world of open-water swimming, and our relay was awarded the WOWSA Performance of the Year 2013 and a Guinness World Record. I had learned to love my secret life. There was a madness about it – experiences that would never be equalled. Anne Marie and I were so lucky to have each other to share our experiences.

I wonder sometimes if I'll be sitting in my nursing home at the age of 90, rocking in my chair, telling people that I swam from Russia to America. I am certain they will smile gently at me and say, 'You did, you did,' and rock me forward.

14

LETTING GO, TAKING HOLD

'Far better it is to dare mighty things, to win glorious triumphs,
even though checkered by failure, than to take rank with those
poor spirits who neither enjoy much nor suffer much, because
they live in the gray twilight that knows not victory nor defeat.'
Theodore Roosevelt

In March 2014, my father passed away. It was unexpected at the end. Grief is never an easy path, but for me it also meant the release of all the emotions I'd held in for the last three years of caring for him. They say that caring for someone is difficult, and it is, but it is a very structured role. You have to be strong for that person – and you are – but underneath is the sorrow of being so close to them, willing them to live, while knowing all the while that they will die. When they are gone, keeping life together without that anchor of strength is the hard part. That space and that silence. Grief stricken.

I had worked so hard to be strong over the last few years, because strong had been my only choice. I held myself together. But the day my father died, I no longer had to be strong. Grief allows us to be weak. Loss takes its toll. My life's energies collapsed. I had drained my well for the last few years, pushing myself through the ice. That was a choice I'd made, trusting that the costs would be worth it. Now, the avalanche of emotion would be the toughest battle for me.

Two weeks after my father died, I was in Rovaniemi, Finland, at the Winter Swimming World Championships, competing in the 450-metre swim. Outside, I was being introduced to the crowd as one of the best swimmers in the world of ice swimming, hearing the rounds of applause and the music, the expectations of the group. Inside, I was broken. I had no idea why I was even doing it. It was a mixture of external pressure and fooling myself that I was able for it. But presenting myself to swim at a world championship, on a world stage, was putting so much pressure on myself. Not only was I exposing my inner self to others, but I was also exposing it to myself. I had not prepared or trained, so I was just showing up. In difficult emotional times we rest, we keep private, we quietly gather ourselves – and yet, here I was.

The ice water was dark – a muddy, peaty brown. I put my face in to try and slow down my anxiety and stress. My breathing was ragged. In about 30 seconds the race would start. As my name was called out, I waved to the group of swimmers from all over the world. I closed my eyes. The water temperature was 0 to −1 degrees, and the water near my feet was coldest, a running river. The surface of the river was frozen over and we were surrounded by ice.

The klaxon sounded. There was a loud roar from the crowd and the competitors on either side of me took off. I could see legs kicking, arms splashing. I put my face in the water and started my swim, but with intense strokes the cold overwhelmed me. As I turned my face and opened my mouth, the gasp reflex resulted in my ingesting water. Again and again, ice-cold water went down my throat.

My face and fingers were tingling, as if pins were being pushed through my skin. At other times in my life, I had been able to tolerate this intense pain, strong enough to drive through the challenges, like my ice mile or the Bering Strait. But today it was just too much. I was vulnerable. Today my opponent exposed my weaknesses and my inability to be strong.

If you can't breathe, you can't swim.

By the time I touched the 125-metre mark and turned, my competitors were already a full length ahead. I was progressively getting slower, swimming with my head up, each attempt to put my face in the water being met with a gasp. I decided my best option was to breaststroke. I don't usually breaststroke, and it made me even slower.

I could hear my name being called with a list of my achievements. I continued to smile.

My eyes picked up the faces of friends. Some of them were aware that my father had passed away two weeks ago, but the majority were not.

Anne Marie was in lane 5 and I was in lane 2. I had wanted to compete at the world championships but now, surrounded by the crowd and the revelry, I wished I was invisible. I wanted to be at home. I wanted to be by the fire. I was not fit to compete with anyone.

That is the beautiful thing about the ice: extremes keep you honest. Even though we tell ourselves that we can, at times we know that we can't. Today was that day for me. I had to face my reflection; I had to be kind to myself. The ice gave me an arena to fight, to create strength, but it also allowed me a window to myself. Strength was important in our family – strength of character, strength of commitment. Those had been driven into me from a young age. *Be the best version of yourself. Do not wallow in circumstances.*

During the last 100 metres, several times I tried to put my face into the dark water to finish strong, but the darkness was filled with the fear. The tears were seconds from my eyes. I quit trying and went back to the breaststroke. I was back in Tyumen 2012, that first ice swim. The difference this time was that I understood exactly what was stopping me. I knew there was no pressure. I was breathing one breath at a time as my hands reached into the −1-degree ice water. I smiled, reaching out each time until the finish. The organisers, Aleksandr from Latvia and Mariia, the president of the International Winter Swimming Association, were urging me on. I could hear the voice of my good friend Melissa O'Reilly, shouting, 'Go Nuala! Go Ireland!' The voices of many of my Bering Strait Relay team and other friends from around the world filled the air with a round of applause.

Anne Marie and I were the only Irish people competing at 0 degrees. For that reason, I was proud that I tried. But that day, I had no control over my inner self. I didn't have the strength to be in a group where achievement and success were becoming more and more important. Waves of grief were taking over.

Hold on for a few more moments.

My feet stepped on the ladder. I had completed 450 metres at −1 degrees, a running river under the ice.

I am my own greatest critic and being vulnerable was not something I had been able to deal with in public. Being exposed to my weaknesses had been my greatest learning curve, but this was different. This was sheer exhaustion. Allowing people to see me weak and vulnerable was my greatest nightmare.

We rewarmed ourselves, then immediately got on a snowmobile and crossed the frozen river. Two hours later we were on a flight to Helsinki. I was free again – free from the applause and high-octane energy. I was heading home after 24 hours inside the Arctic Circle.

When I reached Dingle and home, I turned the key in my door and opened it to the deafening sound of silence. An empty house. No one shouting, 'Is that you? Put the kettle on.' This was my first time coming home to a house without Dad and it was overwhelming.

I was reckoning with the feeling of emptiness in the house, the echoes of silence, the knowledge that a life had departed, but also the fact that my own energy and purpose had changed. I knew that I needed to close my door and stay inside my four walls for a while. I needed to allow myself to rest.

One morning in April I was swimming at Sláidín Beach, with Fungie breaking the crisp water and temperatures of 9 degrees. The cold had come and gone, but the sea was so clear. Despite making six attempts to swim 200 metres, each time the need to breathe had been overwhelming. I flipped onto my back and just floated along. I was constantly tired these days.

I sat myself down on the rocks with my hot chocolate and decided that I had to allow the well of energy to replenish. I had nothing left. Any strength I had I needed for myself, so I pressed pause on life. The cold water helped me to control a part of my life that was otherwise out of control. Looking back, I could not remember the pain of freezing my body for hours on end, but I could remember the pain of not being the person I wanted to be and the pride I felt that I fought through.

I tried to return to the basics – to that time two years ago when I had taken it minute by minute. But the tiredness was still overwhelming and my emotions were fragile. I would wake throughout the night, hearing noises. I'd jump up, thinking it was my father going downstairs, then realise he was not there.

After my father's death I became more focused on being happy than on achieving. I was always my own biggest competition. Sometimes I wished I could be happy with an easier route through life, but one of my greatest honours was having the strength and the selflessness to be able to care for my father when he needed me. We are the sum of our parts, and my strength came from the life I was given.

In the following months there was a concerted effort to develop winter swimming around the world. I accepted invitations from friends and used trips to educate myself and just enjoy the experiences. I found myself in Argentina with the swimmer Matías Ola. Anne Marie and Maryann travelled with me and we experienced the wonderful Perito Moreno glacier, where we swam 1,000 metres at 0 to 1 degrees. The swim was stress free, meandering under the commanding frozen stream of the glacier. The atmosphere was electric and Matías treated everyone as family.

The decision came by email that the IISA would host their first world championships in Murmansk, Russia, for the 1,000-metre event. It was such an exciting time for ice swimming. At the time, I was working on safety procedures and developing the constitution of the IISA. Russia had the purest ice and I made a commitment to Dmitry Blokhin that we would have a strong Irish team. The interest was huge, especially from a swimming group in Camlough Lake in County Armagh.

My immediate concern was that the Irish swimmers had no experience of 0-degree ice. There was a world of difference between 0-degree ice and the average winter temperatures they were used to. Despite the years passing, I was still the only Irish swimmer who had completed 1,000 metres at 0 degrees, and I felt that it was a huge ask to send a team of swimmers to a world championships without a clear pathway of understanding.

I developed an Ireland Ice Swim programme and, with Padraig Mallon in Camlough Lake, trained a group of 45 swimmers with the view to completing 1,000 metres at below 5 degrees. Over the next few weeks, I travelled to Armagh and presented on areas of ice swimming – the challenges, the risks – and then took charge of their training. We worked on areas of personal responsibility and mostly on the focus – that we would swim to recover. Once the swim distance of 300 metres or 5 minutes was successful and the recovery was good, only then would we move to 500 metres, and so on, in sub-5-degree temperatures.

The main commitment for the swimmers was that they would agree to the limits of the training programme. Many were used to swimming longer distances at 8 or 9 degrees, but I needed a commitment to limiting their swims to our agreed time limits in the cold water. It was about discipline. Medicals were completed. As the time in the water increased and the temperatures decreased, the swimmers would all be exposed to risks in remote areas. All of our swims were completed in open water.

In March, the Irish team of 10 swimmers headed to Murmansk, inside the Arctic Circle. Frances Lynch took her first swim, 50 metres at 0 degrees, and raced so fast. I was starting in the first heat. This was the first time ever in the world that 45 swimmers would take on 1,000 metres in 0-degree ice. I was so excited to swim.

The searing Arctic wind peeled my face. I pulled my hood tight as I walked to the poolside, my emotions all over the place. I kept my eyes closed, blocking out the noise as my name was called out. Flanked by team members Jacqueline and Frances, I was like a boxer heading to the ring. I was swimming at a world championships in the same swimming pool – the same space and the same lane – where two years earlier I had made my own history.

A final smile and I shut myself away into my hood, face tilted downward. I was quite good at locking myself into my world and locking others out. A calm had come over me in which nothing else mattered.

'Enjoy yourself,' Frances whispered into my ear. 'These women are all trying to get to where you are. They are all following you, arm over arm. Now, what do you want the music to be? What song will we sing?' she said, arms raised and dance moves at the ready.

Easing myself down the steps of the ladder, the freezing water felt familiar as it moved its path through my body. I splashed my face. There was no pressure. I had prepared as much as I could in the last few months – 500 metres at 0 degrees in Tyumen 3 months ago; 750 metres at 1 degree in Estonia 4 weeks ago (I'd done that one in 16 minutes); my mind was as ready as it could be. I was sharp and free to swim.

I reached into the darkness. I focused once again on being on the cusp of my own greatness. My friend, the ice, showed my reflection, that familiar pain. I was the noise. I was the competition. I loved that moment. The atmosphere was partylike.

My eyes focused on Frances and Jacqueline at each length, pushing me forward as my hands reached into the stabbing cold water. I was so proud of how the sport had evolved and how we had worked to make it so. The cameras flashed.

With 20 lengths to go, I noticed Frances swinging her arms in the air. Was there a problem? I lifted my head a little higher and music filled the air. 'La Bamba' was blaring and 'Nuala Moore' was being shouted over the speakers as snow fell on the water. The colour and the atmosphere were thrilling.

Frances was now in full flight, with a crowd of people dancing at the end of my lane, like they were at a disco. She had requests being played for me while I was swimming. Who does that? Only a friend who knows it isn't about the medals. People who play together stay together, as my friend Mags would say.

Climbing up the ladder, I felt strong – 23 minutes at 0 degrees. That was the same time I had swum two years ago. I smiled at the crowd. I always swam the same pace. My arms knew no different rhythm. The attendants grasped me from both sides and I was immediately walked to the recovery area. I walked there, strong, and was met by Dr Irina Zhidkova and Vicki Brylin. I loved the hot towels.

My body looked and felt strong, and within a few minutes the cold started to leave my body, without any shivering. My mind was clear and being in the ice for the 23 minutes had not had an impact. That day, Frances was crucial to clearing my mind – the music and the understanding that, if I failed, I was safe to do so. The team was perfect. There was no weakness.

In Tyumen 2012 and in Murmansk 2013, the average time for the 1,000 metres at 0 degrees had been 18–20 minutes, even for the men. Today, in 2015, there was talk of 13 minutes for the men and 15 minutes for the women. The sport was being deemed safer; we had procedures in place. The distances were now being covered by ex-champion sprinters. Once the Olympians come in, any sport is on the cusp of change. I felt so proud that I was there at the crossover, central to the safety and the progress, as I watched my great friend Melissa 'Mo' O'Reilly cruise through the 1,000 metres. She had such power and grace through my camera lens. Beyond her, my eyes went to the inside lane, where I noticed a Russian swimmer becoming quite slow, to the point that her arm raised itself as if to grasp for the sky. I jolted myself alert and shouted to the rescue divers and the referee, who were already responding. I moved to the top of the lane.

Immediately, two men in heavy drysuits leapt into the icy water and grasped the swimmer. She rolled onto her back. It was very quick. The divers had her lying backwards in their arms and her airway secured within 10 seconds. The other swimmers were aware of the situation, but the noise and the music dulled the activities and they kept swimming. The woman was taken out and placed on a stretcher and taken to a full medical tent, with an ambulance standing by.

This was the reality of ice swimming and I was transfixed. I immediately started to think about how assessment swims might prevent this. It was panic, it was anxiety, but it could have escalated in a short period to a cardiac incident, which I had previously witnessed in Finland, or even drowning. The toughest part of a rescue is often getting the athlete out of the water, especially in inside lanes. Ultimately, the expertise of the Russians meant Olga's recovery was swift, but if her rescue had taken place in the middle lanes it would have presented a greater challenge. I walked over to the tent and eased myself into the medical area. The referee, Vitaly Poborchiy, knew me well enough to know my interests were safety.

Olga, the woman who was rescued earlier, was sitting up and smiling, embarrassed, with two Russian medical-team members working with her. We had all experienced that moment. It was a good outcome, but my mind was now calculating the risks attached to extreme swim distances. There were recovery procedures in the world of ice we would need to develop.

As the wind and snow fell over the next few hours, seven swimmers collapsed after exiting the water. After they climbed the ladder, on completing the 1,000 metres, their frozen bodies began to walk, supported on both sides, maybe moving faster than their minds could contemplate, then their bodies went limp in the arms of their team members. All were immediately moved to the medical tent a short few metres away and all recovered brilliantly, but I was wondering how that could work if the event was less well organised. What if the event organisers were not prepared, or if it was organised by groups inexperienced? All of this, if managed or handled wrongly, could result in a disastrous outcome. There was so much work still to do.

Later that afternoon, I chatted with Drs Irina and Nataliya. They were pleased to email me my cardiac files from the Bering Strait Relay and agreed to send me information on the medicals and risks of this event and other valuable information. Dmitry Blokhin was also happy to assist. I chatted safety procedures with Ram Barkai, Henri Kaarma, Petar Stoychev, a four-time Olympian and one of the greatest marathon swimmers of all time, and Christof Wandratsch, the new world champion. My work on safety procedures in the world of ice swimming was becoming my journey. I was never going to be the fastest, but I was determined to keep the sport as safe as we could so others could succeed. I had decided to write a manual of ice-swimming safety. It was important to protect the integrity of ice swimming.

I heard my name being called. I had won a silver medal at the world championships. It presented a bit of a dilemma: mentally, I was beginning to ease myself out of the sport itself. As the numbers of competitors increased, so would the need to develop the safety side of it, which excited me; but winning a silver medal in the world championships made me feel the pull back to the ice. I knew I was still fast enough to push harder and do better.

'How could I possibly be faster in this race?' I asked Henri afterwards when a few of us stood chatting.

'Well, your turns are slow. You take about 5 seconds to turn instead of 2 seconds. If you saved 3 seconds every turn and you have 38 turns, that's nearly 2 minutes you would save. And you wouldn't even have to swim faster!' Henri was clinical – a financial analyst, a numbers man. I regretted asking him!

There was no denying that he was right, but secretly I was not looking to be faster.

Later that night, at 2.00 a.m., as many continued the party, I packed my bags in the darkness, only telling my friend Frances. By breakfast time, when my team were waking up, I had already reached Frankfurt – two flights behind me, two more flights from home. I had grown accustomed to leaving in the dark of night.

My time in the extremes placed a mirror before me and gave me an insight into myself. Knowing that strong was my only choice in those years, the ice gave me a means to control my mindset. To achieve at that level, to stay in the ice, there were rules. Not only did I have to be strong, I also had to understand all of my weaknesses. The ocean offered me great battles. I had to fight them.

I was certain that the ice had saved me in those evenings when I sat by the fire, feeling constrained by my circumstances as a carer, yet proud of the choices I had made. Such a contradiction. Others may feel the need to get out, to run away, but the ice gave me a reason to control the pain and challenge of being stuck and to find a way through to find myself. Now, I was not interested in the battle any more. I had no interest in the pain. The race had changed: the stage had changed, the numbers had increased and the party was different. The competition was not for me. The challenge was gone. Now it was just repeat.

I had undertaken to grow the North Channel swim since 2012, developing procedures and safety measures where none had existed, liaising with swimmers and pilots, and managing challenges. The North Channel was listed as one the ocean's seven most difficult channels. My workload increased. There were no swim trackers on the pilot boats, so even travelling across the world, I was running to plug in my computer at airports, checking in with swimmers, organising observers, liaising with pilots.

Being North Channel Secretary and public-relations officer for the Irish Long Distance Swimming Association was a full-time job. It was consuming me, as was my part in developing the ice in my role as IISA Ambassador. I became the first port of call for all things channel swimming and ice swimming.

I found myself trapped in a world I had created but no longer recognised.

By the end of 2015, I was thoroughly exhausted. I was spending hours per week on the phone on swimming related issues to people around the world. Writing articles and promoting and developing standards for marathon, channel and ice swimming. I was facilitating dreams for so many swimmers, but I had lost focus on myself and what I needed to achieve.

I could feel the rumblings of movement inside me again. I had been tucked into the shadows of this world since my father had passed away. My energy had lifted since then, but I was caught in a cycle of being the 'go to' person, a position I'd created for myself. As those around me succeeded and spread their wings, I was stuck in a grey twilight, reaching no more than 70 per cent of my own potential. I could not figure out how to move on.

Nothing excited me. I felt that, no matter what I tried, it would be possible. I was still at a level where I would be capable of achieving things. But I wanted to feel that pushback from the swim, to be challenged. How could I find something that was more than the Bering Strait, more than the Round Ireland Swim, more than 1,000 metres at 0 degrees? I had no desire to collapse in the ice, but I wanted the fear, the jump, the sense of excitement that I was on the cusp of greatness. I had lost my swagger in that grey twilight.

I felt that I was all things to all people, except the one person

I should have been looking after. I was failing her again. My world was filled with emails and phone calls, battles to make swims better for other people. I decided I could not fight all of them.

One day in the shop, having our coffee, I turned to Mary.

'Can you believe that I have been shortlisted for the World Open Water Swimming Woman of the Year for 2014 *and* listed in the World's 50 Most Adventurous Open Water Women 2015? And I have just been awarded IISA Ambassador of the Year 2015 for my work on ice-swimming safety procedures?' But I explained how, despite all this, I still felt that I was wandering in grey twilight. How was it possible that despite all this recognition, I still felt unfulfilled?

We smiled that there was no pleasing me.

'The darkest hour comes before the dawn,' said Mary, and smiled over her glasses.

After that, I decided to step away from all committee duties and focus on me.

In 2016 I decided to travel on my own to Krasnoyarsk and compete as the only non-Russian in the IISA Russian Championships 1,000-metre swim in the River Yenisey. The freezing river originates in Mongolia and runs the length of Russia to the Arctic. It was 0–1-degree ice water, with a cutting wind. The river water was so cold because we were swimming in the area without any flow. The cold was no longer my test. I was now there for the adventure. I travelled alone halfway around the world. I refocused my strength. I was learning and sharing information with ice swimmers worldwide, and I could feel the well replenishing with energy. The previous few years had seen a strange darkness in my life, but a chink of light was starting to show again.

At the shore, I immediately began by seeking out a rescue team who spoke English. I needed to know I could get help if I needed it. We discussed the hand signals and how they would get me from the water. Dr Irina was present, and my seconds were Daniel Brylin and Albert Sobirov, both fabulous ice swimmers in whom I had great trust.

The fresh water was more astringent than the lake, similar to Finland. Immediately, my hands were stinging, but I knew I only had to endure. At the turn point for about 10 minutes, I noticed a lady close to me showing signs of struggling. I stayed with her, stroke for stroke. It was not about racing.

I put my frozen feet under me and walked out of the near-freezing water. Red-skinned, I waited for the lady and smiled when she finished. Standing strong after 25 minutes at 1 degree, I had won the Russian Ice Swimming Championships. My mind was clear.

I finished the race at 3.00 p.m. and my flights were in 14 hours' time. The previous years of flights, collapses and dehydration were in my mind, so I was delighted that Dr Irina gave me three extra ECGs, making sure both blood pressure and heart rate had settled down. I packed my bags, stowing away my trophy from the race.

I sent a WhatsApp message home to Mary: 'Will you wake me at 2.00 a.m.?' I was terrified of missing the flight.

Immediately came a reply: 'Yes. What time is your flight? And what time is it in Krasnoyarsk now? What airport and what time?'

I had forgotten to ask what time it was in Dingle and felt guilty. Then I realised it was only seven hours ahead and relaxed.

The ringing jolted me from a deep sleep at 1.50 a.m. Mary's voice: 'Now so, are you up?' I was.

I jumped out of the bed, having slept for 3 hours. After 8,000 kilometres travelled in 26 hours, Mary picked me up in Cork Airport. Then I was back to Dingle and straight back to work. I felt the energy flow back into my veins.

The following months I focused on the education again, to sharpen my mind, and used courses to mentor and teach. I took survival training with RNLI Portsmouth, attended an extreme ocean-medicine course and completed writing a manual on the safety of ice swimming, which I presented at a conference in Krasnoyarsk and shared with Dr Irina Zhidkova. I printed the manual and sold it worldwide.

In January 2017 I again travelled to the IISA World Championships in Burghausen, Germany. I knew this would be my final competition. It was difficult, emotionally, to feel myself navigate away from the group, like a relationship breakup. Many of my friends who had begun the ice journey with me had already left. The competition was fierce and so exciting.

My own 1,000 metres at 3 degrees was mechanical – 22 minutes and I placed fourth. An American lady, a first timer to the ice, came third in my category and was 7 minutes faster than me. One or two minutes faster and you can still think about competing, but not seven. She was a pool competitor and had skills in racing. The value of the sport was changing. It was now all about competition, which was the future for professional athletes.

We must always face reality and our own expectations for ourselves. The new breed of ice swimmer gave me the freedom to leave the ice swimming world. I had no idea what the future held, but I knew the ice competitions were behind me. I had left my imprint on the sport's history. Now it was my time to be strong enough to stand alone and move on to other things.

One grey Sunday in December, my friend Paul Britten was over visiting from the UK. Paul would sit on his boat for hours, winter and summer; he had a wonderful relationship with Fungie the dolphin. The water temperature that day was 8 degrees. The bite in the air was so severe that taking off my clothes caused me to shudder. Today I had come to freeze my thoughts.

I knew that Fungie would come and that Paul would stay, that I would not be alone with my thoughts. I stuck my face into that dark, grey water and began my circuits. My plan was always to swim from the beach to the lighthouse, turning back to make a triangle towards the green harbour-marker buoys and back over to the bathing boxes – roughly a 400-metre circuit, the same circuit I had completed for the last 4 decades. The location where, as a young child, I'd leapt from my father's boat and the place I'd learned all my skills in the sea. Despite being so close to the harbour's mouth, it was my safe space. I felt that my hands needed to be exposed to pull and feel the water.

On my third circuit, the humming sound of an approaching engine distracted me; then a beautiful, large, shimmering, grey body passed underneath me. He was huge in size but graceful as he glided, and there was a momentary pause when his eye reached mine. Fungie turned on his back, his belly facing mine, as he took that moment, his smile ever present. No matter what emotions were going through my mind, in that moment everything stopped. Life stopped, and a rush of happiness flooded through my body.

I was not alone. That look, where his eyes poured deep into mine. That pause, that moment where I was taken from the present and allowed myself to dream. I often tried to dive down with him, but I had neither the grace nor the ability, so I would stop instead and wait for his return.

This was about spending time in the water, not necessarily swimming, so as soon as Paul came close I stopped to have a chat, freezing as it was. It didn't matter. This was being in the water, exposed to the cold, and not quitting.

As I approached the lighthouse, the green headlands of south Kerry were no longer visible, which meant that the rain was coming in the heavy sky. I could feel the engines ticking behind me. I turned to swim to shore. Fungie sprang into his somersaults, graceful with his splashing, as if somebody had electrocuted him. He jumped high over and back, his huge body propelling itself out of the water, stopping for a pregnant pause and smiling as he went backwards. His eye twisted in its socket, as if to say, 'Look at me! Look at me!' He always stopped us in our tracks. My eyes focused on the lighthouse and I imagined Paddy Ferriter standing, looking down, and his words: 'Where he goes, nobody knows.'

Through all my swimming life, nearly four decades, Fungie the dolphin was my training partner. Each time I rolled my body on that stretch, I would take an extra moment to have a look and see if he was nearby. Today was a great day to hear those sounds and see that face. How he smiled at me.

The rolling clouds, the freezing waters. And through the darkness this dolphin's beautiful, graceful movement as he eased his body under mine and distracted me from moments when I felt that things were difficult, when I allowed my head to get in my own way. Moments when I couldn't keep going, when I felt the pain of my challenges was too much. Whenever I felt my effort and not my calm, he would appear in front of me with that now-old gentleman's smile, those eyes sometimes stopping to stare. Meeting his eye was my magic moment. That lazy gaze of wisdom. Just him and me, at Sláidín Beach, in the water where he'd spent close to 37 years.

The day I did my first big swim around the lighthouse was the first day I saw him, and here we were, all these years later. Fungie recognised people – their voices, their sounds. He loved laughter, people playing. Did he also sense my anxiety and my stress?

I often wondered if he noticed my growth from a child to woman, if he felt my energy change. Dolphins are so intelligent. I wondered if he watched me grow up from the teenager swimming around the lighthouse, scrambling, trying to find her way out of this water, and saw me now, three decades later, still scrambling to find my way. His eyes looked tired recently; so did mine. Did he know? Did he know that I knew? Maybe that was why he would take that second and pose when I took photos with my water camera.

We had shared so much in the last 30 years, and now here he was, that shadow passing under me, that sound as he breached the water. I giggled to myself when he broke the surface and smiled. His huge head, long and shiny.

He too bore the scars of the last few decades. There were marks on his back from the risks he had taken, scars on his head where engines and propellers had cut through his skin. But it was his grin that had aged. His face had aged: insight was now clear in his eyes. I lifted my head and he was there, with his usual pause on the surface, his eye meeting mine. He was watching and moving slowly, gliding through the surface. No speed or erratic movements. That gaze was so peaceful – tired but calm – and it stopped for me. I stood vertical, motionless in the deep water, my breathing relaxed. Even though my hands were cramping and my face hurt, I smiled. I was always home when I was here. Thirty-seven years swimming in the same space with the same dolphin. We both smiled. A few tears began to build and I immediately decided to focus. I thought about this privilege I'd had all my life. How blessed I was.

We had everything we needed to stay for another hour on the beach, to recover and rest: hot chocolate, jellies, cake and chat. That hour post-immersion was now as important to me as the swim itself. It was about pushing and recovering so I could find my limits, live within them and push again. I knew I was close to my personal edge.

Close to the edges of pain I was willing to endure for achievement. I would work my way out of this grey twilight, back to greatness.

One day in May 2017, Mary came into the shop. She was now working in America and her role of international brand manager was exciting. She loved the world stage but it meant she had to travel a lot.

'I'm making bacon and cabbage for the boys behind at the distillery. They've had a busy week. Will I drop you over some?'

'Of course,' was the answer, as always. Mary's bacon and cabbage was her forte. It was hilarious to think that the general manager of the distillery would make a big pot of bacon and cabbage, cook it in the kitchen upstairs and serve it up to the staff to thank them for a good week's work. Recognising everyone and ensuring they felt valued were two of her greatest talents. That and making sure you were fed so that you could work harder. The founding mother.

I was dying to tell her something. Even though I felt invisible to the world of open-water swimming because I had stepped back into the shadows to focus on myself, I was being seen.

'I have just been listed among the World's 50 Most Adventurous Open Water Women 2017 again and shortlisted for the World Open Water Swimming Woman of the Year 2016. Can you believe it?' I was so energised.

Sometimes we are so caught up in our journeys we don't take the time to appreciate our successes. I was always my own biggest fan, with Mary a close second. Standing back and seeing how others viewed me – top 50 in the world – was incredible. Shortlisted to the top 14 in the WOWSA awards. Thinking I was not achieving, thinking I was alone, thinking no one was watching, and there it was all along – the world was watching – but I had to open my eyes and focus outside the space I was in.

I had to embrace the approval. I was being looked at on the world stage as one of the most adventurous women in the world. A calm had come over me; a smile had come into my soul.

'I'm thinking of taking on a swim at Cape Horn. Tierra del Fuego, where the Pacific, Atlantic and Southern Oceans meet. The swim at the end of the world,' I told her now. 'No one has completed this swim before. It's a costly swim, but I think I would be the first swimmer in the world to succeed if I do it. Imagine the location – the Drake Passage. What do you think?'

I was a little nervous of her response.

'Patrick would love to go with you,' she replied. My nephew was so adventurous. 'That's brilliant! That's a fabulous idea! Could we bring two bottles of gin and vodka down to the end of the world? Is that the start of the Wild Atlantic Way? Dingle Vodka on its world tour. Go for it. If you need anything, give me a call.'

With that, her phone rang and Mary stood up to leave.

'I'll drop the bacon and cabbage to the house on my way through later,' she said, and she was gone. The hurricane that was Mary.

There are times in our lives where we cruise along, where we can achieve things without ever being that strong, when we have enough skills to get through, but we know all the same that we could have done better. I had felt that way in the last few years. Over the years, it was not possible to be at 100 per cent all the time, but I scared myself on many occasions when I was happy with being mediocre, when I was content with knowing I could achieve something rather than actually achieving it, when I was able to hide behind my experience and convince others of my brilliance.

I was no longer able to hide from myself. I hadn't yet emerged from the grey twilight. I needed to find that greatness again, that moment when I knew I was better. I needed to find another master.

I needed to find a challenge that would scare me so much that, if I was not the best version of myself, my mask would slip. I could never fool myself. I could see it in my eyes.

Being forced to see every one of my flaws, every one of my weaknesses, was a gift, but it was also a burden. I never feared what I needed to do; I never feared the darkness; I never feared failure. But I did fear the grey twilight. I loved those moments when I could see a glimpse of my own greatness.

Not disappointing myself had becoming my greatest challenge. I had seen the best of myself, but the last few years had taken that from me. There was only one way to be able to look myself in the mirror now, and that was to take this chance. To face my reflection as someone brave and strong was important. It was about courage. I would have to prepare to fail, to risk everything.

For the last year or so, I had started to feel anxious about becoming a passenger in my own world. I was afraid of becoming complacent. I was afraid of not finding my true reflection again. I had to find something so huge that it would frighten me, make me step up to find my greatness. Cape Horn was that something. It was my new master. It would force me to focus again. But it was costly.

Time was passing. I needed to get out of the grey twilight. I needed to let go and focus on myself again.

We often say that safety is not the absence of accidents and incidents. It is the presence of barriers and defences and the ability to fail safely. But to truly fail safely we have to understand why the system failed. It's a constant evolution of processes. As risks occur, sometimes risks we did not know existed, we adjust our plans, change our performance, improve our response. We fail better each time.

It's so important to brief and debrief after every swim. That is standard in scuba diving, but not done in swimming. Risk is always evolving so, until we can create a culture where we learn from incidents and accidents, progress is limited. What was lacking then was a just culture, where reporting and learning from the outcomes was present. It still is today. When those commenting have incomplete stories, such as after some channel swims and after my ice mile, they produce a poor analysis, which is nonetheless accepted by the masses due to traditional and social media. This can lead to incidents being ignored or wrongly reported – instances of swimming-induced pulmonary oedema, for example, are sometimes reported as jellyfish stings. The end result is an environment of confusion. Judgement is a huge challenge and judgement from others can be detrimental to our journey. This social media commentary had rumbled on over the last few years.

I learned the hard way that there are some storms I could not endure – where the path I was travelling was not safe, not designed to weather the storm, and there were casualties. I recognised, too, that some storms were just too fierce for me to battle. To save myself I chose to step away. I used that time to rest. Regardless, learning must not stop. When teams have to make the call for rescue, it is important that there is no judgement, that the call is made with good intent.

I was always afraid that the pressure of judgement would cause people not to make the call.

During the following years, the incidence of swimmers getting into difficulty was greatly on the increase. The impact of swimming in cold water was still proving a challenge. In particular, in relation to the North Channel swim and cold-water swimming. The cold-water swimming community had now grown exponentially and, as the numbers increased, so did the incidents. I had developed Ocean Remote, Recovery, Rescue Emergency Care (Ocean Triple R), an interagency platform where different services could meet and interact with the aim of making people safer in and on the water.

It was about creating value to knowing the information regarding safety in and on the water. Procedures and safety information around the impact of cold-water swimming needed more development.

I invited the crew of Rescue 115, based in Shannon Airport, to attend our weekend. The helicopter arrived onsite and shared in some training with Q and A sessions with the team. We asked Davitt Ward, search-and-rescue technical airman, hoist operator and winchman, about judgement in making the call. I shared my personal experiences of the online attacks after calling for assistance from rescue services, in which I had been accused of wasting resources.

'If we're not entirely certain that someone is in trouble, should we make the call? What is your opinion?' Gary Crawford asked. Gary was attending the weekend in his scuba-diving underwater-rescue capacity. We needed to hear the answer directly from those who responded to such calls.

'Calls with good intent, those are the calls we love. Get us early. If you get us late, it's usually at the recovery end of things. If we're required, time will be key.' Davitt said. 'Making the call is vital. We'd far rather get there and be stood down than get there too late,' he assured us all.

The main message was to make the call. We should not be swayed by opinion, and time was important. We would continue to work hard to create that culture. It might save lives.

I was starting to surround myself with professionals who worked in extreme environments, people who shared my sense of adventure. I developed presentations around cold-water swimming, focusing on areas of cold-water incapacitation, I worked with the lifesaving association and presented on areas of drowning, but my priority was always to create a culture of safety where we would push deeper into our limits and achieve in the extremes.

I was gaining strength again.

15

JOURNEY TO THE END OF THE WORLD: TIERRA DEL FUEGO

*'Ní chuir an fharraige aithne ar éinne riamh, más é do chéad
lá é, nó do mhíliú lá. Má thugann tú seans di, tógfaidh sí thú,
ní le droch mhéin, ach sin é a dheineann sí.'*
*(The sea never made friends with anyone, if it's your first day or
your thousandth day. If you give her a chance she will take you.
Not out of badness, it's just that is what she does.)*
Pat Connor, Baile Dháith, duine dos na caipíní

'I want to swim a mile across the meridian south of Cape Horn, in
the Drake Passage, between the Pacific Ocean and the Atlantic
Ocean,' I said, looking at Catherine and Chris.

At that time, Catherine Buckland and Chris Booker were
working as dive professionals in Antarctic waters. My statement
was met with a mixture of smiles and serious frowns. I had been
invited by World Extreme Medicine founder Mark Hannaford to
share my expertise on cold-water swimming. We chatted about the
prospect of their acting as my rescue team.

'It's an official swim offered by Patagonia Swim – Cristian
Vergara and Julieta Nuñez – based in Chile. If I'm successful, I'll be

the first swimmer in the world to achieve it.' I was reassuring them I was not merely going to head south on my own, drop into the Drake Passage and start swimming. I explained my friendship with both Cristian and Julieta; it was a legit swim. 'Patagonia Swim is a ratifying body for the area. I would have a pilot and crew.'

'So, you would be paying for the privilege of lowering your body voluntarily into the Drake Passage, when sailors do their best not to fall in?' a comment came across the table from Dr Nick Carter, himself a veteran of rounding the southern tip of Cape Horn on yachts.

I showed them the website and the swim route: specific GPS coordinates, starting in the Pacific Ocean and finishing across the meridian in the Atlantic. The significant part would be the GPS of locations where I would be south of all land mass, at the meeting of the oceans.

'In that location, there is no land east or west, as the world turns on its axis,' I finished.

The extreme nature of the swim might have been lost on many, but it certainly was not lost on the group of people I was chatting with over a glass of wine, in Plymouth, at the Ocean Extreme Medicine course in 2017. Swims like this piqued curiosity and more than a few stories. All of them had experienced the Drake Passage.

To my right was Dr Nick Carter, who had sailed around Cape Horn, and Dr Claire Bailey, an accomplished sailor with experience in the southern oceans.

For Catherine and Chris, the Drake Passage, passing Cape Horn, was their commute to and from work in the freezing waters of Antarctica. I had met them all the previous year on the same course, when they were on the teaching faculty. Since then I had struggled to find a swim to excite and challenge me. I felt lost, so education became my go-to comfort. My way of keeping in touch with the extremes.

Last year had been so exciting. I had worked on the extreme areas of acute water-related hypothermia and developing casualty recovery on boats, watching the speed and the proficiency of their extraction techniques. So, to be invited back as faculty to share with the professionals was another step on my journey back to myself. I was working my way out of the grey twilight.

I had been searching for the confidence to let go of the emotions and energy of last few years and work my way back to achieving. Chris, a marine biologist, professional diver and Catherine's partner, had shown us videos of the Drake Passage. It had seemed like serendipity. Their job involved areas that were life threatening, with risks from leopard seals and extreme ice-diving injuries. I felt they would be a great match for me. We shared a huge interest in all things safety and water.

'En route home from our work in Antarctica, we could stop off for a week in Puerto Williams and work with you on the swim. If the dates line up, I don't see any problem,' Catherine said. She was a strong-willed and professional woman and her can-do attitude was something to behold. She and Chris passed through the Drake Passage perhaps 20 times a year. They knew its energy more than most, and their respect was reasoned and not based in fear.

'Let's stay in contact,' Catherine finished as we returned to our course.

At last, I could see the way forward.

My father had rarely applauded my ice swims, but he had been proud that I'd had the courage to swim the Bering Strait. Swimming at Cape Horn was something we had talked about often.

'Sailors' graveyard,' he said of the Drake Passage, staring at the fire one December evening in 2011. 'The roughest, most dangerous water in the world. Below 40 degrees south there is no law. Below 50 degrees there is no god. That's what they say, anyway.'

I always wondered what he meant by that. My proposed swim would be 56 degrees south.

My father would give a few deep breaths and a few shakes of the head when he was thinking about the areas in oceans where the water will always be master. I knew we could never understand what fishermen had experienced, but the one thing they all shared was respect for the power of the sea and a disrespect for those who were reckless in their approach. 'Foolish behaviour,' my father would call it. My priority was to be as well prepared as I could be, to respect my fishing heritage.

He would say. 'The waves can hit you from all sides down there – there will be nowhere to hide when the engine is ticking over.' His voice would be stern. His hands would describe how the boat would be vulnerable without power if one of the rogue waves were to hit it. Then his tone would change. 'You'd have a good crew, though?'

'It would be a fully organised swim.' I replied, knowing I had lots to think about.

That was then.

If anything was to jumpstart my life, to get to that girl inside, to reawaken the spirit, this was it. This was my time to test myself. I knew that choosing the right team was the first step. I owed it to my family and friends to do my best to cover each risk and uncertainty as we knew it.

I broke the swim apart to see what it was, to see where the challenges lay. Every water has its heartbeat – some pattern, even if it's chaotic. This waterway connecting the Pacific Ocean to the Atlantic Ocean is 800 kilometres wide, and the ocean floor is thought to reach depths of over 5,000 metres. The Antarctic Circumpolar

Current spans 8 degrees of latitude or more; its northern boundary occurs between latitudes 48 and 58 degrees south. I would be swimming close to 56 degrees. The Antarctic Circumpolar Current separates the Southern Ocean from the Pacific and Atlantic Oceans. Warm water mixing with cold water, warm fronts meeting cold fronts, conflicting waves, monstrous seas. It was the Bering Strait multiplied by 100.

Where the Pacific and Atlantic Oceans meet is the most dangerous place. There the wave patterns are confused, angry, even foolish. It was not that the team might lose sight of me, it was that they might not be able to get to me. I could get swept away on the wings of the waves and drown. I needed to prepare for all outcomes. I needed to prepare to fail.

'The boys will bring us home,' had always been Anne Marie's phrase. There was a reality to that sentence now. I needed to create a team who could bring me home. Subconsciously, I was putting the puzzle together and planning my escape from the grey twilight.

Chris and Catherine and their skills immediately came to my mind. Another piece of my puzzle was Dr Patrick Buck, a professional in the management of hypothermic casualties in a remote setting. In the event of failure, how could we manage the outcomes? I had connected with Dr Buck a few years earlier on the issue of swim failure and an incident I'd experienced as a crew member. This was the one haunting image I had not dealt with and needed to prepare for.

In 2012, I had been overjoyed to crew for one of the best and most experienced open-water swimmers in the world. A perfect, textbook swim. After 9 hours swimming in water no warmer than 12 degrees, there had been a reduction per minute in the rotation rate of the swimmer's arms. After 10 hours, the stroke rate continued to drop, but the arms continued rotating. Like an electric shock, the swimmer's eyes through their goggles hit me: large and dilated, vacant. The entire physical being of the swimmer had changed, yet they continued to rotate the arms in a way that would not cause any alarm. I felt a sense of panic and dread and immediately turned to the team and said, 'We need to get the swimmer out.'

The *how* we had not discussed at all – how we could extract a swimmer – we were so confident of success. We were on a big timber pilot boat and we had not discussed our safety plan with the swimmer. We did not have any relevant information about the swimmer – their medical requirements or their next-of-kin numbers. I had accepted that role with excitement. How could I have failed to prepare? I had underestimated the challenge. We had not contemplated any negative outcomes because we had been blinded by the swimmer's experience. We had not been prepared for someone to override all the signs and symptoms of a swimmer in difficulty, nor had we been able to properly identify the risks of the cold-water swim.

I had immediately stripped to get into the water. When I reached the swimmer, their slurred voice was one of the creepiest things I ever experienced. Yet they had continued to rotate their arms, even as they had begun to sink without power. In silence and maintaining eye contact with the pilot, who had followed in a rowboat, killing the engines of the pilot boat, I had reached for the rope and, in a split-second, looped it around the arm of the swimmer so they would not sink or get away from me. Up close, the eyes had been large, searching and blank, the voice now slow, the head unable to support itself. Once the rope was secured, I had grabbed the swimmer from the water and, with the help of the pilot, hauled them into the small rowboat we had with us.

The next few hours changed so much for me as we acted to rewarm and recover the swimmer en route back to port. I had never been exposed to such an incident, to manage an acutely hypothermic casualty in a remote setting before. I had never been exposed to this level of personal risk. I had not questioned the responsibilities of the role I undertook as a team member and I was ill prepared. That swimmer could have swum to unconsciousness and drowned.

What we had experienced that day was the slow and insidious danger of cold-water immersion, the manner in which swimmers can fall unconscious and collapse. I can say with a great degree of certainty that we were lucky that day. As experienced swimmers, we had the skills necessary to manage our outcomes. Now I needed my team to accept that risk.

I had reached out to Patrick to discuss that situation, in order to understand more of what had occurred. Since then, we had stayed in touch, sharing experiences of ice-swimming safety.

Now, I made the call.

'I want to swim south of Cape Horn in the Drake Passage. Would you be interested in coming on board as a team member?' I asked Patrick one day on the phone.

'That's a very interesting project – certainly one of the most extreme adventures I have heard about. It's much more than just swimming. We should meet up,' he said.

He felt that the management of the swim was possible, but he wanted to think about it. He wanted me to focus on remote recovery management.

In December 2017 I arranged to swim the meeting of the oceans with Patagonia Swim and my good friend Cristian Vergara. I spoke with Cristian multiple times and discussed the options. He confirmed that no other swimmer had ever taken on this route, let alone completed it. The swim route was created by Cristian and Julieta and the swim would be observed, ratified and authenticated by their association. The gold-standard evidence would be signoff on the swim by the Chilean Navy, with coordinates verified by Adan Otaiza Caro on the Cape Horn Lighthouse. This was a swim to specific GPS routes – meaning no protection from land – 2 miles south of the southern tip. It was the most extreme location in the world for any open-water swim.

If oceanic conditions did not allow me to swim, there was also a swim option in the Bahía Leon on the north side of the island, a bay other swimmers had swum, plus the swim at Roca Negro on the South side of the Island, lighthouse to lighthouse, within the protection of the land. But, with land as protection, it was just cold water in another bay. These swim options, to me, were a swim I could do at home. I wanted the gold standard; I needed the exposure to the risk. Swimming inside a bay had a certain outcome.

I booked the swim and gave my commitment, then emailed Catherine and Chris in Antarctica. I had four weeks to pay my deposit of $5,000. The balance of $7,000 would have to be paid in the next 12 weeks. My focus changed.

'Now so, can I give you a giggle?' Mary bounced into the shop. I was staring at the computer.

I smiled, but my tense face gave the story away. We never got to the giggle. I was emotionally drained by my decision. I felt so alone, with the risk of failing so high in my mind.

'I can't believe I'm after committing to Cape Horn,' I said to Mary. I outlined the financial costs, that sense of being exposed to my own choices.

She stared at me over the rim of her glasses.

'It's a lot of money to get to the end of the world,' I said.

Turning the laptop around, I showed her the map of the famous Tierra del Fuego.

'As the world turns on its axis, there is no land east or west, so the three oceans – the Atlantic, the Pacific and the Antarctic – rush together at this point. It's 100 nautical miles off the southern tip of South America. It has to be at this location. It is a very tight weather window. If it works, I could be the first in the world to lower my body off a boat at that point in the world. But if anything happens, there is no helicopter coming!' I finished, closing my laptop.

We laughed, equal parts amusement and bemusement. Mary gave a sigh that meant, 'Why?'

I explained my chat with Patrick Buck.

'What can I do to help?'

Mary undertook to contact companies for sponsorship. This immediately removed so much pressure. She never once asked me if it was safe or what the risks were. Her only response was: 'How can I help to get you there?'

Two days later, Mary and I drove to Killarney to meet with Patrick. His smile said it all as we sat down for coffee in the lobby of a hotel.

Patrick discusses swims on a different level. Together we peeled the skin off the bones and exposed the inner workings and challenges.

'The fact is that no one has done this before, Nuala. Humans do not like the unknown. The fact that you are willing to risk it is daring. The fact that you are willing to take it on impresses me as it is,' Patrick said. I smiled.

We discussed the high probability of failing and what the cost of failing at this swim would or could look like. We talked about the remote setting, what the team would need and what the team would need to be aware of. We also discussed the need to prepare – not only physically, but also psychologically.

'The psychological side of this swim is most likely going to be the greatest challenge for you – that and the remote management of any outcome in that setting. You will need to be strong,' he said.

I was enthralled. Survival instincts began to rise inside me. My breathing elevated. This was the most alive I'd felt in the last few years. This was me we were talking about. This was me being exposed to these risks. This was me being asked to let go. Cape Horn was my new master. I had to be the best casualty I could be. I had to train for the challenge.

'There is a big difference between your previous expeditions and this one, in that you know absolutely nothing about the waters of the Drake Passage. It will be about the support team and understanding the challenge, but also accepting the possibility of failure. There are so many scary things there, Nuala. This is extreme swimming at its utmost. You may not even be able to swim forward.'

Dr Buck agreed to come on board and help me with remote management of outcomes. The one area that was starting to become a real emotional challenge was the setting. There would be nobody coming to rescue me – it was simply too far away. It would be like being above 6,000 metres on Mount Everest. I needed to be realistic. The easier option of the swim near the land was always open to me.

In January 2018, Catherine Buckland and Patrick Buck arrived in Dingle. Our plan was to work on recovery from a drowning scenario and remote recovery of an acutely hypothermic casualty. The day's work involved cold-water immersion after immersion, discussing risks, casualty recovery and remote management, and letting them see first-hand how I was able to handle extreme cold. They both wanted to witness my responses to swimming in freezing waters, to figure out how to handle me in a hypothermic condition in a remote setting. We revisited Peddler's Lake, in wind and 3-degree water. We set up scenarios and procedures. It was happening.

Catherine was very thorough, which was what I most respected about her. She and Chris needed to know exactly what their role was – what an 'unlikely event' could mean in the remote waters of Cape Horn. Would they be willing to stop the swim in the event of a risk to life? Catherine was very sure that, if such a call had to be made, they would make it. We also had to have a difficult conversation: how would they manage a drowning outcome?

When alone with my thoughts, I knew I had to train to be the strongest I could be, mainly because an 'unlikely event' could mean their losing sight of me, or worse, my drowning. I was determined to be bulletproof. I was determined to find the strength to face my reflection and be the person I knew I could be. Creating a team to work with me was vital.

My friends and family had developed a silent way of trying to keep my perimeter clear, taking away the small problems in order to support me. This was my moment to let go, follow my heart and accept their support. Everyone was rooting for me.

It was as if I was rebuilding again, the best version of myself. Who gets to see themselves stripped bare, torn apart, and rebuilt again and again? It felt great to know that I was capable of rebuilding. I was willing to stand apart.

I began to find joy in effort, comfort in darkness, knowing that there was always a way forward. The waves and the ocean had taught me that. The calm would come later, but now it was time to release the doubt and take risks again. To feel that moment of survival.

In February my training reached its peak, with four weeks to departure. Unfortunately, for the first time in years, the sea temperature had fallen to 6 degrees, with the air temperature close to zero. With stiff easterly winds, the air dropped to −6 or −7 degrees. I was swimming for two hours one day a week and one hour every other day. The pressure of the commitment left me no choice but to spend that time in the water at these incredibly low temperatures. There is nothing that focuses the mind more than the sacrifices you have to make. I had some close calls during training, where the cold caused fatigue and I made poor decisions, staying in the water too long, making rewarming and my journey home too challenging.

After that, I made the decision to wait on the beach for an hour after each swim, until the tiredness associated with hypothermia passed. Driving post-immersion can be very risky, especially with fatigue and yawning. Patrick brought me huge military-grade thermal trilaminate foil jackets and bags that covered me head to foot to prevent heat loss. I needed to reheat slowly.

One of the areas we worked on was the personal responsibility of the swimmer and the team. Patrick designed the REST acronym to determine what safety equipment we needed to bring with us and how to plan. The REST acronym is role specific, so we needed to answer the questions as they related to our roles. It allowed me to plan for my team and create the best options around our outcomes. Everybody had a duty of care to themselves.

The **REST** system works like this:

Risk – analysing the risks and the outcomes.

Equipment – equipment based on risk quantification.

Skill – equipment based on available skill sets.

Time – equipment based on time window to definitive care.

By using the REST acronym and Patrick's help, I set up my training programme and planned to be well prepared for most eventualities. This allowed me to work on the level of professionalism that Catherine and Chris expected from me. However, nothing in this world is 100 per cent predictable, so we had to be able to improvise too.

I was used to discussing the outcomes and risks in open-water swimming and extreme cold and ice waters as if they were something to be managed. Here, the primary goal was staying alive. We were training to keep me from drowning, in the understanding of what losing sight of me would mean. People only see the end result – success or failure. They don't see the dedication, perseverance, pain management, sacrifice, judgement, disappointment, injury and emotional challenges – personal battles on all levels – needed to bring it about.

One day Patrick and I spent a few hours brainstorming the risks of taking on the meeting of the oceans. It was very clear that, if anything went wrong and there was an incident, we would be alone out there. There would be no support coming and my survival time in the water would be no more than a few hours. If I chose the swim closer to the island at the Roca Negro, this risk would greatly reduce, and the certainty would increase.

Patrick added, 'While the human body is an amazing piece of evolutionary engineering, it does have survival limits, especially in cold water. We can tolerate only so much abuse before problems arise and, if our tolerances are breached, we run the very real risk of sustaining injury. Understanding our physiological limits in water not only allows us to perform at our optimum level, but also prevents us overloading our systems so that complications arise.'

Because we are not designed to be in the water, we have to keep fighting to stay safe. In doing that we have to understand the risks and the rules of playing in the ocean and the ice.

Two hours at 6 degrees, in –4-degree air, was stripping cold. I was training to be strong. To take everything that I chose to throw at myself. I was seeking out the pain. I would sit in my large survival bag on the beach and drink hot chocolate, text home, chat with Maryann and reheat naturally. My body heat recovered so quickly wrapped in these huge jackets. Some days I wore them around the house for hours to encourage my body to warm up to the point of overheating.

My hands were a different story. Freezing and reheating after the swims and holding hot cups of tea and hot-water bottles after being in freezing temperatures had resulted in damage to my peripheral circulation. The circulation had broken down and as a result my fingers had developed chilblains. These were softened and opened by the salt water and became open sores, some ulcerated, the saltwater inhibiting healing. Four of my fingers had open and infected ulcers. The pain was intense. I could not wear neoprene gloves when swimming, because the neoprene would tighten over the raw skin and pull it open. The only other medical direction was to stay out of the water, but that was not an option. I could not entertain it. If I stopped swimming, I would lose my acclimatisation.

I hid my hands from people. There was no other way forward. I was in too deep.

The weeks rolled by, and, in March, the Beast from the East arrived. It was one of the coldest springs in years. Although my body was sore, I felt calm. I was not conscious of the hardship or the pain of staying in these temperatures for two hours at a time. The pain of the cold was now my comfort. It was where I went to freeze my mind, to jumpstart my day, to reset my life, to silence the thoughts and to find my greatness.

The swim was not going to be the hard part. I would have to accept all the pain. I was starting to see my reflection, the person

I knew was there all along. Over the last few years, the person looking back at me did not reflect the person I could be. I had not been able to tap into that part of myself. But these extremes forced me to be honest, to silence the voices that had forced me into that grey twilight. I could now see my own strength. I was developing a sniper-like focus through training, allowing me to make myself a priority. I had been buried beneath my own clutter. Now, each day, I was forcing myself to be the best version of myself. That was the objective.

The reason I chose the swim was that it would force me to be at my peak mentally. This was so personal. As with the Bering Strait, no one would ever understand this mile that I would swim. I was tired of coasting and tired of being able to fool myself into believing. I had to let go.

When we break a challenge down for ourselves, in the privacy of our own rooms, our own circles, our own space, we need to share our deepest fears and then decide. This swim had allowed me to have these deep discussions with myself.

The cost of any event is the amount of your life you are willing to exchange for it.

'Get local honey or strong manuka honey, put it on the open sores and wrap your hands with clingfilm. Allow the honey to soak into the infected areas, keeping them sterile,' Patrick suggested.

He had accepted my decision not to take vasodilators to allow my circulation to reopen. I did not want to take medication because it risked interfering with my body's natural response to hypothermia. My blood pressure was perfect, my medicals were strong and I did not want anything to jeopardise that. I was in too deep. I would suffer on and it would be over soon. I would pay my dues. At least the honey wrap helped.

On 20 March 2018 at 4.00 a.m., I jumped into Mary's car and we headed for Cork Airport.

'It only takes 36 hours to get to the end of the world?' Mary laughed at my destination. 'Tierra del Fuego.' Where the Atlantic Ocean begins.

'Have you everything? Passport, money everything?' she said as she handed me a Ziploc plastic bag and another bag. Mary was in her pyjamas and had her big cup of coffee. The morning, when most of us struggled to function, was her time.

She handed me the bag with the two empty bottles of Dingle Gin and Dingle Vodka for my photoshoot, having agreed that I would not carry full bottles because of the luggage weight involved in four flights. Cork to Paris to Buenos Aires to Punta Arenas to Puerto Williams. I would have to pray that my luggage would arrive safely in each destination.

'I put five miniature bottles into this one. They're 100-millilitre bottles of vodka and gin – perfect for photos. They fit perfectly,' she said as she proudly displayed the five small bottles zipped into the bag I would normally use for my toiletries. She then handed me €50 to buy some beauty creams when I got to my destination.

At the top, squeezed in, were two breakfast-portion jars and a tube of hand cream.

'That's two small jars of manuka honey. I cut a roll of clingfilm into a hand-width size for you to wrap your hands.'

At the airport, saying goodbye, I was strangely emotional. I was heading off on my own, in charge of my own destiny, not quite knowing what was ahead, or whether, after investing so much money, I would succeed or fail.

'Travel safe and may the Force be with you,' Mary said. We laughed. 'Give me a call when you get to the end of the world.' With that I turned and started my marathon journey to Tierra del

Fuego. All alone. I smiled at how my family embraced risk.

My bags and I arrived safely in Puerto Williams, Chile, the southernmost town in the world. We were now officially off the South American mainland, on Isla Navarino. Chris and Catherine had freed up their schedule – we had seven days to secure our swim. It was lovely to walk around and breathe and see everything, even through the constant excitement of what I was here to do. The prow of the *Yelcho*, the actual ship that arrived on Elephant Island to rescue Shackleton and his crew, including Tom Crean, stood firmly bolted at the naval base. You could feel the sense of history and knowing that Tom Crean, a giant of an explorer, born 10 miles from my home, once stood in this spot was a huge emotional support.

Discussions began immediately with Julieta and Cristian, our pilot Roni and the rest of my team. We talked about swim logistics and the paperwork that needed to be completed. The weather window would be about 36 hours in exposed water, including 12 hours to steam south over 100 nautical miles to the southern tip of Cape Horn. That meant we'd have only a few hours at Cape Horn. The boat could only be south of that point for the bare minimum time.

The weather forecast for the week was not favourable and we had to work with the limits of the vessel. It was vital that our small fishing boat could steam north in rogue conditions to secure shelter behind the islands and evade weather risks. I would not have a navy ship with me this time. We may not even get down to Cape Horn.

Roni informed us that there was a pending cold front forecast. This would cause the wind to turn suddenly, flip from the north-west, which would be behind me to the south-west, right on the meeting of the oceans, right where the warm and cold waters meet, directly against me. There was also a regional forecast. Areas like

Cape Horn have their own weather systems, like where I live in west Kerry.

At the office in this tiny town, the peace commissioner explained that I would have to personally accept the risk of swimming south of Cape Horn.

We are in the game. I could feel my heartbeat inside my chest. That need to risk it all was so great.

We got the call to leave the port and set sail. The crab boat was heavy and square, the bunks small for eight people, considering all the hours we would remain inside. It's so important to be calm with your team in confined spaces. The boat was no bigger than boats at home. I wondered about steaming 100 miles from the mainland in this vessel. Then I silenced those voices.

Several times, when the waves were too heavy, I tied myself to the door, stepping outside only to take in some air as the boat bounced and dipped her way south. When the waves increased, the boat had to fill its tanks with water to remain stable. We lost speed but gained control and safety. When the waves dropped again, the tanks would empty and our speed increase.

We steamed south through the Beagle Channel, where Chile and Argentina are a mere 5 kilometres apart. The wind funnelled its way through, gusting from the north-west, across the waterway. Today's swim would take place at Italy Glacier, a towering wall of ice that looked as if it had stopped in full flow as it eased into the waterway, frozen in time. The anchor dropped onsite at 10.30 a.m. The conditions were challenging.

'We have to be leaving at 1.30 p.m. for Cape Horn, so your swim window is tomorrow lunchtime, give or take,' Cristian said. There was huge pressure.

I put on the blizzard jacket over my swimming togs and immersion suit and four of us loaded into the Zodiac, the wind and freezing waves hitting me in the face as we navigated to the start point.

The towering glacier was bearing down on the water, with pieces of it calving into the water. The water temperature was 3 degrees. The air was cutting. Chris and Catherine in their drysuits struggled to get the boat to shore to the start point. The engines had to be cut and lifted because of the rocks and the seaweed, so it was down to the team to row the boat to the start point. They paddled against the crushing wind tunnelling through the Beagle Channel. After 10 minutes, unable to reach the start point, my anxiety was building again. The water was 3 degrees, too cold for a 5-kilometre swim. The wind was pushing the boat backwards. I thought about the cost on my body, and on my mindset if I was unsuccessful.

My mind drifted to the voice of Brendan Proctor, who was our command-boat skipper for the Round Ireland Swim. He was always decisive. I could hear him now, as if his voice was on the wind: 'Stand down, stand down. None of you will risk a bad swim. If you risk a bad swim, that risk could destroy a really good swim tomorrow. Stand down.'

In that split second, I made my call.

'I'm not going to risk a bad swim. I'm going to save everything I have for the meeting of the oceans. I'm not going beyond 2 kilometres in these conditions – not in 3-degree water, not in this wind.'

I got into the icy waters, swam to shore and began my 2-kilometre swim with Chris, in his drysuit and fins, camera in hand, in the water beside me. Catherine was on the Zodiac. It was cold. I stayed protected from the wind under the solid wall of glacier ice.

I pushed my hands into the soapy, freezing water as it froze my body and focused my mind. With each breath, I stared up at Italy Glacier and watched the pure ice calve. It was the first time I'd been alone with my thoughts since we'd arrived in Puerto Williams. The pain of the last few months eased away. I was thinking the glacier wall would be a lovely photoshoot location for Mary's Dingle Vodka and Dingle Gin. The purest of ice for the purest of drinks. I was marketing and not worrying about the outcome. My breathing was balanced. My mind was relaxed.

Once out of the water and reheated, I asked Chris and Catherine to return to the glacier with me before we headed south, with the bottles of Dingle Gin and Dingle Vodka. I had to use the opportunity. Chris came from the water in his dive gear onto a shelf of ice, where he pretended to grab the purple bottle of Dingle Vodka and took photos. It was such fun, and I knew Mary would be happy. It was the first time in months that my mind was calm.

The boat hauled anchor and headed south the 110 miles to Cape Horn through the Drake Passage. I decided to stay in the wheelhouse and absorb the reality of our journey, watching the plotter and radar heading south and seeing the Antarctic on the charts, thinking this was the route that Shackleton and Crean used to return from their expeditions. We were travelling the same journey south on the route of history.

Once between the islands of Navarino and Hermite, there were about 30 miles of open oceans, all mixing, trailing, rolling waves from the north-west. We charted our path through these islands with one inhabitant – truly the end of the world. The waves were threatening, short, powerful waves, filled with emotion and passion. I just kept thinking, *I did not give this swim the respect it deserves.* A genuine sense of fear began to build. The feeling that the power was shifting from me to the ocean.

Twenty-four hours later we were still steaming our way through the archipelago of Tierra del Fuego. Three oceans rushed around us as we descended further and further south and the water got larger and darker. There was a sense that we, in our vessel, were truly getting smaller. A feeling of humility, a sense of our own insignificance, the knowledge that we were at the mercy of these oceans – that nothing could stop or even slow down their movement. That feeling of isolation.

Thirty-six hours later we arrived at the back of Isla Hornos, a hundred miles south of the mainland of South America.

Roni and Adan Otaiza Caro chatted on the VHF. 'Sí, sí,' was all I understood. We waited. Their discussion was to decide if conditions were suitable for the vessel to take the journey 2 miles beyond the southern tip to the location of the meeting of the oceans, where there is no land east or west. It would be dangerous in itself for a crab boat of our size to be exposed to the waves that were in the area. The lighthouse keeper, the admiral of Cape Horn, would have the final say.

Silence, then a conversation in Spanish with Julieta and Cristian. I stood waiting with Catherine and Chris, who both spoke Spanish too. Finally, a nod confirmed the approval.

'So, the admiral has confirmed that you can swim the meeting of the oceans at our agreed GPS coordinates, but we must go now. You must go into the water in the next hour. The risk changes in two hours. We must be inside the protection of Cabo de Hornos by 4.00 p.m., before the cold front comes in, as our boat needs to be clear of that area.'

Cristian and Roni continued to chat. My mind went to the thought that a boat our size, steaming around, standing off me in these waves, having to turn in to water to track me, was high risk. With low or no engine power, she was at the mercy of the oceans.

It was close to 1.40 p.m.

'It is 30 minutes south of here, so one hour preparing for your swim and that will give us time to get back into the shelter of the island. We go now or not at all.'

I nodded. We were steaming south.

The iconic headland bore down on us. It resembled Sybil Head – a tall, commanding landmass, withstanding the tests of time, taking beating after beating and holding its own. Above my head an albatross circled on the winds of the oceans. East and west of here was only ocean. I looked at the location where the easier swims took place and for a brief second wondered if I should just take that option instead.

'A sign,' Catherine said, pointing to the rainbow that suddenly arched across the Drake Passage.

I held on to the door as we headed south-west, to water as deep as 4,000 metres, a sea floor I could not imagine, all rising to climb up onto the shelf at Cape Horn. The wave sets were as high as 4 and 5 metres, with troughs of up to 4 metres, and they kept coming. They were like the waves I had seen in the Bering Strait, but bigger and stronger, their power evident in their rolling size, not their shape. It was at this meridian that the oceans met, the Pacific and the Atlantic, circling the globe with the Antarctic Circumpolar Current close to 56 degrees south.

I held on to the door and watched the waves rolling into each other – no pattern, but enough time and space between them to allow the boat to drop and rise. As a swimmer, I would be so low between them. How would they see me from the boat? I would be swimming up and down these walls of water. I would be caught in the troughs. I suddenly understood with crystal clarity the immenseness of this swim, of the challenge that faced me. We passed the lighthouse and the Roca Negra, I looked at the other swim. We steamed south for another 2 miles to clear all land and then cross over to the Pacific Ocean. The GPS markings had to be reached.

I needed to withdraw, to close my world down. I needed to take the location away, to focus solely on the swim and not on the big picture or the location. Just on the moment.

I stepped downstairs to put Vaseline in my armpits and on my feet to protect against the cold. I put my thermals on over the Vaseline, the heat allowing the ointment to soak into my pores, giving me some thermal protection.

I had a chat with myself. I talked myself through the swim as the belly of the boat was hit with some serious thuds. I could tell from my childhood the sounds when the engines were being pulled back and when the power was given to drive through. The vessel was at its limits. I could hear its sounds, the engine's reduced power.

Catherine called to me to come up.

'Commanding officer Otaiza Caro has just radioed from the lighthouse. You can do the swim and you must go now, but Chris and I cannot take the Zodiac with you. We must stay on the command boat.'

I stared at her, trying to process what this meant. How could I visualise this new procedure? How would this affect my plan? How could I do this without my safety cover?

'There is no way that the Zodiac with Chris and me can be in the water with you – it's too dangerous. We'll follow you on this boat.' Catherine had a definite way of communication. It carried certainty. 'We will get to you,' she finished.

I was unable to speak, trying to process how to work this new option. The large boat would not be able to travel alongside me. Roni would have to be ahead or behind. I would be alone. I knew these boats. It took minutes to turn them and even longer to stop and change direction. My face showed all my emotion and my heart raced as a huge wave hit the side – bang! – and the boat dropped low in the water. The sound was magnified in the hold of the boat – the waves were just outside the timber walls. I looked at our nurse and the defibrillator, which now took on a new focus.

'You can also swim inside the bay, from the lighthouse, point to point, where others have also completed their swims. We can go with you into that water and bring the Zodiac.' Her voice trailed off.

'What if I am pushed backwards by the current and can't get any distance at all? How quickly could you get to me? How far away would you be? What if I can't cross the meridian and lose everything?' I asked. I was so confused. I could not process the questions. I looked around the group, from Roni to Cristian to Julieta to Chris and back to Catherine.

'We would get you from the water, we would not lose sight of you,' Catherine said. 'Your call.'

Words in Spanish over the VHF as the boat took another wallop from the waves. They had to get their engines moving.

'We have to go now,' Cristian said. 'We have a tight window. The swim is yours – Roni will stay with you. It is not safe for us to sit here in the fishing boat.'

'How far away? I won't be able to see anyone through the waves,' I said, looking at the oceans and where we were.

'A few hundred metres, maximum,' Chris replied.

That was a long way. My mind went to the Bering Strait. I could be flipped in the waves, pulled under. Lost.

'Give me a minute,' I said. Terrified that I might swim for an hour and not be able to cross the meridian of the meeting of the oceans, what if I fail to swim the required distance? What does failure look like down here?

I took a step back down the ladder, reversing downstairs. I could not read their faces.

What if they lose me? What is their plan? There will be no one else coming to help. The waves were monsters and they twisted and turned on themselves. *These are the feared southern oceans. What am I doing here?* I was saying all this out loud to myself, trying to make sense of it.

These were some of the most dangerous waters in the world and I was about to jump into them and swim, all on my own.

Catherine appeared and looked at me down the ladder.

'This is what you came for,' she said. 'We will not take our eyes off you, I promise.'

This was no longer about being the first swimmer in the world. This was about staying alive. But I believed her, and I trusted myself. All I had to do was swim.

A few deep breaths.

I will do it.

This is why I am here.

This is who I am.

TRUE NORTH

'The more you head into the maelstrom, the more vulnerable you are, of course. But it's what you owe to whatever gift you have.'
Ellen McLaughlin

I let go.

Cape Horn stood high in the distance, commanding. It was dark. The sun was behind the clouds, directly behind the island. I could have been anywhere in the world, but I wasn't. I was nearly 56 degrees south, 100 nautical miles off mainland South America. At this exact latitude, the Pacific, Atlantic and Antarctic Oceans found freedom. I was between the devil and the deep blue sea.

The wind was spinning from north-west to south-west, meaning only one thing – that the cold front was coming towards us. The boat and the crew had to be out of this location in two hours. Our boat was not equipped to manage these waves, to be steaming around at up to 2–4 knots.

I uncurled my fingers from the rope that kept me anchored to the boat and released my body into the oceans. In a second, my body was pulled away as the engines revved. It was a frustrated, twisted sea, walls and walls of water 3 to 4 metres high, rolling around the world. For those moments my breathing had become incredibly elevated – ragged, even. I was so nervous. My breaths were short and sharp, a mixture of cold shock and anxiety, a dangerous combination for my heart.

The water temperature was 7 degrees – I knew that. It was vital to be able to breathe through the cold shock. If I didn't get control of my breathing, there were immediate risks at play. My panic could trigger a cardiac incident before I even had a chance to get lost.

Breathe. If you can't breathe, you can't swim. Plan your swim, swim your plan.

Closing my eyes, I went into my own dark world, breathing long, deep breaths. I visualised myself at 30 metres on a deep dive, the pressure creating limits. Right now, I could hear my inhalations, the effort to gasp each breath.

At 30 metres deep the breath is slow and steady, measured by the pressure. I had to get to the place where everything slows, where that urge to inhale is calmed. I took an extra moment to focus on the still water underneath me before I turned to see the turmoil of the surface. Then back to the calm. The gasp passed. Long exhalations of bubbles.

I called out every mantra that came to my mind.

Pain is an indication your body is working.
If you ask yourself why, you have no place here.
This is what you are built for.
This is why you are here.

I didn't turn my head back as the engines fell silent. I knew they were gone. I could hear the boat steaming away on my blind side. My face was tingling as the freezing water made contact with my skin. My mouth filled, stroke after stroke, because I could not find a pocket to breathe. *Try again. Go slower and pull harder under your armpit. Stay calm.* Walls of water were hitting me.

The first few minutes were stressful. I could not hear the engines, which would normally be loud underwater. I had a moment of panic as I could not remember what the crew's plan was – would they circle me? I needed to know that they could see me in the water. I knew I could not see them, even if I tried. I was swimming deep into the trenches of these colossal waves.

There was only me now.

A huge wave walloped me head on and pulled my arm backwards, nearly jerking it out of its socket. I bolted backwards and yelped as another wave turned me on my back. My goggles were still on. I reached and tightened the strap and immediately dug deep under the next wall coming from the side. This swim would be as much about getting air as it would be about lifting my arms. The cold was no longer the challenge. This was raw survival.

Every push forward of my right arm, I turned my head from the water, my eyes focused on the headland of Cape Horn. Cabo de Hornos, the graveyard of sailors, withstanding every storm; the sea around it the most feared body of water in the world. Above my head were albatross, gliding gracefully on the screaming winds of the Furious Fifties between the Pacific and Atlantic Oceans. They swooped low to check me out, their 3-metre wingspan beating on the edge of time.

Wild and pure nature. I was home. This was where I could find my freedom. I let go. There was no more standing still, no more questioning what I was capable of. This was it.

If the boat lost sight of me in these waves, no one would come to rescue me. In these temperatures and conditions, I would stay alive for two hours maximum. I was too far away to make land. *What am I doing here?* said a fragile voice inside me. *I have to be home for work on Monday.* I gave a little giggle.

I didn't choose this location because of the swim; I chose this swim because of the location. I wanted to be the first swimmer in the world to take on this huge challenge, the first swimmer in the world to swim from the Pacific Ocean to the Atlantic Ocean in the Drake Passage, the first swimmer in the world to conquer this mile south of Cape Horn. Yet at this moment, facing the belly of the beast, it all seemed so irrelevant, so insignificant, so insane. In my head the words screaming out: *Give me passage. Let me pass through your oceans.*

I chose to tackle my storm head on, mainly as I was at its centre. There was no other way to find out if I was the person I thought I was, if I could trust myself. This was not about the swim: this was personal. For the last few years, my reflection in the mirror had scared me – a face and eyes that did not show the strength of the woman inside. An absence of energy. I knew that I was so strong, but I could not reach my strength. I knew I was powerful, but my drive was lost inside. I could see what I wanted to be, but it was just beyond my reach. My reflection haunted me. I knew I was the sum of my parts, of my life's experiences. But, try as I might for the last few years, I had been unable to find my way to my true reflection. I had lost my swagger.

This moment was about putting myself into an environment that would challenge every fibre of my being. I had every skill necessary to survive, if I could just trust myself. The last few years had challenged me on every level, and what I respected most about taking on anything extreme was that it required me to step up and be the best version of myself. In that moment, when strength was my only choice, I could be strong. I needed my true self to steer my ship.

'No storm can hit you on all four sides. The wind turns. Rotate and find your shelter. If you can't find shelter, take the only other option. Gather steam and drive directly into the storm. That is the only place where you have control. Take that wave head on.' My father would repeat this so many times. It was what he had learned from a life on the sea.

Right now, it was chaotic. The waves were crashing, breaking. I was swimming like I was dancing at a disco to a song I'd never heard before. I could not sort out my rhythm. I was being tossed and turned – there was no shelter. I needed to build power and drive straight through the waves.

This was not about the swim. This was about letting go and knowing I could trust myself and my team, that I could stand over my choices and my decisions. I was never comfortable with being fragile or weak.

Slow down and listen to the music.

This was the most remote I would ever be, at the mercy of a storm even greater than the one inside me. This was the most alone I would ever be, the most vulnerable I would ever be. Letting go of that boat and turning my face away from my team was one of the hardest things I had ever done – not because the swim was impossible, but because I risked absolute catastrophe. I had chosen the path of most risk. I had chosen to be vulnerable.

So, it's up to you, Nuala. Strength or weakness? Trust or panic? Hero or zero?

Right now, I could scream and scream and no one would hear me. The wind would drown out my cries, the waves would hide my presence in their troughs. No one would come. I couldn't see. I couldn't hear. I was a tiny dot amidst these rolling, freezing oceans. I was completely alone.

Suddenly I was back in a memory, drifting through time.

'What is wrong with you?' Mary asked one afternoon in my shop when I was knee-deep in preparations for this swim. She was on the bed, glasses on her nose, writing an email, with a coffee, and I was on the computer.

'I don't know. I can't figure out what's scaring me. I think I've underestimated the challenge of Cape Horn. I can't get my head clear. I'm afraid I will panic. It's so much money and risk.'

'Why do you do it?' she demanded. 'Because you can. Life has trained you to hold on. She who suffers remembers, Nuala. Isn't that what you say? You come from a long line of strong women. You are a sniper in your approach. You've a good team. Just don't think about it. Trust yourself. It's in our blood.' Mary was just not someone who wallowed in things.

I hated that feeling of doubt that crept in. I often thought, if the other struggles had not existed, would I have been freer to take risks?

'Just do it now,' she said, eyes over the rims of her glasses, in a tone that made us both laugh.

'Well now, Mary, if I could just remind you that your commit-and-go approach is a little different to mine!'

She laughed, her eyes and nose scrunching behind the rims of her glasses.

On holiday in South Africa, Mary had wanted to try a bungee jump. She did not tell her kids as she did not want to scare them. The highest she could find was 216 metres high, over a river at Bloukrans Bridge. On the bridge, the crew tied the straps around her ankles and gave her a thumbs-up. As they turned to do their final check, Mary bunny-hopped away from them, ankles strapped together, and jumped off the bridge, to the screams of the team and everyone else present as her body flew through the air without her final safety check. The video was hysterical. Their faces.

'They gave me a thumbs-up,' was her defence. Her usual shrug of her shoulders. 'It wasn't great value for money.'

Laughter filled the shop, tears streaming down our faces. I followed years later to do the same bungee jump. We agreed on how well we both bounced up and down on that rope, with all our extra body weight!

'Nothing is as bad as it seems. You've had enough tests, you are well able for this and you will come home safe. Think of our breeding and look at what we battle,' she said firmly.

As she walked out the door, she turned back and looked at me, both of us still laughing.

'Just bunny-hop off your bridge now and jump, let go,' she said. With that she gave a little jump out the door, followed by a whoop. 'If you need anything, give me a call.'

It was her swagger, her confidence. Mary knew how to work a room. She knew how to let go, how to break and rebuild, how to lead and how to follow. She was fearless of judgement and she chased storms. She trusted.

This was about holding on. I needed to find strength in these sacrifices to find the swagger I could feel when I closed my eyes and saw that reflection that only came to the surface when I was surrounded by those I loved. I needed to find that giggle again.

Mary was always taking chances, being fearless and being strong. Her voice came strongly into my head: 'What a fabulous opportunity to see Cape Horn!'

I let go.

I gave in to the beauty of the extremes. I committed to the ocean. I gave it the honesty it deserved. I was the first swimmer in the world to lower my body off the side of a boat in the Drake Passage this far south of Cape Horn.

The albatross circled above my head. I wondered how strong they were, whether they could lift me. If they worked as a team, could they pick me up? *Last seen flying north over Cape Horn.* I laughed to myself so much that I heard my bubbles.

I had found a rhythm in the chaos. I was free.

You are on the cusp of greatness. The words tumbled into the blue waves, words I had not uttered freely in a long time.

The hum of the engines came and went, rumbling underwater, revving forward and back. I tilted my head a few times between the waves, but it was stressful to see the vessel steaming away again. I battled. I was tumbled. I disappeared; they disappeared. I knew why others did not take on this swim. Who travels halfway around the world to risk it all for so little glory? People pay for certainty, not risk. No one would understand my journey. But the magic for me lay in the insanity of this moment. I was no longer fighting the swim. I was surfing and diving, my face focusing on the still, calm water under my body, shadows of blue. I found a rhythm in the chaos. The crew's job was more stressful than mine. They had to keep finding me, looking for me, this tiny head. I only had to be strong.

The pain in my hands and face from the 7-degree water was no longer an issue. My thoughts were frozen in time. I had mended my nets. I had rebuilt. I was exactly who I thought I was. How powerful I was! How powerful I had to be to hold my focus on this thin edge. Maybe I was foolish. I thought of my fishing family and the risks they took daily. I was the sum of my parts. I was now dancing with the oceans, accepting their rhythm, and this was the most alive I had felt for years.

I could have stayed there, swimming, for a longer distance than the mile. But time was our enemy. The small timber boat had been steaming around the Drake Passage for the last half an hour, engines powered low in gravely dangerous waters. I knew I had to leave. I had to protect the team and the vessel. The window in which we could safely be so far south of Cape Horn was closing. I hoped I'd made it over the meridian and into the Atlantic Ocean. It was hard to know if I was making progress or just being tossed around.

The growling of the engines came closer and then the sound stalled. Engines in reverse, the sounds revved up again, powering backwards. I could hear their intention, although I could not see the vessel. These were sounds I had grown accustomed to over the years. My team were steadying their ship in the Drake Passage. I looked up, focusing on the horizon, staying high, and with the wave drop I could see the Zodiac tied to the side of the boat. I had to push hard – the waves were now coming from the sides of the boat. She was rocking. They were vulnerable. The risks had shifted.

My father's words were scrolling through my mind: 'Do not be weak out there. Do not add to their problems. They have the biggest job.' Energy rose inside me.

Catherine was on her knees on the boat and Chris was in the water, holding on to the rope. I could make out Roni's head through the wheelhouse window. I dug deep, kicked hard and pushed towards him. My power had dropped off with the cold-water impact. My legs were stiff but I gave it everything. Thinking about breathing was no longer a necessity. *Think of an emergency ascent on one breath, hear your bubbles and get there. Gather steam and push on. Drive into the storm.* My hands drove deep under my body. I had to aim directly for Chris and Catherine and hope the momentum of the wave would drive me on top of them.

A hand grabbed me and tied me to the side of the Zodiac. I wrapped the rope around my arm as my hands were too cold to grasp it. I held on for dear life as the ocean waves tossed us from side to side. We were tied together. The fishing vessel was in neutral and she was broadside to the waves, taking their force. *Breathe.* The Zodiac was tied to the boat and I was tied to the Zodiac.

In a few seconds, Chris was in the Zodiac and, as we'd trained for time and again, within seconds Chris and Catherine had me airborne, both planted on their knees, as my frozen body was hauled in. I was out.

'We're not there yet!' Anne Marie's words came into my mind. We had to move quickly to get their engines in power. To gain control. We had to shelter.

It was the strangest feeling. I was not cold. All the emotions that I had experienced – the fear, the anxiety, the stress – seemed to have faded so that I had no memory of them. I don't remember the weakness; I remember the power, the strength and the privilege. There were only the excitement and adrenaline of what I had just achieved. It was the biggest water I had ever been in, like a crazy ride in a theme park. The risks had evaporated and the reward was great. I wanted to ring home, but that would have to wait. We had been out of signal for days now.

Now that it was done, I wanted to sit and relax and breathe for a few minutes and take it all in. Location and concept. I had swum 1,700 metres across the meeting of the oceans. There was no major sense of achievement, just a few deep breaths and gratitude that I had been given passage across the Drake Passage.

As we steamed close to the land, towards the lighthouse-to-lighthouse swim at Roca Negra, I was delighted that I'd had courage enough to take the risk.

I was exhausted, but I had a sense of finally being able to breathe, to be able to strike free of the grey twilight that had engulfed me for so long. I had found my greatness again. I wanted to stare at the sun. *I am strong. I can hold on.* It was possible to silence the monsters in the mind.

I had the perfect team and they had my back. Catherine and Chris, Cristian, Julieta and Roni. They held that vessel so I could reach it. The risks had been so great, but they had never taken their eyes off me.

So much had flowed from swimming around Ireland. My smile was so huge. *I am built for this.* I always thought that sentence meant I was heavy and strong, but it didn't. It meant that I was designed for these moments, these storms.

I moved beyond fear. I moved beyond anxiety. I moved beyond stress. The emotion that filled my core was an appreciation of privilege. How honoured I was to be here, to be able to look up at this monumental headland, knowing the lives it had taken, knowing that rounding this point remains one of the greatest achievements in sailing, let alone swimming. And now I had swum it – not on a calm day, but on a day when there was huge risk.

I wondered what my father would say if he were alive. No doubt he would shake his head and spin a story about a time he rounded Cape Horn himself, a time when he had chosen not to use the Strait of Magellan but to travel instead these waters, the most dangerous waters in the world. I closed my eyes as tears welled up and fell. I thought of my journey across the oceans of life to this point – the grief and the greatness, the loss and the growth.

Many people ask me: how do you do what you do?

My family. It was they who taught me to stare at the sea, never to take my eyes off it, to be grateful for passage, knowing that it would always be my greatest adversary.

Wherever I was going, my father had already been. Whether his stories were tall tales or true tales, he knew the geography of the oceans, but he also embedded into my psyche the respect and the humility necessary to survive.

My mother taught me to be happy, to prepare and to push to be the best. Not to fear too much, not to get too cocky and not to claim wins. We were all winners. The oceans had all lined up. I had been given passage.

I thought about the young child jumping off the *Bridget* at

Sláidín Beach, not really knowing how to swim, but knowing how to not drown. Studying how to get around the lighthouse for no other reason than wanting not to be left behind. It was only by testing myself that I could truly find my strength. By letting go and trusting myself that I could be my own hero, I found my path to survival.

I had given myself the greatest challenge of my life. This was about the higher power, about my journey back to trusting myself. This was a huge risk for me. I didn't fit into today's model of winning and losing. The reward was personal. I found myself again. I learned that my strength in the face of adversity is steel-like. That I seek out storms and that I find value in the battle. Sometimes too much. In those moments when I was at my weakest, I found a strength that was there all along. Skills learned from childhood were my tools to survive. I discovered I have a need to celebrate everyone and everything, recognition is important for me, as is finding the value. I thrived on achievement and being the best version of myself. I wanted everyone to succeed and not fear the storm. But I also found the world of success and failure and winning and losing deeply challenging. Team was everything to me. Through accepting support and trusting ourselves we could find our swagger and dance to our own tunes. By rising up and building strength and courage, we bring those around us with us.

Few would or could know the costs of the journey – what these swims took from me emotionally, what it took to train my body and how hard it was to let go of control, in a world where control is all we have. But the gain was greater than any award. It was life beyond the grey twilight. If it was achievement I was seeking, there were much easier options. I had needed to test myself, to expose myself to my weaknesses. In that I found resilience. Extremes demand honesty. I had to be honest with my preparation, honest with my training and honest with myself. I had won my battle. Team is everything. Risk and reward are opposite sides of the same coin. I opened my eyes to the monument of Cape Horn, to the albatross, staring south to the oceans. I honoured the souls lost in the winds of time. I honoured the significance of the location and the significance of the statement I was making.

Once home, I cried for the first time. Reading the articles, I was so proud of my courage.

Cristian Vergara explained:

Last Easter Sunday, Nuala Moore under the guidance of Patagonia Swim became the first swimmer in history to swim the maritime boundary between the Pacific and Atlantic Oceans defined as LONG 67°16′W. The swim received the go-ahead by the commanding officer, keeper of the lighthouse of Cape Horn, Adan Otaiza Caro.

In my family, storms were not feared. They were the natural energy of the oceans. Storms in the fishing world were used as a time to rest. Some storms are beautiful; some storms we stand off. My brother often welcomes a storm because it's the time to steady the ship, to go to the protection of the land, of home, of his family. During such times, fishermen gather their energy. We seafarers welcome rest because we can't always battle the persistent powerful nature of the waves. Some storms show our character. In other storms, we close our doors, breathe and wait it out, safe in the knowledge that all of them pass. I needed to be tested by my greatest adversary, myself.

In the very worst of storms, though, we must drive straight ahead, because it is only by facing the waves head-on that we can gain control. When waves come from the side or the stern, they can unsteady our ship or even take it. We have to understand the journey into the storm, bide our time, find our moment, gather steam and take control of the winds and waves.

As a child, I would watch as the skippers threw their ropes from the pier. I remember the excitement and urgency as the fishermen steamed away and left the land behind. I knew they would crave that moment of leaving shore again. As a family, such moments can be scary. I remember times of waiting, wondering how the fishermen navigated through the winds and oceans so far from shore. Trusting and being patient. For us, it was a way of life. When they lost sight of the shore, that was when the magic happened. As Mary used to say, 'My needs are simple – I only want the best.'

The last few stormy years had been scary, but now I was home. I had allowed too much noise into my world, I had spread myself too thin, creating a path for many when I should have sought calm for my own world. I was privileged to have the calm of the underwater world, the extremes of the ice and the magnificence of the storms. I had truly been one on one with nature. What did it mean to be the first person in the world to attempt something, let alone succeed? The path less travelled takes more courage than the better-trodden path. *The cost of any event is the amount of your life you are willing to exchange for it.* I was always drawn to that statement.

Extremes had stripped me bare emotionally, exposed my weaknesses and allowed me to recover and rebuild by choosing my path forward. Pain is always a choice in sport, but it imitates life. I always felt that letting go was necessary to find that person inside of me. I chose events with huge costs, and my successes and failures have exposed a person I am proud to be. I am limited and limitless, opposite sides of the same coin. By going south, I found my true north.

I faced my reflection and smiled.

Mairimid ar a bhfaighimid
agus bláthaimid ar a dtugaimid.

This book is to celebrate the inimitable memory of my
beautiful sister Mary Moore Ferriter
(1959–2020)

You were diplomatic, charismatic and glamorous. You were full
of empathy, warmth, compassion, determination and just the
right amount of crazy.

I am the albatross that awaits you
at the end of the world.
I am the forgotten soul of the dead mariners
who passed Cape Horn
from all the seas of the world.
But they did not die
in the furious waves.
Today they soar on my wings
towards eternity
in the last crack
of the Antarctic winds.

SARA VIAL

ACKNOWLEDGEMENTS

It truly takes a village. I always knew I would write a book, just not this one.

I had a fabulous childhood growing up in Dingle, surrounded by a wonderful community. The love and support of my family were central to that. My father gave me my love of the sea, strength, work ethic and resilience. My beautiful mother Bridget showed incredible emotional intelligence, courage, humanity and humility. At age ten, she told me that I could run for president, she taught me to dream and showed me the value of patience.

To my brother Edward, your strength and fearlessness in the face of adversity is something to behold. You would run through fire and steam and through the fiercest storms to ensure everyone around you is safe. Kate, my sister-in-law, you are one of the most determined, inexhaustible and resilient women I know. Paddyjoe, the last few years have been so difficult, Mary will always be shining in our lives. My nieces and nephews, Bridget, Christopher, Christine, Ciara, Patrick and Cathal, I hope you take strength from this book. Mary, you were everything I wanted to be, you pushed us all to be the best version of ourselves. I hope I will always do you proud. Beau, welcome.

Friendship and love of adventure are the threads that weave through my life. Joan O'Shea, Claire Walsh, Mary Murphy and Sharon Ashe, we met as children and, to this day, our circle of friendship is gold. Mags O'Sullivan, Frances Lynch and Sandra Fitzgibbon, our lives have been entwined for decades as we laughed, achieved and mostly created an environment where everyone was celebrated. Maryann Heidtke, you supported me to achieve the highest standards for myself. Ger Moore, Tricia Taylor, Maura Bawn, JEF, Máire Uí Chonchúir and my great friend Nora Murphy – always a tower of strength to me. To Jean Sheehy, I am sorry you are not here to see this.

Thank you to the triathletes and swimmers I had the opportunity to lead, be led by and be inspired by. Thank you to Cathal O'Brien, Roger Harty, Robert Whyte, Paul Tanner, Lisa Staplebrook, Ellen Vitting, Paul Kelly, Garry Kavanagh, Ciara Lynch, Sandra Lynch, Robyn Fitzgibbon, Brendan Condon, Pat and Ronnie Fitzgibbon, John Woulfe and Mallow Search and Rescue Unit. To Ram, Mariia, Aleksandr, Dmitry 3 minutes, Cristian Vergara, Matias Ola, Dr Irina, Vladislav Bykov, Jack Bright, Dr Nataliya and all my friends in Tyumen and around the world, thank you. Lynne Cox, you are my greatest inspiration. Steven Munatones, you always reminded me of my strength.

Thank you to Catherine Buckland, Chris Booker, Patrick Buck, Gary Crawford, Ann Payne, Claire Bailey, David Power, Niamh Feely, Davitt Ward, Sarah Staunton and Ger Beggs. People come into our lives at exactly the right time – thank you for your friendship, you helped me navigate the challenging waters and steady my ship.

To my Round Ireland Swim team – what an adventure – Ryan Ward, Tom Watters, Ian Claxton, Anne Marie Ward, Neil Aherne, Derek Flanagan, Noel Brennan, Brendan Proctor, Kathleen King, all at Sheephaven SAC and Henry O'Donnell, you put the dream together and now we have the story in words. To the original Bond girls, Melissa O'Reilly and Jackie Cobell, your bravery is special. Henri Kaarma, we all need a hero.

A huge thank you to my amazing team at Gill, especially Seán Hayes, my wonderful commissioning editor, my structural editor Rachel Pierce, and Alicia McAuley and Margaret Farrelly, my wonderful editing team.

It is always the strength of the collective that makes the individuals strong.